KT-590-558

COMPLAINTS

COMPLAINTS

EDMUND SPENSER

Edited by
W. L. RENWICK

THE SCHOLARTIS PRESS
30, MUSEUM STREET, LONDON
1928

COMPLAINTS

By EDMUND SPENSER

EDITED WITH COMMENTARY AND NOTES
BY W. L. RENWICK.

PUBLISHED BY THE SCHOLARTIS PRESS,

PRINTED BY THE BOTOLPH PRINTING WORKS,
AT GATE STREET, KINGSWAY, W.C.

THERE ARE TWO EDITIONS: THE ONE OF

95 NUMBERED COPIES ON OLD STYLE HAND-MADE
PAPER,

THE OTHER OF 1660 COPIES ON UNIVERSAL ANTIQUE
LAID PAPER.

CONTENTS

A note of the sundrie Poemes contained in this Volume.

THE PRINTER TO THE GENTLE READER.

SINCE my late setting foorth of the *Faerie Queene*, finding that it hath found a favourable passage amongst you; I have sithence endevoured by all good meanes (for the better encrease and accomplishment of your delights,) to get into my handes such smale Poemes of the same Authors; as I heard were disperst abroad in sundrie hands, and not easie to bee come by, by himselfe; some of them having bene diverslie imbeziled and purloyned from him, since his departure over Sea. Of the which I have by good meanes gathered togeather these fewe parcels present, which I have caused to bee imprinted altogeather, for that they al seeme to containe like matter of argument in them: being all complaints and meditations of the worlds vanitie; verie grave and profitable. To which effect I understand that he besides wrote sundrie others, namelie *Ecclesiastes*, & *Canticum canticorum* translated, *A senights slumber*, *The hell of lovers*, *his Purgatorie*, being all dedicated to Ladies; so as it may seeme he ment them all to one volume. Besides some other Pamphlets looselie scattered abroad: as *The dying Pellican*, *The howers of the Lord*, *The sacrifice of a sinner*, *The seven Psalmes*, *&c.* which when I can either by himselfe, or otherwise attaine too, I meane likewise for your favour sake to set foorth. In the meane time praying you gentlie to accept of these, & graciouslie to entertaine the new Poet. *I take leave.*

THE RUINES OF TIME.

DEDICATED

TO THE RIGHT NOBLE AND BEAUTIFULL LADIE,

THE LA. MARIE COUNTESSE OF PEMBROOKE.

MOST Honourable and bountifull Ladie, there bee long sithens deepe sowed in my brest, the seede of most entire love & humble affection unto that most brave Knight your noble brother deceased; which taking roote began in his life time somewhat to bud forth: and to shew themselves to him, as then in the weakenes of their first spring: And would in their riper strength (had it pleased high God till then to drawe out his daies) spired forth fruit of more perfection. But since God hath disdeigned the world of that most noble Spirit, which was the hope of all learned men, and the Patron of my young Muses; togeather with him both their hope of anie further fruit was cut off: and also the tender delight of those their first blossoms nipped and quite dead. Yet sithens my late cumming into England, some frends of mine (which might much prevaile with me, and indeede commaund me) knowing with howe straight bandes of duetie I was tied to him: as also bound unto that noble house, (of which the chiefe hope then rested in him) have sought ro revive them by upbraiding me: for that I have not shewed anie thankefull remembrance towards him or any of them; but suffer their names to sleep in silence and forgetfulnesse. Whome chieflie to satisfie, or els to avoide that fowle blot of unthankefulnesse, I have conceived this small Poeme, intituled by a generall name of the worlds Ruines: yet speciallie intended to the renowming of that noble race, from which both you and he sprong, and to the eternizing of some of the chiefe of them late deceased. The which I dedicate unto your La. as whome it most speciallie concerneth: and to whome I acknowledge my selfe bounden, by manie singular favours & great graces. I pray for your Honourable happinesse: & so humblie kisse your handes.

Your Ladiships ever
humblie at commaund.
E.S.

THE RUINES OF TIME.

IT chaunced me on day beside the shore
Of silver streaming *Thamesis* to bee,
Nigh where the goodly *Verlame* stood of yore,
Of which there now remaines no memorie,
Nor anie little moniment to see,
By which the travailer, that fares that way,
This once was she, may warned be to say.

There on the other side, I did behold
A Woman sitting sorrowfullie wailing,
Rending her yeolow locks, like wyrie golde, 10
About her shoulders careleslie downe trailing,
And streames of teares from her faire eyes forth
railing.
In her right hand a broken rod she held,
Which towards heaven shee seemd on high to weld.

Whether she were one of that Rivers Nymphes,
Which did the losse of some dere love lament,
I doubt; or one of those three fatall Impes,
Which draw the dayes of men forth in extent;
Or th' auncient *Genius* of that Citie brent:
But seeing her so piteouslie perplexed, 20
I (to her calling) askt what her so vexed.

Ah what delight (quoth she) in earthlie thing,
Or comfort can I wretched creature have?
Whose happines the heavens envying,
From highest staire to lowest step me drave,
And have in mine owne bowels made my grave,
That of all Nations now I am forlorne,
The worlds sad spectacle, and fortunes scorne

Much was I mooved at her piteous plaint,
And felt my heart nigh riven in my brest 30
With tender ruth to see her sore constraint,
That shedding teares a while I still did rest,
And after did her name of her request.
Name have I none (quoth she) nor anie being,
Bereft of both by Fates unjust decreeing.

I was that Citie, which the garland wore
Of *Britaines* pride, delivered unto me
By *Romane* Victors, which it wonne of yore;
Though nought at all but ruines now I bee,
And lye in mine owne ashes, as ye see: 40
Verlame I was; what bootes it that I was,
Sith now I am but weedes and wastfull gras?

O vaine worlds glorie, and unstedfast state
Of all that lives, on face of sinfull earth,
Which from their first untill their utmost date
Tast no one hower of happines or merth,
But like as at the ingate of their berth,
They crying creep out of their mothers woomb,
So wailing backe go to their wofull toomb.

Why then dooth flesh, a bubble glas of breath, 50
Hunt after honour and advauncement vaine,
And reare a trophee for devouring death,
With so great labour and long lasting paine,
As if his daies for ever should remaine?
Sith all that in this world is great or gaie,
Doth as a vapour vanish, and decaie.

Looke backe, who list, unto the former ages,
And call to count, what is of them become:
Where be those learned wits and antique Sages,
Which of all wisedome knew the perfect somme: 60
Where those great warriors, which did overcomme
The world with conquest of their might and maine,
And made one meare of th' earth & of their raine?

What nowe is of th' *Assyrian* Lyonesse,
Of whom no footing now on earth appeares ?
What of the *Persian* Beares outragiousnesse,
Whose memorie is quite worne out with yeares ?
Who of the *Grecian* Libbard now ought heares,
That overran the East with greedie powre,
And left his whelps their kingdomes to devoure ? 70

And where is that same great seven headded beast,
That made all nations vassals of her pride,
To fall before her feete at her beheast,
And in the necke of all the world did ride ?
Where doth she all that wondrous welth nowe hide ?
With her owne weight downe pressed now shee lies,
And by her heaps her hugenesse testifies.

O *Rome* thy ruine I lament and rue,
And in thy fall my fatall overthrowe,
That whilom was, whilst heavens with equall
vewe 80
Deignd to behold me, and their gifts bestowe,
The picture of thy pride in pompous shew :
And of the whole world as thou wast the Empresse,
So I of this small Northerne world was Princesse.

To tell the beawtie of my buildings fayre,
Adornd with purest golde, and precious stone ;
To tell my riches, and endowments rare
That by my foes are now all spent and gone :
To tell my forces matchable to none,
Were but lost labour, that few would beleeve, 90
And with rehearsing would me more agreeve.

High towers, faire temples, goodly theaters,
Strong walls, rich porches, princelie pallaces,
Large streetes, brave houses, sacred sepulchers,
Sure gates, sweete gardens, stately galleries,
Wrought with faire pillours, and fine imageries,
All those (ô pitie) now are turnd to dust,
And overgrowen with blacke oblivions rust.

Theretoo for warlike power, and peoples store,
In *Britannie* was none to match with mee, 100
That manie often did abie full sore:
Ne *Troynouant*, though elder sister shee,
With my great forces might compared bee;
That stout *Pendragon* to his perill felt,
Who in a siege seaven yeres about me dwelt.

But long ere this *Bunduca* Britonnesse
Her mightie hoast against my bulwarkes brought,
Bunduca, that victorious conqueresse,
That lifting up her brave heroick thought
Bove womens weaknes, with the *Romanes* fought, 110
Fought, and in field against them thrice prevailed:
Yet was she foyld, when as she me assailed.

And though at last by force I conquered were
Of hardie *Saxons*, and became their thrall;
Yet was I with much bloodshed bought full deere,
And prizde with slaughter of their Generall:
The moniment of whose sad funerall,
For wonder of the world, long in me lasted;
But now to nought through spoyle of time is wasted.

Wasted it is, as if it never were, 120
And all the rest that me so honord made,
And of the world admired ev'rie where,
Is turnd to smoake, that doth to nothing fade;
And of that brightnes now appeares no shade,
But greislie shades, such as doo haunt in hell
With fearfull fiends, that in deep darknes dwell.

Where my high steeples whilom usde to stand,
On which the lordly Faulcon wont to towre,
There now is but an heap of lyme and sand,
For the Shriche-owle to build her balefull bowre: 130
And where the Nightingale wont forth to powre

Her restles plaints, to comfort wakefull Lovers,
There now haunt yelling Mewes & whining
Plovers.

And where the christall *Thamis* wont to slide
In silver channell, downe along the Lee,
About whose flowrie bankes on either side
A thousand Nymphes, with mirthfull jollitee
Were wont to play, from all annoyance free;
There now no rivers course is to be seene,
But moorish fennes, and marshes ever greene. 140

Seemes, that that gentle River for great griefe
Of my mishaps, which oft I to him plained;
Or for to shunne the horrible mischiefe,
With which he saw my cruell foes me pained,
And his pure streames with guiltles blood oft stained,
From my unhappie neighborhood farre fled,
And his sweete waters away with him led.

There also where the winged ships were seene
In liquid waves to cut their fomie waie,
And thousand Fishers numbred to have been, 150
In that wide lake looking for plenteous praie
Of fish, which they with baits usde to betraie,
Is now no lake, nor anie fishers store,
Nor ever ship shall saile there anie more.

They all are gone, and all with them is gone,
Ne ought to me remaines, but to lament
My long decay, which no man els doth mone,
And mourne my fall with dolefull dreriment.
Yet it is comfort in great languishment,
To be bemoned with compassion kinde, 160
And mitigates the anguish of the minde.

But me no man bewaileth, but in game,
Ne sheddeth teares from lamentable eie:
Nor anie lives that mentioneth my name

To be remembred of posteritie,
Save One that maugre fortunes injurie,
And times decay, and envies cruell tort,
Hath writ my record in true-seeming sort.

Cambden the nourice of antiquitie,
And lanterne unto late succeeding age, 170
To see the light of simple veritie,
Buried in ruines, through the great outrage
Of her owne people, led with warlike rage.
Cambden, though Time all moniments obscure,
Yet thy just labours ever shall endure.

But whie (unhappie wight) doo I thus crie,
And grieve that my remembrance quite is raced
Out of the knowledge of posteritie,
And all my antique moniments defaced?
Sith I doo dailie see things highest placed, 180
So soone as fates their vitall thred have shorne,
Forgotten quite as they were never borne.

It is not long, since these two eyes beheld
A mightie Prince, of most renowmed race,
Whom *England* high in count of honour held,
And greatest ones did sue to gaine his grace;
Of greatest ones he greatest in his place,
Sate in the bosome of his Soveraine,
And *Right and loyall* did his word maintaine.

I saw him die, I saw him die, as one 190
Of the meane people, and brought foorth on beare,
I saw him die, and no man left to mone
His dolefull fate, that late him loved deare:
Scarse anie left to close his eylids neare;
Scarse anie left upon his lips to laie
The sacred sod, or *Requiem* to saie.

O trustlesse state of miserable men,
That builde you blis on hope of earthly thing,

And vainly thinke your selves halfe happie then,
When painted faces with smooth flattering 200
Doo fawne on you, and your wide praises sing,
And when the courting masker louteth lowe,
Him true in heart and trustie to you trow.

All is but fained, and with oaker dide,
That everie shower will wash and wipe away,
All things doo change that under heaven abide,
And after death all friendship doth decaie.
Therefore what ever man bearst worldlie sway,
Living, on God, and on thy selfe relie;
For when thou diest, all shall with thee die. 210

He now is dead, and all is with him dead,
Save what in heavens storehouse he uplaid:
His hope is faild, and come to passe his dread,
And evill men, now dead, his deedes upbraid:
Spite bites the dead, that living never baid.
He now is gone, the whiles the Foxe is crept
Into the hole, the which the Badger swept.

He now is dead, and all his glorie gone,
And all his greatnes vapoured to nought,
That as a glasse upon the water shone, 220
Which vanisht quite, so soone as it was sought:
His name is worne alreadie out of thought,
Ne anie Poet seekes him to revive;
Yet manie Poets honourd him alive.

Ne doth his *Colin*, carelesse *Colin Cloute*,
Care now his idle bagpipe up to raise,
Ne tell his sorrow to the listning rout
Of shepherd groomes, which wont his songs to
praise:
Praise who so list, yet I will him dispraise,
Untill he quite him of this guiltie blame: 230
Wake shepheards boy, at length awake for shame.

And who so els did goodnes by him gaine,
And who so els his bounteous minde did trie,
Whether he shepheard be, or shepheards swaine,
(For manie did, which doo it now denie)
Awake, and to his Song a part applie :
And I, the whilest you mourne for his decease,
Will with my mourning plaints your plaint increase.

He dyde, and after him his brother dyde,
His brother Prince, his brother noble Peere, 240
That whilste he lived, was of none envyde,
And dead is now, as living, counted deare,
Deare unto all that true affection beare :
But unto thee most deare, ô dearest Dame,
His noble Spouse, and Paragon of fame.

He whilest he lived, happie was through thee,
And being dead is happie now much more ;
Living, that lincked chaunst with thee to bee,
And dead, because him dead thou dost adore
As living, and thy lost deare love deplore. 250
So whilst that thou, faire flower of chastitie,
Dost live, by thee thy Lord shall never die.

Thy Lord shall never die, the whiles this verse
Shall live, and surely it shall live for ever :
For ever it shall live, and shall rehearse
His worthie praise, and vertues dying never,
Though death his soule doo from his bodie sever.
And thou thy selfe herein shalt also live ;
Such grace the heavens doo to my verses give.

Ne shall his sister, ne thy father die, 260
Thy father, that good Earle of rare renowne,
And noble Patrone of weake povertie ;
Whose great good deeds in countrey and in towne
Have purchast him in heaven an happie crowne ;
Where he now liveth in eternall blis,
And left his sonne t' ensue those steps of his.

He noble bud, his Grandsires livelie hayre,
Under the shadow of thy countenaunce
Now ginnes to shoote up fast, and flourish fayre
In learned artes and goodlie gouvernaunce, 270
That him to highest honour shall advaunce.
Brave Impe of *Bedford*, grow apace in bountie,
And count of wisedome more than of thy Countie.

Ne may I let thy husbands sister die,
That goodly Ladie, sith she eke did spring
Out of this stocke, and famous familie,
Whose praises I to future age doo sing,
And foorth out of her happie womb did bring
The sacred brood of learning and all honour;
In whom the heavens powrde all their gifts upon
her. 280

Most gentle spirite breathed from above,
Out of the bosome of the makers blis,
In whom all bountie and all vertuous love
Appeared in their native propertis,
And did enrich that noble breast of his,
With treasure passing all this worldes worth,
Worthie of heaven it selfe, which brought it forth.

His blessed spirite full of power divine
And influence of all celestiall grace,
Loathing this sinfull earth and earthlie slime, 290
Fled backe too soone unto his native place,
Too soone for all that did his love embrace,
Too soone for all this wretched world, whom he
Robd of all right and true nobilitie.

Yet ere his happie soule to heaven went
Out of this fleshlie goale, he did devise
Unto his heavenlie maker to present
His bodie, as a spotles sacrifise;
And chose, that guiltie hands of enemies

Should powre forth th' offring of his guiltles blood: 300
So life exchanging for his countries good.

O noble spirite, live there ever blessed,
The worlds late wonder, and the heavens new joy,
Live ever there, and leave me here distressed
With mortall cares, and cumbrous worlds anoy.
But where thou dost that happines enjoy,
Bid me, ô bid me quicklie come to thee,
That happie there I maie thee alwaies see.

Yet whilest the fates affoord me vitall breath,
I will it spend in speaking of thy praise, 310
And sing to thee, untill that timelie death
By heavens doome doo ende my earthlie daies:
Thereto doo thou my humble spirite raise,
And into me that sacred breath inspire,
Which thou there breathest perfect and entire.

Then will I sing, but who can better sing,
Than thine owne sister, peerles Ladie bright,
Which to thee sings with deep harts sorrowing,
Sorrowing tempered with deare delight,
That her to heare I feele my feeble spright 320
Robbed of sense, and ravished with joy,
O sad joy made of mourning and anoy.

Yet will I sing, but who can better sing,
Than thou thy selfe, thine owne selfes valiance,
That whilest thou livedst, madest the forrests ring,
And fields reswownd, and flockes to leap and daunce,
And shepheards leave their lambs unto mischaunce,
To runne thy shrill *Arcadian* Pipe to heare:
O happie were those dayes, thrice happie were.

But now more happie thou, and wretched wee, 330
Which want the wonted sweetnes of thy voice,
Whiles thou now in *Elisian* fields so free,

With *Orpheus*, and with *Linus*, and the choice
Of all that ever did in rimes rejoyce,
Conversest, and doost heare their heavenlie layes,
And they heare thine, and thine doo better praise.

So there thou livest, singing evermore,
And here thou livest, being ever song
Of us, which living loved thee afore,
And now thee worship, mongst that blessed
throng 340
Of heavenlie Poets and Heroes strong.
So thou both here and there immortall art,
And everie where through excellent desart.

But such as neither of themselves can sing,
Nor yet are sung of others for reward,
Die in obscure oblivion, as the thing
Which never was, ne ever with regard
Their names shall of the later age be heard,
But shall in rustie darknes ever lie,
Unles they mentiond be with infamie. 350

What booteth it to have beene rich alive ?
What to be great ? what to be gracious ?
When after death no token doth survive,
Of former being in this mortall hous,
But sleepes in dust dead and inglorious,
Like beast, whose breath but in his nostrels is,
And hath no hope of happinesse or blis.

How manie great ones may remembred be,
Which in their daies most famouslie did florish ;
Of whome no word we heare, nor signe now
see, 360
But as things wipt out with a sponge to perishe,
Because they living, cared not to cherishe
No gentle wits, through pride or covetize,
Which might their names for ever memorize.

Provide therefore (ye Princes) whilst ye live,
That of the *Muses* ye may friended bee,
Which unto men eternitie do give;
For they be daughters of Dame memorie,
And *Jove* the father of eternitie,
And do those men in golden thrones repose, 370
Whose merits they to glorifie do chose.

The seven fold yron gates of grislie Hell,
And horrid house of sad *Proserpina*,
They able are with power of mightie spell
To breake, and thence the soules to bring awaie
Out of dread darknesse, to eternall day,
And them immortall make, which els would die
In foule forgetfulnesse, and nameles lie.

So whilome raised they the puissant brood
Of golden girt *Alcmena*, for great merite, 380
Out of the dust, to which the *Oetæan* wood
Had him consum'd, and spent his vitall spirite:
To highest heaven, where now he doth inherite
All happinesse in *Hebes* silver bowre,
Chosen to be her dearest Paramoure.

So raisde they eke faire *Ledaes* warlick twinnes,
And interchanged life unto them lent,
That when th' one dies, th' other then beginnes
To shew in Heaven his brightnes orient;
And they, for pittie of the sad wayment, 390
Which *Orpheus* for *Eurydice* did make,
Her back againe to life sent for his sake.

So happie are they, and so fortunate,
Whom the *Pierian* sacred sisters love,
That freed from bands of impacable fate,
And power of death, they live for aye above,
Where mortall wreakes their blis may not remove:
But with the Gods, for former vertues meede,
On *Nectar* and *Ambrosia* do feede.

For deeds doe die, how ever noblie donne, 400
And thoughts of men do as themselves decay,
But wise wordes taught in numbers for to runne,
Recorded by the Muses, live for ay;
Ne may with storming showers be washt away,
Ne bitter breathing windes with harmfull blast,
Nor age, nor envie shall them ever wast.

In vaine doo earthly Princes then, in vaine
Seeke with Pyramides, to heaven aspired;
Or huge Colosses, built with costlie paine;
Or brasen Pillours, never to be fired, 410
Or Shrines, made of the mettall most desired;
To make their memories for ever live:
For how can mortall immortalitie give.

Such one *Mausolus* made, the worlds great wonder,
But now no remnant doth thereof remaine:
Such one *Marcellus*, but was torne with thunder:
Such one *Lisippus*, but is worne with raine;
Such one King *Edmond*, but was rent for gaine.
All such vaine moniments of earthlie masse,
Devour'd of Time, in time to nought doo passe. 420

But fame with golden wings aloft doth flie,
Above the reach of ruinous decay,
And with brave plumes doth beate the azure skie,
Admir'd of base-borne men from farre away:
Then who so will with vertuous deeds assay
To mount to heaven, on *Pegasus* must ride,
And with sweete Poets verse be glorifide.

For not to have been dipt in *Lethe* lake,
Could save the sonne of *Thetis* from to die;
But that blinde bard did him immortall make 430
With verses, dipt in deaw of *Castalie*:
Which made the Easterne Conquerour to crie,
O fortunate yong-man, whose vertue found
So brave a Trompe, thy noble acts to sound.

Therefore in this halfe happie I doo read
Good *Melibœ,* that hath a Poet got,
To sing his living praises being dead,
Deserving never here to be forgot,
In spight of envie, that his deeds would spot:
Since whose decease, learning lies unregarded, 440
And men of armes doo wander unrewarded.

Those two be those two great calamities,
That long agoe did grieve the noble spright
Of *Salomon* with great indignities;
Who whilome was alive the wisest wight.
But now his wisedom is disprooved quite;
For he that now welds all things at his will,
Scorns th' one and th' other in his deeper skill.

O griefe of griefes, ô gall of all good heartes,
To see that vertue should dispised bee 450
Of him, that first was raisde for vertuous parts,
And now broad spreading like an aged tree,
Lets none shoot up, that nigh him planted bee:
O let the man, of whom the Muse is scorned,
Nor alive, nor dead be of the Muse adorned.

O vile worlds trust, that with such vaine illusion
Hath so wise men bewitcht, and overkest,
That they see not the way of their confusion,
O vainesse to be added to the rest,
That do my soule with inward griefe infest: 460
Let them behold the piteous fall of mee:
And in my case their owne ensample see.

And who so els that sits in highest seate
Of this worlds glorie, worshipped of all,
Ne feareth change of time, nor fortunes threate,
Let him behold the horror of my fall,
And his owne end unto remembrance call;
That of like ruine he may warned bee,
And in himselfe be moov'd to pittie mee.

Thus having ended all her piteous plaint, 470
With dolefull shrikes shee vanished away,
That I through inward sorrowe wexen faint,
And all astonished with deepe dismay,
For her departure, had no word to say :
But sate long time in sencelesse sad affright,
Looking still, if I might of her have sight.

Which when I missed, having looked long,
My thought returned greeved home againe,
Renewing her complaint with passion strong,
For ruth of that same womans piteous paine ; 480
Whose wordes recording in my troubled braine,
I felt such anguish wound my feeble heart,
That frosen horror ran through everie part.

So inlie greeving in my groning brest,
And deepelie muzing at her doubtfull speach,
Whose meaning much I labored foorth to wreste,
Being above my slender reasons reach ;
At length by demonstration me to teach,
Before mine eies strange sights presented were,
Like tragicke Pageants seeming to appeare. 490

1.

I SAW an Image, all of massie gold,
Placed on high upon an Altare faire,
That all, which did the same from farre beholde,
Might worship it, and fall on lowest staire.
Not that great Idoll might with this compaire,
To which th' *Assyrian* tyrant would have made
The holie brethren, falslie to have praid,

But th' Altare, on the which this Image staid,
Was (ô great pitie) built of brickle clay,
That shortly the foundation decaid, 500
With showres of heaven and tempests worne away,
Then downe it fell, and low in ashes lay,

Scorned of everie one, which by it went;
That I it seing, dearelie did lament.

2.

Next unto this a statelie Towre appeared,
Built all of richest stone, that might bee found,
And nigh unto the Heavens in height upreared,
But placed on a plot of sandie ground:
Not that great Towre, which is so much renownd
For tongues confusion in holie writ, 510
King *Ninus* worke might be compar'd to it.

But ô vaine labours of terrestriall wit,
That buildes so stronglie on so frayle a soyle,
As with each storme does fall away, and flit,
And gives the fruit of all your travailes toyle,
To be the pray of Tyme, and Fortunes spoyle:
I saw this Towre fall sodainlie to dust,
That nigh with griefe thereof my heart was brust.

3.

Then did I see a pleasant Paradize,
Full of sweete flowres and daintiest delights, 520
Such as on earth man could not more devize,
With pleasures choyce to feed his cheerefull sprights;
Not that, which *Merlin* by his Magicke flights
Made for the gentle squire, to entertaine
His fayre *Belphœbe*, could this gardine staine.

But ô short pleasure bought with lasting paine,
Why will hereafter anie flesh delight
In earthlie blis, and joy in pleasures vaine,
Since that I sawe this gardine wasted quite,
That where it was scarce seemed anie sight? 530
That I, which once that beautie did beholde,
Could not from teares my melting eyes with-holde.

4.

Soone after this a Giaunt came in place,
Of wondrous power, and of exceeding stature,
That none durst vewe the horror of his face,
Yet was he milde of speach, and meeke of nature.
Nor he, which in despight of his Creatour
With railing tearmes defied the Jewish hoast,
Might with this mightie one in hugenes boast.

For from the one he could to th' other coast, 540
Stretch his strong thighes, and th' Occæan overstride,
And reatch his hand into his enemies hoast.
But see the end of pompe and fleshlie pride;
One of his feete unwares from him did slide,
That downe hee fell into the deepe Abisse,
Where drownd with him is all his earthlie blisse.

5.

Then did I see a Bridge, made all of golde,
Over the Sea from one to other side,
Withouten prop or pillour it t' upholde,
But like the coulored Rainbowe arched wide: 550
Not that great Arche, which *Trajan* edifide,
To be a wonder to all age ensuing,
Was matchable to this in equall vewing.

But (ah) what bootes it to see earthlie thing
In glorie, or in greatnes to excell,
Sith time doth greatest things to ruine bring?
This goodlie bridge, one foote not fastned well,
Gan faile, and all the rest downe shortlie fell,
Ne of so brave a building ought remained,
That griefe thereof my spirite greatly pained. 560

6.

I saw two Beares, as white as anie milke,
Lying together in a mightie cave,

Of milde aspect, and haire as soft as silke,
That salvage nature seemed not to have,
Nor after greedie spoyle of blood to crave:
Two fairer beasts might not elswhere be found,
Although the compast world were sought around.

But what can long abide above this ground
In state of blis, or stedfast happinesse?
The Cave, in which these Beares lay sleeping sound, 570
Was but earth, and with her owne weightinesse
Upon them fell, and did unwares oppresse,
That for great sorrow of their sudden fate,
Henceforth all worlds felicitie I hate.

¶ Much was I troubled in my heavie spright,
At sight of these sad spectacles forepast,
That all my senses were bereaved quight,
And I in minde remained sore agast,
Distraught twixt feare and pitie; when at last
I heard a voyce, which loudly to me called, 580
That with the suddein shrill I was appalled.

Behold (said it) and by ensample see,
That all is vanitie and griefe of minde,
Ne other comfort in this world can be,
But hope of heaven, and heart to God inclinde;
For all the rest must needs be left behinde:
With that it bad me, to the other side
To cast mine eye, where other sights I spide!

1.

¶ UPON that famous Rivers further shore,
There stood a snowie Swan of heavenly hiew, 590
And gentle kinde, as ever Fowle afore;
A fairer one in all the goodlie criew
Of white *Strimonian* brood might no man view:
There he most sweetly sung the prophecie
Of his owne death in dolefull Elegie.

At last, when all his mourning melodie
He ended had, that both the shores resounded,
Feeling the fit that him forewarnd to die,
With loftie flight above the earth he bounded,
And out of sight to highest heaven mounted: 600
Where now he is become an heavenly signe;
There now the joy is his, here sorrow mine.

2.

Whilest thus I looked, loe adowne the *Lee*,
I saw an Harpe stroong all with silver twyne,
And made of golde and costlie yvorie,
Swimming, that whilome seemed to have been
The harpe, on which *Dan Orpheus* was seene
Wylde beasts and forrests after him to lead,
But was th' Harpe of *Philisides* now dead.

At length out of the River it was reard 610
And borne above the cloudes to be divin'd,
Whilst all the way most heavenly noyse was heard
Of the strings, stirred with the warbling wind,
That wrought both joy and sorrow in my mind:
So now in heaven a signe it doth appeare,
The Harpe well knowne beside the Northern Beare.

3.

Soone after this I saw on th' other side,
A curious Coffer made of *Heben* wood,
That in it did most precious treasure hide,
Exceeding all this baser worldes good: 620
Yet through the overflowing of the flood
It almost drowned was, and done to nought,
That sight thereof much griev'd my pensive thought.

At length when most in perill it was brought,
Two Angels downe descending with swift flight,
Out of the swelling streame it lightly caught,

And twixt their blessed armes it carried quight
Above the reach of anie living sight:
So now it is transform'd into that starre,
In which all heavenly treasures locked are. 630

4.

Looking aside I saw a stately Bed,
Adorned all with costly cloth of gold,
That might for anie Princes couche be red,
And deckt with daintie flowres, as if it shold
Be for some bride, her joyous night to hold:
Therein a goodly Virgine sleeping lay;
A fairer wight saw never summers day.

I heard a voyce that called farre away
And her awaking bad her quickly dight,
For lo her Bridegrome was in readie ray 640
To come to her, and seeke her loves delight:
With that she started up with cherefull sight,
When suddeinly both bed and all was gone,
And I in languor left there all alone.

5.

Still as I gazed, I beheld where stood
A Knight all arm'd, upon a winged steed,
The same that was bred of *Medusaes* blood,
On which *Dan Perseus* borne of heavenly seed,
The faire *Andromeda* from perill freed:
Full mortally this Knight ywounded was, 650
That streames of blood foorth flowed on the gras.

Yet was he deckt (small joy to him alas)
With manie garlands for his victories,
And with rich spoyles, which late he did purchas
Through brave atcheivements from his enemies:
Fainting at last through long infirmities,
He smote his steed, that straight to heaven him bore,
And left me here his losse for to deplore.

6.

Lastly I saw an Arke of purest golde
Upon a brazen pillour standing hie, 660
Which th' ashes seem'd of some great Prince to hold,
Enclosde therein for endles memorie
Of him, whom all the world did glorifie:
Seemed the heavens with the earth did disagree,
Whether should of those ashes keeper bee.

At last me seem'd wing footed *Mercurie*,
From heaven descending to appease their strife,
The Arke did beare with him above the skie,
And to those ashes gave a second life,
To live in heaven, where happines is rife: 670
At which the earth did grieve exceedingly,
And I for dole was almost like to die.

L: Envoy.

Immortall spirite of *Philisides*,
Which now art made the heavens ornament,
That whilome wast the worlds chiefst riches;
Give leave to him that lov'de thee to lament
His losse, by lacke of thee to heaven hent,
And with last duties of this broken verse,
Broken with sighes, to decke thy sable Herse.

And ye faire Ladie th' honor of your daies, 680
And glorie of the world, your high thoughts scorne;
Vouchsafe this moniment of his last praise,
With some few silver dropping teares t' adorne:
And as ye be of heavenlie off-spring borne,
So unto heaven let your high minde aspire,
And loath this drosse of sinfull worlds desire.

FINIS.

THE TEARES OF THE MUSES.

TO THE RIGHT HONORABLE

THE LADY STRANGE.

MOST brave and noble Ladie, the things that make ye so much honored of the world as ye bee, are such, as (without my simple lines testimonie) are throughlie knowen to all men; namely, your excellent beautie, your vertuous behavior, & your noble match with that most honourable Lord the verie Paterne of right Nobilitie: But the causes for which ye have thus deserved of me to be honoured (if honour it be at all) are, both your particular bounties, and also some private bands of affinitie, which it hath pleased your Ladiship to acknowledge. Of which whenas I found my selfe in no part worthie, I devised this last slender meanes, both to intimate my humble affection to your Ladiship and also to make the same universallie knowen to the world; that by honouring you they might know me, and by knowing me they might honor you. Vouchsafe noble Lady to accept this simple remembrance, thogh not worthy of your self, yet such, as perhaps by good acceptance thereof, ye may hereafter cull out a more meet & memorable evidence of your own excellent deserts. So recommending the same to your Ladiships good liking, I humbly take leave.

Your La: humbly ever,

Ed. Sp.

THE TEARES OF THE MUSES.

REHEARSE to me ye sacred Sisters nine:
The golden brood of great *Apolloes* wit,
Those piteous plaints and sorrowful sad tine,
Which late ye powred forth as ye did sit
Beside the silver Springs of *Helicone*,
Making your musick of hart-breaking mone.

For since the time that *Phœbus* foolish sonne
Ythundered through *Joves* avengefull wrath,
For traversing the charret of the Sunne
Beyond the compasse of his pointed path, 10
Of you his mournfull Sisters was lamented,
Such mournfull tunes were never since invented

Nor since that faire *Calliope* did lose
Her loved Twinnes, the dearlings of her joy,
Her *Palici*, whom her unkindly foes
The fatall Sisters, did for spight destroy,
Whom all the Muses did bewaile long space;
Was ever heard such wayling in this place.

For all their groves, which with the heavenly noyses
Of their sweete instruments were wont to
sound, 20
And th' hollow hills, from which their silver voyces
Were wont redoubled Echoes to rebound,
Did now rebound with nought but rufull cries,
And yelling shrieks throwne up into the skies.

The trembling streames which wont in chanels
cleare
To romble gently downe with murmur soft,
And were by them right tunefull taught to beare

A Bases part amongst their consorts oft;
Now forst to overflowe with brackish teares,
With troublous noyse did dull their daintie
eares. 30

The joyous Nymphes and lightfoote Faeries
Which thether came to heare their musick sweet,
And to the measure of their melodies
Did learne to move their nimble shifting feete;
Now hearing them so heavily lament,
Like heavily lamenting from them went.

And all that els was wont to worke delight
Through the divine infusion of their skill,
And all that els seemd faire and fresh in sight,
So made by nature for to serve their will, 40
Was turned now to dismall heavinesse,
Was turned now to dreadfull uglinesse.

Ay me, what thing on earth that all thing breeds,
Might be the cause of so impatient plight?
What furie, or what feend with felon deeds
Hath stirred up so mischievous despight?
Can griefe then enter into heavenly harts,
And pierce immortall breasts with mortall smarts?

Vouchsafe ye then, whom onely it concernes,
To me those secret causes to display; 50
For none but you, or who of you it learnes
Can rightfully aread so dolefull lay.
Begin thou eldest Sister of the crew,
And let the rest in order thee ensew.

Clio.

HEARE thou great Father of the Gods on hie
That most art dreaded for thy thunder darts:
And thou our Syre that raignst in *Castalie*
And mount *Parnasse*, the God of goodly Arts:

Heare and behold the miserable state
Of us thy daughters, dolefull desolate. 60

Behold the fowle reproach and open shame,
The which is day by day unto us wrought
By such as hate the honour of our name,
The foes of learning, and each gentle thought;
They not contented us themselves to scorne,
Doo seeke to make us of the world forlorne.

Ne onely they that dwell in lowly dust,
The sonnes of darknes and of ignoraunce;
But they, whom thou great *Jove* by doome unjust
Didst to the type of honour earst advaunce; 70
They now puft up with sdeignfull insolence,
Despise the brood of blessed Sapience.

The sectaries of my celestiall skill,
That wont to be the worlds chiefe ornament,
And learned Impes that wont to shoote up still,
And grow to hight of kingdomes government
They underkeep, and with their spredding armes
Do beat their buds, that perish through their harmes.

It most behoves the honorable race
Of mightie Peeres, true wisedome to sustaine, 80
And with their noble countenaunce to grace
The learned forheads, without gifts or gaine:
Or rather learnd themselves behoves to bee;
That is the girlond of Nobilitie.

But (ah) all otherwise they doo esteeme
Of th' heavenly gift of wisdomes influence,
And to be learned it a base thing deeme;
Base minded they that want intelligence:
For God himselfe for wisedome most is praised,
And men to God thereby are nighest raised. 90

But they doo onely strive themselves to raise
Through pompous pride, and foolish vanitie;
In th' eyes of people they put all their praise,
And onely boast of Armes and Auncestrie:
But vertuous deeds, which did those Armes first give
To their Grandsyres, they care not to atchive.

So I, that doo all noble feates professe
To register, and sound in trump of gold;
Through their bad dooings, or base slothfulnesse,
Finde nothing worthie to be writ, or told: 100
For better farre it were to hide their names,
Than telling them to blazon out their blames.

So shall succeeding ages have no light
Of things forepast, nor moniments of time,
And all that in this world is worthie hight
Shall die in darknesse, and lie hid in slime:
Therefore I mourne with deep harts sorrowing,
Because I nothing noble have to sing.

With that she raynd such store of streaming teares,
That could have made a stonie heart to weep, 110
And all her Sisters rent their golden heares,
And their faire faces with salt humour steep.
So ended shee: and then the next anew,
Began her grievous plaint as doth ensew.

Melpomene.

O WHO shall powre into my swollen eyes
A sea of teares that never may be dryde,
A brasen voice that may with shrilling cryes
Pierce the dull heavens and fill the ayer wide,
And yron sides that sighing may endure,
To waile the wretchednes of world impure? 120

Ah wretched world the den of wickednesse,
Deformd with filth and fowle iniquitie;

Ah wretched world the house of heavinesse,
Fild with the wreaks of mortall miserie ;
Ah wretched world, and all that is therein
The vassals of Gods wrath, and slaves of sin.

Most miserable creature under sky
Man without understanding doth appeare ;
For all this worlds affliction he thereby,
And Fortunes freakes is wisely taught to beare : 130
Of wretched life the onely joy shee is,
And th' only comfort in calamities.

She armes the brest with constant patience,
Against the bitter throwes of dolours darts,
She solaceth with rules of Sapience
The gentle minds, in midst of worldlie smarts :
When he is sad, shee seeks to make him merie,
And doth refresh his sprights when they be werie.

But he that is of reasons skill bereft,
And wants the staffe of wisedome him to stay, 140
Is like a ship in midst of tempest left
Withouten helme or Pilot her to sway,
Full sad and dreadfull is that ships event :
So is the man that wants intendiment.

Whie then doo foolish men so much despize
The precious store of this celestiall riches ?
Why doo they banish us, that patronize
The name of learning ? Most unhappie wretches,
The which lie drowned in deep wretchednes,
Yet doo not see their owne unhappines. 150

My part it is and my professed skill
The Stage with Tragick buskin to adorne,
And fill the Scene with plaint and outcries shrill
Of wretched persons, to misfortune borne :
But none more tragick matter I can finde
Then this, of men depriv'd of sense and minde.

For all mans life me seemes a Tragedy,
Full of sad sights and sore Catastrophees;
First comming to the world with weeping eye,
Where all his dayes like dolorous Trophees, 160
Are heapt with spoyles of fortune and of feare,
And he at last laid forth on balefull beare.

So all with rufull spectacles is fild
Fit for *Megera* or *Persephone*;
But I that in true Tragedies am skild,
The flowre of wit, finde nought to busie me:
Therefore I mourne, and pitifully mone,
Because that mourning matter I have none.

Then gan she wofully to waile, and wring
Her wretched hands in lamentable wise; 170
And all her Sisters thereto answering,
Threw forth lowd shrieks and drerie dolefull cries.
So rested she: and then the next in rew,
Began her grievous plaint as doth ensew.

Thalia.

WHERE be the sweete delights of learnings treasure,
That wont with Comick sock to beautefie
The painted Theaters, and fill with pleasure
The listners eyes, and eares with melodie;
In which I late was wont to raine as Queene,
And maske in mirth with Graces well beseene? 180

O all is gone, and all that goodly glee,
Which wont to be the glorie of gay wits,
Is layd abed, and no where now to see;
And in her roome unseemly Sorrow sits,
With hollow browes and greisly countenaunce,
Marring my joyous gentle dalliaunce.

And him beside sits ugly Barbarisme,
And brutish Ignorance, ycrept of late

Out of dredd darknes of the deepe Abysme,
Where being bredd, he light and heaven does
hate: 190
They in the mindes of men now tyrannize,
And the faire Scene with rudenes foule disguize.

All places they with follie have possest,
And with vaine toyes the vulgare entertaine;
But me have banished, with all the rest
That whilome wont to wait upon my traine,
Fine Counterfesaunce and unhurtfull Sport,
Delight and Laughter deckt in seemly sort.

All these, and all that els the Comick Stage
With seasoned wit and goodly pleasance graced;
200
By which mans life in his likest image
Was limned forth, are wholly now defaced;
And those sweete wits which wont the like to
frame,
Are now despizd, and made a laughing game.

And he the man, whom Nature selfe had made
To mock her selfe, and Truth to imitate,
With kindly counter under Mimick shade,
Our pleasant *Willy*, ah is dead of late:
With whom all joy and jolly meriment
Is also deaded, and in dolour drent. 210

In stead thereof scoffing Scurrilitie,
And scornfull Follie with Contempt is crept,
Rolling in rymes of shameles ribaudrie
Without regard, or due Decorum kept,
Each idle wit at will presumes to make,
And doth the Learneds taske upon him take.

But that same gentle Spirit, from whose pen
Large streames of honnie and sweete Nectar flowe,
Scorning the boldnes of such base-borne men,

Which dare their follies forth so rashlie throwe; 220
Doth rather choose to sit in idle Cell,
Than so himselfe to mockerie to sell.

So am I made the servant of the manie,
And laughing stocke of all that list to scorne,
Not honored nor cared for of anie;
But loath'd of losels as a thing forlorne:
Therefore I mourne and sorrow with the rest,
Untill my cause of sorrow be redrest.

Therewith she lowdly did lament and shrike,
Pouring forth streames of teares abundantly, 230
And all her Sisters with compassion like,
The breaches of her singulfs did supply.
So rested she: and then the next in rew
Began her grievous plaint, as doth ensew.

Euterpe.

LIKE as the dearling of the Summers pryde,
Faire *Philomele*, when winters stormie wrath
The goodly fields, that earst so gay were dyde
In colours divers, quite despoyled hath,
All comfortlesse doth hide her chearlesse head
During the time of that her widowhead: 240

So we, that earst were wont in sweet accord
All places with our pleasant notes to fill,
Whilest favourable times did us afford
Free libertie to chaunt our charmes at will:
All comfortlesse upon the bared bow,
Like wofull Culvers doo sit wayling now.

For far more bitter storme than winters stowre
The beautie of the world hath lately wasted,
And those fresh buds, which wont so faire to flowre,

Hath marred quite, and all their blossoms blasted: 250
And those yong plants, which wont with fruit t' abound,
Now without fruite or leaves are to be found.

A stonie coldnesse hath benumbd the sence
And livelie spirits of each living wight,
And dimd with darknesse their intelligence,
Darknesse more than *Cymerians* daylie night!
And monstrous error flying in the ayre,
Hath mard the face of all that semed fayre.

Image of hellish horrour Ignorance,
Borne in the bosome of the black *Abysse*, 260
And fed with furies milke, for sustenaunce
Of his weake infancie, begot amisse
By yawning Sloth on his owne mother Night;
So hee his sonnes both Syre and brother hight.

He armd with blindnesse and with boldnes stout,
(For blind is bold) hath our fayre light defaced;
And gathering unto him a ragged rout
Of *Faunes* and *Satyres*, hath our dwellings raced
And our chast bowers, in which all vertue rained,
With brutishnesse and beastlie filth hath stained. 270

The sacred springs of horsefoot *Helicon*,
So oft bedeawed with our learned layes,
And speaking streames of pure *Castalion*,
The famous witnesse of our wonted praise,
They trampled have with their fowle footings trade,
And like to troubled puddles have them made.

Our pleasant groves, which planted were with paines,
That with our musick wont so oft to ring,
And arbors sweet, in which the Shepheards swaines
Were wont so oft their Pastoralls to sing, 280

They have cut downe and all their pleasaunce mard,
That now no pastorall is to bee hard.

In stead of them fowle Goblins and Shriekowles,
With fearfull howling do all places fill;
And feeble *Eccho* now laments and howles,
The dreadfull accents of their outcries shrill.
So all is turned into wildernesse,
Whilest Ignorance the Muses doth oppresse.

And I whose joy was earst with Spirit full
To teach the warbling pipe to sound aloft, 290
My spirits now dismayd with sorrow dull,
Doo mone my miserie with silence soft.
Therefore I mourne and waile incessantly,
Till please the heavens affoord me remedy.

Therewith shee wayled with exceeding woe
And pitious lamentation did make,
And all her Sisters seeing her doo soe,
With equall plaints her sorrowe did partake.
So rested shee : and then the next in rew,
Began her grievous plaint as doth ensew. 300

Terpsichore.

WHO so hath in the lap of soft delight
Beene long time luld, and fed with pleasures sweet,
Feareles through his own fault or Fortunes spight,
To tumble into sorrow and regreet,
Yf chaunce him fall into calamitie,
Finds greater burthen of his miserie.

So wee that earst in joyance did abound
And in the bosome of all blis did sit,
Like virgin Queenes with laurell garlands cround,
For vertues meed and ornament of wit, 310
Sith ignorance our kingdome did confound,
Bee now become most wretched wightes on ground :

And in our royall thrones which lately stood
In th' hearts of men to rule them carefully,
He now hath placed his accursed brood,
By him begotten of fowle infamy;
Blind Error, scornefull Follie, and base Spight,
Who hold by wrong, that wee should have by right.

They to the vulgar sort now pipe and sing,
And make them merrie with their fooleries, 320
They cherelie chaunt and rymes at randon fling,
The fruitfull spawne of their ranke fantasies:
They feede the eares of fooles with flattery,
And good men blame, and losels magnify:

All places they doo with their toyes possesse,
And raigne in liking of the multitude,
The schooles they fill with fond new fanglenesse,
And sway in Court with pride and rashnes rude;
Mongst simple shepheards they do boast their skill,
And say their musicke matcheth *Phœbus* quill. 330

The noble hearts to pleasures they allure,
And tell their Prince that learning is but vaine,
Faire Ladies loves they spot with thoughts impure,
And gentle mindes with lewd delights distaine:
Clerks they to loathly idlenes entice,
And fill their bookes with discipline of vice.

So every where they rule and tyrannize,
For their usurped kingdomes maintenaunce,
The whiles we silly Maides, whom they dispize,
And with reprochfull scorne discountenance, 340
From our owne native heritage exilde,
Walk through the world of every one revilde.

Nor anie one doth care to call us in,
Or once vouchsafeth us to entertaine,
Unlesse some one perhaps of gentle kin,
For pitties sake compassion our paine,

And yeeld us some reliefe in this distresse,
Yet to be so reliev'd is wretchednesse.

So wander we all carefull comfortlesse,
Yet none doth care to comfort us at all; 350
So seeke we helpe our sorrow to redresse,
Yet none vouchsafes to answere to our call:
Therefore we mourne and pittilesse complaine,
Because none living pittieth our paine.

With that she wept and wofullie waymented,
That naught on earth her griefe might pacifie;
And all the rest her dolefull din augmented,
With shrikes and groanes and grievous agonie.
So ended shee: and then the next in rew,
Began her piteous plaint as doth ensew. 360

Erato.

YE gentle Spirits breathing from above,
Where ye in *Venus* silver bowre were bred,
Thoughts halfe devine full of the fire of love,
With beawtie kindled and with pleasure fed,
Which ye now in securitie possesse,
Forgetfull of your former heavinesse:

Now change the tenor of your joyous layes,
With which ye use your loves to deifie,
And blazon foorth an earthlie beauties praise,
Above the compasse of the arched skie: 370
Now change your praises into piteous cries,
And Eulogies turne into Elegies.

Such as ye wont whenas those bitter stounds
Of raging love first gan you to torment,
And launch your hearts with lamentable wounds
Of secret sorrow and sad languishment,
Before your Loves did take you unto grace;
Those now renew as fitter for this place.

For I that rule in measure moderate
The tempest of that stormie passion, 380
And use to paint in rimes the troublous state
Of Lovers life in likest fashion,
Am put from practise of my kindlie skill,
Banisht by those that Love with leawdnes fill.

Love wont to be schoolmaster of my skill,
And the devicefull matter of my song;
Sweete Love devoyd of villanie or ill,
But pure and spotles, as at first he sprong
Out of th' Almighties bosome, where he nests;
From thence infused into mortall brests. 390

Such high conceipt of that celestiall fire,
The base-borne brood of blindnes cannot gesse,
Ne ever dare their dunghill thoughts aspire
Unto so loftie pitch of perfectnesse,
But rime at riot, and doo rage in love;
Yet little wote what doth thereto behove.

Faire *Cytheree* the Mother of delight,
And Queene of beautie, now thou maist go pack;
For lo thy Kingdome is defaced quight,
Thy scepter rent, and power put to wrack; 400
And thy gay Sonne, that winged God of Love,
May now goe prune his plumes like ruffed Dove.

And ye three Twins to light by *Venus* brought,
The sweete companions of the Muses late,
From whom what ever thing is goodly thought
Doth borrow grace, the fancie to aggrate;
Go beg with us, and be companions still
As heretofore of good, so now of ill.

For neither you nor we shall anie more
Find entertainment, or in Court or Schoole: 410
For that which was accounted heretofore
The learneds meed, is now lent to the foole,

He sings of love, and maketh loving layes,
And they him heare, and they him highly prayse.

With that she powred foorth a brackish flood
Of bitter teares, and made exceeding mone;
And all her Sisters seeing her sad mood,
With lowd laments her answered all at one.
So ended she: and then the next in rew
Began her grievous plaint, as doth ensew. 420

Calliope.

To whom shall I my evill case complaine,
Or tell the anguish of my inward smart,
Sith none is left to remedie my paine,
Or deignes to pitie a perplexed hart;
But rather seekes my sorrow to augment
With fowle reproach, and cruell banishment.

For they to whom I used to applie
The faithfull service of my learned skill,
The goodly off-spring of *Joves* progenie,
That wont the world with famous acts to fill; 430
Whose living praises in heroïck style,
It is my chiefe profession to compyle.

They all corrupted through the rust of time,
That doth all fairest things on earth deface,
Or through unnoble sloth, or sinfull crime,
That doth degenerate the noble race;
Have both desire of worthie deeds forlorne,
And name of learning utterly doo scorne.

Ne doo they care to have the auncestrie
Of th' old Heroës memorizde anew, 440
Ne doo they care that late posteritie
Should know their names, or speak their praises dew:
But die forgot from whence at first they sprong,
As they themselves shalbe forgot ere long.

What bootes it then to come from glorious
Forefathers, or to have been nobly bredd?
What oddes twixt *Irus* and old *Inachus*,
Twixt best and worst, when both alike are dedd;
If none of neither mention should make,
Nor out of dust their memories awake? 450

Or who would ever care to doo brave deed,
Or strive in vertue others to excell;
If none should yeeld him his deserved meed,
Due praise, that is the spur of dooing well?
For if good were not praised more than ill,
None would choose goodnes of his owne freewill.

Therefore the nurse of vertue I am hight,
And golden Trompet of eternitie,
That lowly thoughts lift up to heavens hight,
And mortall men have powre to deifie: 460
Bacchus and *Hercules* I raisd to heaven,
And *Charlemaine*, amongst the Starris seaven.

But now I will my golden Clarion rend,
And will henceforth immortalize no more:
Sith I no more find worthie to commend
For prize of value, or for learned lore:
For noble Peeres whom I was wont to raise,
Now onely seeke for pleasure, nought for praise.

Their great revenues all in sumptuous pride
They spend, that nought to learning they may
spare; 470
And the rich fee which Poets wont divide,
Now Parasites and Sycophants doo share:
Therefore I mourne and endlesse sorrow make,
Both for my selfe and for my Sisters sake.

With that she lowdly gan to waile and shrike,
And from her eyes a sea of teares did powre,
And all her sisters with compassion like,

Did more increase the sharpnes of her showre.
So ended she: and then the next in rew
Began her plaint, as doth herein ensew. 480

Urania.

WHAT wrath of Gods, or wicked influence
Of Starres conspiring wretched men t' afflict,
Hath powrd on earth this noyous pestilence,
That mortall mindes doth inwardly infect
With love of blindnesse and of ignorance,
To dwell in darkenesse without sovenance?

What difference twixt man and beast is left,
When th' heavenlie light of knowledge is put out,
And th' ornaments of wisdome are bereft?
Then wandreth he in error and in doubt, 490
Unweeting of the danger hee is in,
Through fleshes frailtie and deceipt of sin.

In this wide world in which they wretches stray,
It is the onelie comfort which they have,
It is their light, their loadstarre and their day;
But hell and darkenesse and the grislie grave
Is ignorance, the enemie of grace,
That mindes of men borne heavenlie doth debace.

Through knowledge we behold the worlds creation,
How in his cradle first he fostred was; 500
And judge of Natures cunning operation,
How things she formed of a formelesse mas:
By knowledge wee doo learne our selves to knowe,
And what to man, and what to God wee owe.

From hence wee mount aloft unto the skie,
And looke into the Christall firmament,
There we behold the heavens great *Hierarchie*,
The Starres pure light, the Spheres swift movement,
The Spirites and Intelligences fayre,

And Angels waighting on th' Almighties chayre. 510

And there with humble minde and high insight,
Th' eternall Makers majestie wee viewe,
His love, his truth, his glorie, and his might,
And mercie more than mortall men can vew.
O soveraigne Lord, ô soveraigne happinesse
To see thee, and thy mercie measurelesse :

Such happines have they, that do embrace
The precepts of my heavenlie discipline ;
But shame and sorrow and accursed case
Have they, that scorne the schoole of arts divine, 520
And banish me, which do professe the skill
To make men heavenly wise, through humbled will.

How ever yet they mee despise and spight,
I feede on sweet contentment of my thought,
And please my selfe with mine owne selfe-delight,
In contemplation of things heavenlie wrought :
So loathing earth, I looke up to the sky,
And being driven hence I thether fly.

Thence I behold the miserie of men,
Which want the blis that wisedom would them breed, 530
And like brute beasts doo lie in loathsome den,
Of ghostly darkenes, and of gastlie dreed :
For whom I mourne and for my selfe complaine,
And for my Sisters eake whom they disdaine.

With that shee wept and waild so pityouslie,
As if her eyes had beene two springing wells :
And all the rest her sorrow to supplie,
Did throw forth shrieks and cries and dreery yells.
So ended shee, and then the next in rew,
Began her mournfull plaint as doth ensew. 540

Polyhymnia.

A DOLEFULL case desires a dolefull song,
Without vaine art or curious complements,
And squallid Fortune into basenes flong,
Doth scorne the pride of wonted ornaments.
Then fittest are these ragged rimes for mee,
To tell my sorrowes that exceeding bee:

For the sweet numbers and melodious measures,
With which I wont the winged words to tie,
And make a tunefull Diapase of pleasures,
Now being let to runne at libertie 550
By those which have no skill to rule them right,
Have now quite lost their naturall delight.

Heapes of huge words uphoorded hideously,
With horrid sound though having little sence,
They thinke to be chiefe praise of Poëtry;
And thereby wanting due intelligence,
Have mard the face of goodly Poësie,
And made a monster of their fantasie:

Whilom in ages past none might professe
But Princes and high Priests that secret skill, 560
The sacred lawes therein they wont expresse,
And with deepe Oracles their verses fill:
Then was shee held in soveraigne dignitie,
And made the noursling of Nobilitie.

But now nor Prince nor Priest doth her maintayne,
But suffer her prophaned for to bee
Of the base vulgar, that with hands uncleane
Dares to pollute her hidden mysterie.
And treadeth under foote hir holie things,
Which was the care of Kesars and of Kings. 570

One onelie lives, her ages ornament,
And myrrour of her Makers majestie;

That with rich bountie and deare cherishment,
Supports the praise of noble Poësie:
Ne onelie favours them which it professe,
But is herselfe a peereles Poëtresse.

Most peereles Prince, most peereles Poëtresse,
The true *Pandora* of all heavenly graces,
Divine *Elisa*, sacred Emperesse:
Live she for ever, and her royall P'laces 580
Be fild with praises of divinest wits,
That her eternize with their heavenlie writs.

Some few beside, this sacred skill esteme,
Admirers of her glorious excellence,
Which being lightned with her beawties beme,
Are thereby fild with happie influence:
And lifted up above the worldes gaze,
To sing with Angels her immortall praize.

But all the rest as borne of salvage brood,
And having beene with Acorns alwaies fed; 590
Can no whit favour this celestiall food,
But with base thoughts are into blindnesse led,
And kept from looking on the lightsome day:
For whome I waile and weepe all that I may.

Eftsoones such store of teares shee forth did powre,
As if shee all to water would have gone;
And all her sisters seeing her sad stowre,
Did weep and waile and made exceeding mone,
And all their learned instrument did breake:
The rest untold no loving tongue can speake.

FINIS.

VIRGILS GNAT.

VIRGILS GNAT.

LONG SINCE DEDICATED

TO THE MOST NOBLE AND EXCELLENT LORD,

THE EARLE OF LEICESTER, late deceased.

WRONG'D, yet not daring to expresse my paine,
To you (great Lord) the causer of my care,
In clowdie teares my case I thus complaine
Unto yourselfe, that onely privie are :
But if that any Oedipus *unware*
Shall chaunce, through power of some divining spright,
To reade the secrete of this riddle rare,
And know the purporte of my evill plight,
Let him rest pleased with his owne insight,
Ne further seeke to glose upon the text :
For griefe enough it is to grieved wight
To feele his fault, and not be further vext.
But what so by my selfe may not be showen,
May by this Gnatts complaint be easily knowen.

VIRGILS GNAT.

WE now have playde (*Augustus*) wantonly,
Tuning our song unto a tender Muse,
And like a cobweb weaving slenderly,
Have onely playde : let thus much then excuse
This Gnats small Poeme, that th' whole history
Is but a jest, though envie it abuse :
But who such sports and sweet delights doth blame,
Shall lighter seeme than this Gnats idle name.

Hereafter, when as season more secure
Shall bring forth fruit, this Muse shall speak to
thee 10
In bigger notes, that may thy sense allure,
And for thy worth frame some fit Poesie,
The golden offspring of *Latona* pure,
And ornament of great *Joves* progenie,
Phœbus shall be the author of my song,
Playing on ivorie harp with silver strong.

He shall inspire my verse with gentle mood
Of Poets Prince, whether he woon beside
Faire *Xanthus* sprincled with *Chimæras* blood ;
Or in the woods of *Astery* abide ; 20
Or whereas mount *Parnasse*, the Muses brood,
Doth his broad forhead like two hornes divide,
And the sweete waves of sounding *Castaly*
With liquid foote doth slide downe easily.

Wherefore ye Sisters which the glorie bee
Of the *Pierian* streames, fayre *Naiades*,
Go too, and dauncing all in companie,
Adorne that God : and thou holie *Pales*,
To whome the honest care of husbandrie

Returneth by continuall successe, 30
Have care for to pursue his footing light;
Throgh the wide woods, & groves, with green leaves
dight.

Professing thee I lifted am aloft
Betwixt the forrest wide and starrie sky:
And thou most dread (*Octavius*) which oft
To learned wits givest courage worthily,
O come (thou sacred childe) come sliding soft,
And favour my beginnings graciously:
For not these leaves do sing that dreadfull stound,
When Giants bloud did staine *Phlegræan*
ground. 40

Nor how th' halfe horsy people, *Centaures* hight,
Fought with the bloudie *Lapithaes* at bord,
Nor how the East with tyranous despight
Burnt th' *Attick* towres, and people slew with sword;
Nor how mount *Athos* through exceeding might
Was digged downe, nor yron bands abord
The *Pontick* sea by their huge Navy cast,
My volume shall renowne, so long since past.

Nor *Hellespont* trampled with horses feete,
When flocking *Persians* did the *Greeks* affray; 50
But my soft Muse, as for her power more meete,
Delights (with *Phœbus* friendly leave) to play
An easie running verse with tender feete.
And thou (dread sacred child) to thee alway,
Let everlasting lightsome glory strive,
Through the worlds endles ages to survive.

And let an happie roome remaine for thee
Mongst heavenly ranks, where blessed soules do rest;
And let long lasting life with joyous glee,
As thy due meede that thou deservest best, 60
Hereafter many yeares remembred be
Amongst good men, of whom thou oft are blest;

Live thou for ever in all happinesse :
But let us turne to our first businesse.

The fiery Sun was mounted now on hight
Up to the heavenly towers, and shot each where
Out of his golden Charet glistering light ;
And fayre *Aurora* with her rosie heare,
The hatefull darknes now had put to flight,
When as the shepheard seeing day appeare, 70
His little Goats gan drive out of their stalls,
To feede abroad, where pasture best befalls.

To an high mountaines top he with them went,
Where thickest grasse did cloath the open hills :
They now amongst the woods and thickets ment,
Now in the valleies wandring at their wills,
Spread themselves farre abroad through each descent ;
Some on the soft greene grasse feeding their fills ;
Some clambring through the hollow cliffes on hy,
Nibble the bushie shrubs, which growe thereby. 80

Others the utmost boughs of trees doe crop,
And brouze the woodbine twigges, that freshly bud
This with full bit doth catch the utmost top
Of some soft Willow, or new growen stud ;
This with sharpe teeth the bramble leaves doth lop,
And chaw the tender prickles in her Cud ;
The whiles another high doth overlooke
Her owne like image in a christall brooke.

O the great happines, which shepheards have,
Who so loathes not too much the poor estate, 90
With minde that ill use doth before deprave,
Ne measures all things by the costly rate
Of riotise, and semblants outward brave ;
No such sad cares, as wont to macerate
And rend the greedie mindes of covetous men,
Do ever creepe into the shepheards den.

Ne cares he if the fleece, which him arayes,
Be not twice steeped in Assyrian dye,
Ne glistering of golde, which underlayes
The summer beames, doe blinde his gazing eye. 100
Ne pictures beautie, nor the glauncing rayes
Of precious stones, whence no good commeth by;
Ne yet his cup embost with Imagery
Of *Bætus* or of *Alcons* vanity.

Ne ought the whelky pearles esteemeth hee,
Which are from Indian seas brought far away:
But with pure brest from carefull sorrow free,
On the soft grasse his limbs doth oft display,
In sweete spring time, when flowres varietie
With sundrie colours paints the sprincled lay; 110
There lying all at ease, from guile or spight,
With pype of fennie reedes doth him delight.

There he, Lord of himselfe, with palme bedight,
His looser locks doth wrap in wreath of vine:
There his milk dropping Goats be his delight,
And fruitefull *Pales*, and the forrest greene,
And darkesome caves in pleasaunt vallies pight,
Wheras continuall shade is to be seene,
And where fresh springing wells, as christall neate,
Do alwayes flow, to quench his thirstie heate. 120

O who can lead then a more happie life,
Than he, that with cleane minde and heart sincere,
No greedy riches knowes nor bloudie strife,
No deadly fight of warlick fleete doth feare,
Ne runs in perill of foes cruell knife,
That in the sacred temples he may reare,
A trophee of his glittering spoyles and treasure,
Or may abound in riches above measure.

Of him his God is worshipt with his sythe,
And not with skill of craftsman polished: 130
He joyes in groves, and makes himselfe full blythe,

With sundrie flowers in wilde fieldes gathered;
Ne frankincens he from *Panchæa* buyth,
Sweete quiet harbours in his harmeles head,
And perfect pleasure buildes her joyous bowre,
Free from sad cares, that rich mens hearts devowre.

This all his care, this all his whole indevour,
To this his minde and senses he doth bend,
How he may flow in quiets matchles treasour,
Content with any food that God doth send; 140
And how his limbs, resolu'd through idle leisour,
Unto sweete sleepe he may securely lend,
In some coole shadow from the scorching heat,
The whiles his flock their chawed cuds do eate.

O flocks, O Faunes, and O ye pleasaunt springs
Of *Tempe*, where the countrey Nymphs are rife,
Through whose not costly care each shepheard sings
As merrie notes upon his rusticke Fife,
As that *Ascræan* bard, whose fame now rings
Through the wide world, and leads as joyfull life. 150
Free from all troubles and from worldly toyle,
In which fond men doe all their dayes turmoyle.

In such delights whilst thus his carelesse time
This shepheard drives, upleaning on his batt,
And on shrill reedes chaunting his rustick rime,
Hyperion throwing foorth his beames full hott,
Into the highest top of heaven gan clime,
And the world parting by an equall lott,
Did shed his whirling flames on either side,
As the great *Ocean* doth himselfe divide. 160

Then gan the shepheard gather into one
His stragling Goates, and drave them to a foord,
Whose cærule streame, rombling in Pible stone,
Crept under mosse as greene as any goord.
Now had the Sun halfe heaven overgone,

When he his heard back from that water foord,
Drave from the force of *Phœbus* boyling ray,
Into thick shadowes, there themselves to lay.

Soone as he them plac'd in thy sacred wood
(O *Delian* Goddesse) saw, to which of yore 170
Came the bad daughter of old *Cadmus* brood,
Cruell *Agave*, flying vengeance sore
Of king *Nictileus* for the guiltie blood,
Which she with cursed hands had shed before;
There she halfe frantick having slaine her sonne,
Did shrowd her selfe like punishment to shonne.

Here also playing on the grassy greene,
Woodgods, and Satyres, and swift Dryades,
With many Fairies oft were dauncing seene.
Not so much did Dan *Orpheus* represse, 180
The streames of *Hebrus* with his songs I weene,
As that faire troupe of woodie Goddesses
Staied thee, (O *Peneus*) powring foorth to thee,
From cheereful lookes great mirth & gladsome glee.

The verie nature of the place, resounding
With gentle murmure of the breathing ayre,
A pleasant bowre with all delight abounding
In the fresh shadowe did for them prepayre,
To rest their limbs with wearines redounding.
For first the high Plaine trees with braunches
faire, 190
Out of the lowly vallies did arise,
And high shoote up their heads into the skyes

And them amongst the wicked Lotos grew,
Wicked, for holding guilefully away
Ulysses men, whom rapt with sweetenes new,
Taking to hoste, it quite from him did stay,
And eke those trees, in whose transformed hew
The Sunnes sad daughters waylde the rash decay
Of *Phaeton*, whose limbs with lightening rent,

They gathering up, with sweete teares did
lament. 200

And that same tree, in which *Demophoon*,
By his disloyalty lamented sore,
Eternall hurte left unto many one:
Whom als accompanied the Oke, of yore
Through fatall charmes transformd to such an one:
The Oke, whose Acornes were our foode, before
That *Ceres* seede of mortall men were knowne,
Which first *Triptoleme* taught how to be sowne.

Here also grew the rougher rinded Pine,
The great *Argoan* ships brave ornament 210
Whom golden Fleece did make an heavenly signe;
Which coveting, with his high tops extent,
To make the mountaines touch the starres divine,
Decks all the forrest with embellishment,
And the blacke Holme that loves the watrie vale,
And the sweete Cypresse signe of deadly bale.

Emongst the rest the clambring Yvie grew,
Knitting his wanton armes with grasping hold,
Least that the Poplar happely should rew
Her brothers strokes, whose boughes she doth
enfold 220
With her lythe twigs, till they the top survew,
And paint with pallid greene her buds of gold.
Next did the Myrtle tree to her approach,
Not yet unmindfull of her olde reproach.

But the small Birds in their wide boughs embowring,
Chaunted their sundrie tunes with sweete consent,
And under them a silver Spring forth powring
His trickling streames, a gentle murmure sent;
Thereto the frogs, bred in the slimie scowring
Of the moist moores, their jarring voyces bent; 230
And shrill grashoppers chirped them around:
All which the ayrie Echo did resound.

In this so pleasant place this Shepheards flocke
Lay everie where, their wearie limbs to rest,
On everie bush, and everie hollow rocke
Where breathe on them the whistling wind mote best;
The whiles the Shepheard self tending his stocke,
Sate by the fountaine side, in shade to rest,
Where gentle slumbring sleep oppressed him,
Displaid on ground, and seized everie lim. 240

Of trecherie or traines nought tooke he keep,
But looslie on the grassie greene dispredd,
His dearest life did trust to careles sleep;
Which weighing down his drouping drowsie hedd,
In quiet rest his molten heart did steep,
Devoid of care, and feare of all falshedd:
Had not inconstant fortune, bent to ill,
Bid strange mischance his quietnes to spill.

For at his wonted time in that same place
An huge great Serpent all with speckles pide, 250
To drench himselfe in moorish slime did trace,
There from the boyling heate himselfe to hide:
He passing by with rolling wreathed pace,
With brandisht tongue the emptie aire did gride,
And wrapt his scalie boughts with fell despight,
That all things seem'd appalled at his sight.

Now more and more having himselfe enrolde,
His glittering breast he lifteth up on hie,
And with proud vaunt his head aloft doth holde;
His creste above spotted with purple die, 260
On everie side did shine like scalie golde,
And his bright eyes glauncing full dreadfullie,
Did seeme to flame out flakes of flashing fyre,
And with sterne lookes to threaten kindled yre.

Thus wise long time he did himselfe dispace
There round about, when as at last he spide

Lying along before him in that place,
That flocks grand Captaine, and most trustie guide :
Eftsoones more fierce in visage, and in pace,
Throwing his firie eyes on everie side, 270
He commeth on, and all things in his way
Full stearnly rends, that might his passage stay.

Much he disdaines, that anie one should dare
To come unto his haunt ; for which intent
He inly burns, and gins straight to prepare
The weapons, which Nature to him hath lent ;
Fellie he hisseth, and doth fiercely stare,
And hath his jawes with angrie spirits rent,
That all his tract with bloudie drops is stained,
And all his foldes are now in length outstrained. 280

Whom thus at point prepared, to prevent,
A litle noursling of the humid ayre,
A Gnat unto the sleepie Shepheard went,
And marking where his ey-lids twinckling rare,
Shewd the two pearles, which sight unto him lent,
Through their thin coverings appearing fayre,
His little needle there infixing deep,
Warnd him awake, from death himselfe to keep.

Wherewith enrag'd, he fiercely gan upstart,
And with his hand him rashly bruzing, slewe 290
As in avengement of his heedles smart,
That streight the spirite out of his senses flew,
And life out of his members did depart :
When suddenly casting aside his vew,
He spide his foe with felonous intent,
And fervent eyes to his destruction bent.

All suddenly dismaid, and hartles quight,
He fled abacke, and catching hastie holde
Of a yong alder hard beside him pight,
It rent, and streight about him gan beholde, 300
What God or Fortune would assist his might.

But whether God or Fortune made him bold
Its hard to read: yet hardie will he had
To overcome, that made him lesse adrad.

The scalie backe of that most hideous snake
Enwrapped round, oft faining to retire,
And oft him to assaile, he fiercely strake
Whereas his temples did his creast-front tyre;
And for he was but slowe, did slowth off shake,
And gazing ghastly on (for feare and yre 310
Had blent so much his sense, that lesse he feard;)
Yet when he saw him slaine, himselfe he cheard.

By this the night forth from the darksome bowre
Of *Herebus* her teemed steedes gan call,
And laesie *Vesper* in his timelie howre
From golden *Oeta* gan proceede withall;
Whenas the Shepheard after this sharpe stowre,
Seing the doubled shadowes low to fall,
Gathering his straying flocke, does homeward fare,
And unto rest his wearie joynts prepare. 320

Into whose sense so soone as lighter sleepe
Was entered, and now loosing everie lim,
Sweete slumbring deaw in carelesnesse did steepe,
The Image of that Gnat appeard to him,
And in sad tearmes gan sorrowfully weepe,
With greislie countenaunce and visage grim,
Wailing the wrong which he had done of late,
In steed of good hastning his cruell fate.

Said he, what have I wretch deserv'd, that thus
Into this bitter bale I am outcast, 330
Whilest that thy life more deare and precious
Was than mine owne, so long as it did last?
I now in lieu of paines so gracious,
Am tost in th' ayre with everie windie blast:
Thou safe delivered from sad decay,
Thy careles limbs in loose sleep dost display.

So livest thou, but my poore wretched ghost
Is forst to ferrie over *Lethes* River,
And spoyld of *Charon* too and fro am tost.
Seest thou, how all places quake and quiver 340
Lightned with deadly lamps on everie post?
Tisiphone each where doth shake and shiver
Her flaming fire brond, encountring me,
Whose lockes uncombed cruell adders be.

And *Cerberus*, whose many mouthes doo bay,
And barke out flames, as if on fire he fed;
Adowne whose necke in terrible array,
Ten thousand snakes cralling about his hed
Doo hang in heapes, that horribly affray,
And bloodie eyes doo glister firie red; 350
He oftentimes me dreadfullie doth threaten,
With painfull torments to be sorely beaten.

Ay me, that thankes so much should faile of meed,
For that I thee restor'd to life againe,
Even from the doore of death and deadlie dreed.
Where then is now the guerdon of my paine?
Where the reward of my so piteous deed?
The praise of pitie vanisht is in vaine,
And th' antique faith of Justice long agone
Out of the land is fled away and gone. 360

I saw anothers fate approaching fast,
And left mine owne his safetie to tender;
Into the same mishap I now am cast,
And shun'd destruction doth destruction render:
Not unto him that never hath trespast,
But punishment is due to the offender.
Yet let destruction be the punishment,
So long as thankfull will may it relent.

I carried am into waste wildernesse,
Waste wildernes, amongst *Cymerian* shades, 370
Where endles paines and hideous heavinesse

Is round about me heapt in darksome glades.
For there huge *Othos* sits in sad distresse,
Fast bound with serpents that him oft invades;
Far of beholding *Ephialtes* tide,
Which once assai'd to burne this world so wide.

And there is mournfull *Tityus* mindefull yet
Of thy displeasure, O *Latona* faire;
Displeasure too implacable was it,
That made him meat for wild foules of the ayre: 380
Much do I feare among such fiends to sit;
Much do I feare back to them to repayre,
To the black shadowes of the *Stygian* shore,
Where wretched ghosts sit wailing evermore.

There next the utmost brinck doth he abide,
That did the bankets of the Gods bewray,
Whose throat through thirst to nought nigh being
 dride
His sense to seeke for ease turnes every way:
And he that in avengement of his pride,
For scorning to the sacred Gods to pray, 390
Against a mountaine rolls a mightie stone,
Calling in vaine for rest, and can have none.

Go ye with them, go cursed damosells,
Whose bridale torches foule *Erynnis* tynde,
And *Hymen* at your Spousalls sad, foretells
Tydings of death and massacre unkinde:
With them that cruell *Colchid* mother dwells,
The which conceiv'd in her revengefull minde,
With bitter woundes her owne deere babes to slay,
And murdred troupes upon great heapes to lay. 400

There also those two *Pandionian* maides,
Calling on *Itis*, *Itis* evermore,
Whom wretched boy they slew with guiltie blades;
For whome the *Thracian* king lamenting sore,
Turn'd to a Lapwing, fowlie them upbraydes,

And flattering round about them still does sore;
There now they all eternally complaine
Of others wrong, and suffer endles paine.

But the two brethren borne of *Cadmus* blood,
Whilst each does for the Soveraignty contend, 410
Blinde through ambition, and with vengeance wood
Each doth against the others bodie bend
His cursed steele, of neither well withstood,
And with wide wounds their carcases doth rend;
That yet they both doe mortall foes remaine,
Sith each with brothers bloudie hand was slaine.

Ah (waladay) there is no end of paine,
Nor chaunge of labour may intreated bee:
Yet I beyond all these am carried faine,
Where other powers farre different I see, 420
And must passe over to th' *Elisian* plaine:
There grim *Persephone* encountring mee,
Doth urge her fellow Furies earnestlie,
With their bright firebronds me to terrifie.

There chast *Alceste* lives inviolate,
Free from all care, for that her husbands daies
She did prolong by changing fate for fate,
Lo there lives also the immortall praise
Of womankinde, most faithfull to her mate,
Penelope: and from her farre awayes 430
A rulesse rout of yongmen, which her woo'd
All slaine with darts, lie wallowed in their blood.

And sad *Eurydice* thence now no more
Must turne to life, but there detained bee,
For looking back, being forbid before:
Yet was the guilt thereof, *Orpheus*, in thee.
Bold sure he was, and worthie spirite bore,
That durst those lowest shadowes goe to see,
And could beleeve that anie thing could please
Fell *Cerberus*, or Stygian powres appease. 440

Ne feard the burning waves of *Phlegeton*,
Nor those same mournfull kingdomes, compassed
With rustie horrour and fowle fashion,
And deep digd vawtes, and Tartar covered
With bloodie night, and darke confusion,
And judgement seates, whose Judge is deadlie dred,
A judge, that after death doth punish sore
The faults, which life hath trespassed before.

But valiant fortune made *Dan Orpheus* bolde:
For the swift running rivers still did stand, 450
And the wilde beasts their furie did withhold,
To follow *Orpheus* musicke through the land:
And th' Okes deep grounded in the earthly molde
Did move, as if they could him understand;
And the shrill woods, which were of sense bereav'd,
Through their hard barke his silver sound receav'd.

And eke the Moone her hastie steedes did stay,
Drawing in teemes along the starrie skie,
And didst (ô monthly Virgin) thou delay
Thy nightly course, to heare his melodie? 460
The same was able with like lovely lay
The Queene of hell to move as easily,
To yeeld *Eurydice* unto her fere,
Backe to be borne, though it unlawfull were.

She (Ladie) having well before approoved,
The feends to be too cruell and severe,
Observ'd th' appointed way, as her behooved,
Ne ever did her ey-sight turne arere,
Ne ever spake, ne cause of speaking mooved:
But cruell *Orpheus*, thou much crueller, 470
Seeking to kisse her, brok'st the Gods decree,
And thereby mad'st her ever damn'd to be.

Ah but sweete love of pardon worthie is,
And doth deserve to have small faults remitted;
If Hell at least things lightly done amis

Knew how to pardon, when ought is omitted:
Yet are ye both received into blis,
And to the seates of happie soules admitted.
And you, beside the honourable band
Of great Heroës doo in order stand. 480

There be the two stout sonnes of *Aeacus*,
Fierce *Peleus*, and the hardie *Telamon*,
Both seeming now full glad and joyeous
Through their Syres dreadfull jurisdiction,
Being the Judge of all that horrid hous:
And both of them by strange occasion,
Renown'd in choyce of happie marriage
Through *Venus* grace, and vertues cariage.

For th' one was ravisht of his owne bondmaide,
The faire *Hesione* captiv'd from *Troy*: 490
But th' other was with *Thetis* love assaid,
Great *Nereus* his daughter, and his joy.
On this side them there is a yongman layd,
Their match in glorie, mightie, fierce and coy;
That from th' Argolick ships, with furious yre,
Bett back the furie of the Trojan fyre.

O who would not recount the strong divorces
Of that great warre, which Trojanes oft behelde,
And oft beheld the warlike Greekish forces,
When *Teucrian* soyle with bloodie rivers swelde, 500
And wide *Sigæan* shores were spred with corses,
And *Simois* and *Xanthus* blood outwelde,
Whilst *Hector* raged with outragious minde,
Flames, weapons, wounds, in *Greeks* fleete to have tynde.

For *Ida* selfe, in ayde of that fierce fight,
Out of her mountaines ministred supplies,
And like a kindly nourse, did yeeld (for spight)
Store of firebronds out of her nourseries,
Unto her foster children, that they might

Inflame the Navie of their enemies, 510
And all the *Rhætean* shore to ashes turne,
Where lay the ships, which they did seeke to burne.

Gainst which the noble sonne of *Telamon*
Opposd' himselfe, and thwarting his huge shield,
Them battell bad, gainst whom appeard anon
Hector, the glorie of the *Trojan* field:
Both fierce and furious in contention
Encountred, that their mightie strokes so shrild,
As the great clap of thunder, which doth ryve
The ratling heavens, and cloudes asunder dryve. 520

So th' one with fire and weapons did contend
To cut the ships, from turning home againe
To *Argos*, th' other strove for to defend
The force of *Vulcane* with his might and maine.
Thus th' one *Aeacide* did his fame extend:
But th' other joy'd, that on the *Phrygian* playne
Having the blood of vanquisht *Hector* shedd,
He compast *Troy* thrice with his bodie dedd.

Againe great dole on either partie grewe,
That him to death unfaithfull *Paris* sent, 530
And also him that false *Ulysses* slewe,
Drawne into danger through close ambushment:
Therefore from him *Laërtes* sonne his vewe
Doth turne aside, and boasts his good event
In working of *Strymonian Rhæsus* fall,
And efte in *Dolons* slye surprysall.

Againe the dreadfull *Cycones* him dismay,
And blacke *Læstrigones*, a people stout:
Then greedie *Scilla*, under whom there bay
Manie great bandogs, which her gird about: 540
Then doo the *Aetnean* Cyclops him affray,
And deep *Charybdis* gulphing in and out:
Lastly the squalid lakes of *Tartarie*,
And griesly Feends of hell him terrifie.

There also goodly *Agamemnon* bosts,
The glorie of the stock of *Tantalus*,
And famous light of all the Greekish hosts,
Under whose conduct most victorious,
The *Dorick* flames consum'd the *Iliack* posts.
Ah but the *Greekes* themselves more dolorous, 550
To thee, ô *Troy*, paid penaunce for thy fall,
In th' *Hellespont* being nigh drowned all.

Well may appeare by proofe of their mischaunce,
The chaungfull turning of mens slipperie state,
That none, whom fortune freely doth advaunce,
Himselfe therefore to heaven should elevate:
For loftie type of honour through the glaunce
Of envies dart, is downe in dust prostrate;
And all that vaunts in worldly vanitie,
Shall fall through fortunes mutabilitie. 560

Th' *Argolicke* power returning home againe,
Enricht with spoyles of th' *Ericthonian* towre,
Did happie winde and weather entertaine,
And with good speed the fomie billowes scowre:
No signe of storme, no feare of future paine,
Which soone ensued them with heavie stowre.
Nereïs to the Seas a token gave,
The whiles their crooked keeles the surges clave.

Suddenly, whether through the Gods decree,
Or haplesse rising of some froward starre, 570
The heavens on everie side enclowded bee:
Black stormes and fogs are blowen up from farre,
That now the Pylote can no loadstarre see,
But skies and seas doo make most dreadfull warre;
The billowes striving to the heavens to reach,
And th' heavens striving them for to impeach.

And in avengement of their bold attempt,
Both Sun and starres and all the heavenly powres
Conspire in one to wreake their rash contempt,

And downne on them to fall from highest
towres : 580
The skie in pieces seeming to be rent,
Throwes lightning forth, & haile, & harmful
showres
That death on everie side to them appeares
In thousand formes, to worke more ghastly feares.

Some in the greedie flouds are sunke and drent,
Some on the rocks of *Caphareus* are throwne ;
Some on th' *Euboick* Cliffs in pieces rent ;
Some scattred on the *Heræan* shores unknowne ;
And manie lost, of whom no moniment
Remaines, nor memorie is to be showne : 590
Whilst all the purchase of the *Phrigian* pray
Tost on salt billowes, round about doth stray.

Here manie other like Heroës bee,
Equall in honour to the former crue,
Whom ye in goodly seates may placed see,
Descended all from *Rome* by linage due,
From *Rome*, that holds the world in sovereigntie,
And doth all Nations unto her subdue :
Here *Fabij* and *Decij* doo dwell,
Horatij that in vertue did excell. 600

And here the antique fame of stout *Camill*
Doth ever live, and constant *Curtius*,
Who stifly bent his vowed life to spill
For Countreyes health, a gulph most hideous
Amidst the Towne with his owne corps did fill,
T' appease the powers ; and prudent *Mutius*,
Who in his flesh endur'd the scorching flame,
To daunt his foe by ensample of the same.

And here wise *Curius*, companion
Of noble vertues, lives in endles rest ; 610
And stout *Flaminius*, whose devotion
Taught him the fires scorn'd furie to detest ;

And here the praise of either *Scipion*
Abides in highest place above the best,
To whom the ruin'd walls of *Carthage* vow'd,
Trembling their forces, sound their praises lowd.

Live they for ever through their lasting praise:
But I poore wretch am forced to retourne
To the sad lakes, that *Phœbus* sunnie rayes
Doo never see, where soules doo alwaies mourne, 620
And by the wayling shores to waste my dayes,
Where *Phlegeton* with quenchles flames doth burne;
By which just *Minos* righteous soules doth sever
From wicked ones, to live in blisse for ever.

Me therefore thus the cruell fiends of hell
Girt with long snakes, and thousand yron chaynes,
Through doome of that their cruell Judge, compell
With bitter torture and impatient paines,
Cause of my death, and just complaint to tell.
For thou art he, whom my poore ghost complaines 630
To be the author of her ill unwares,
That careles hear'st my intollerable cares.

Them therefore as bequeathing to the winde,
I now depart, returning to thee never,
And leave this lamentable plaint behinde.
But doo thou haunt the soft downe rolling river,
And wilde greene woods, and fruitful pastures minde,
And let the flitting aire my vaine words sever.
Thus having said, he heavily departed
With piteous crie, that anie would have smarted. 640

Now, when the sloathful fit of lifes sweete rest
Had left the heavie Shepheard, wondrous cares
His inly grieved minde full sore opprest;

That balefull sorrow he no longer beares,
For that Gnats death, which deeply was imprest:
But bends what ever power his aged yeares
Him lent, yet being such, as through their might
He lately slue his dreadfull foe in fight.

By that same River lurking under greene,
Eftsoones he gins to fashion forth a place, 650
And squaring it in compasse well beseene,
There plotteth out a tombe by measured space:
His yron headed spade tho making cleene,
To dig up sods out of the flowrie grasse,
His worke he shortly to good purpose brought,
Like as he had conceiv'd it in his thought.

An heape of earth he hoorded up on hie,
Enclosing it with banks on everie side,
And thereupon did raise full busily
A little mount, of greene turffs edifide; 660
And on the top of all, that passers by
Might it behold, the toomb he did provide
Of smoothest marble stone in order set,
That never might his luckie scape forget.

And round about he taught sweete flowres to growe,
The Rose engrained in pure scarlet die,
The Lilly fresh, and Violet belowe,
The Marigolde, and cherefull Rosemarie,
The *Spartan* Mirtle, whence sweet gumb does flowe,
The purple Hyacinthe, and fresh Costmarie, 670
And Saffron sought for in *Cilician* soyle,
And Lawrell th' ornament of *Phœbus* toyle.

Fresh *Rhododaphne*, and the *Sabine* flowre
Matching the wealth of th' auncient Frankincence,
And pallid Yvie building his owne bowre,
And Box yet mindfull of his olde offence,
Red *Amaranthus*, lucklesse Paramour,
Oxeye still greene, and bitter Patience;

Ne wants there pale *Narcisse*, that in a well
Seeing his beautie, in love with it fell, 680

And whatsoever other flowre of worth,
And whatso other hearb of lovely hew
The joyous Spring out of the ground brings forth,
To cloath her selfe in colours fresh and new;
He planted there, and reard a mount of earth,
In whose high front was writ as doth ensue.

To thee, small Gnat, in lieu of his life saved,
The Shepheard hath thy deaths record engraved.

FINIS.

PROSOPOPOIA:

OR

MOTHER HUBBERDS TALE.

MOTHER HUBBERDS TALE.

TO THE RIGHT HONOURABLE, THE

LADIE COMPTON AND MOUNTEGLE.

MOST faire and vertuous Ladie; having often sought opportunitie by some good meanes to make knowen to your Ladiship, the humble affection and faithfull duetie, which I have alwaies professed, and am bound to beare to that House, from whence yee spring, I have at length found occasion to remember the same, by making a simple present to you of these my idle labours; which having long sithens composed in the raw conceipt of my youth, I lately amongst other papers lighted upon, and was by others, which liked the same, mooved to set them foorth. Simple is the device, and the composition meane, yet carrieth some delight, even the rather because of the simplicitie & meannesse thus personated. The same I beseech your Ladiship take in good part, as a pledge of that profession which I have made to you, and keepe with you untill with some other more worthie labour, I do redeeme it out of your hands, and discharge my utmost dutie. Till then wishing your Ladiship all increase of honour and happinesse, I humblie take leave.

Your La: ever
humbly; *Ed. Sp.*

PROSOPOPOIA:

OR

MOTHER HUBBERDS TALE.

It was the month, in which the righteous Maide,
That for disdaine of sinfull worlds upbraide,
Fled back to heaven, whence she was first conceived,
Into her silver bowre the Sunne received;
And the hot *Syrian* Dog on him awayting,
After the chafed Lyons cruell bayting,
Corrupted had th' ayre with his noysome breath,
And powr'd on th' earth plague, pestilence, and
death.
Emongst the rest a wicked maladie
Raign'd emongst men, that manie did to die, 10
Depriv'd of sense and ordinarie reason;
That it to Leaches seemed strange and geason.
My fortune was mongst manie others moe,
To be partaker of their common woe;
And my weake bodie set on fire with griefe,
Was rob'd of rest, and naturall reliefe.
In this ill plight, there came to visite mee
Some friends, who sorie my sad case to see,
Began to comfort me in chearfull wise,
And meanes of gladsome solace to devise. 20
But seeing kindly sleep refuse to doe
His office, and my feeble eyes forgoe,
They sought my troubled sense how to deceave
With talke, that might unquiet fancies reave;
And sitting all in seates about me round,
With pleasant tales (fit for that idle stound)
They cast in course to waste the wearie howres:
Some tolde of Ladies, and their Paramoures;
Some of brave Knights, and their renowned Squires;

Some of the Faeries and their strange attires; 30
And some of Giaunts hard to be beleeved,
That the delight thereof me much releeved.
Amongst the rest a good old woman was,
Hight Mother *Hubberd*, who did farre surpas
The rest in honest mirth, that seem'd her well:
She when her turne was come her tale to tell,
Tolde of a strange adventure, that betided
Betwixt the Foxe and th' Ape by him misguided;
The which for that my sense it greatly pleased,
All were my spirite heavie and diseased, 40
Ile write in termes, as she the same did say,
So well as I her words remember may.
No Muses aide me needs heretoo to call;
Base is the style, and matter meane withall.
¶ Whilome (said she) before the world was civill,
The Foxe and th' Ape disliking of their evill
And hard estate, determined to seeke
Their fortunes farre abroad, lyeke with his lyeke:
For both were craftie and unhappie witted;
Two fellowes might no where be better fitted. 50
The Foxe, that first this cause of griefe did finde,
Gan first thus plaine his case with words unkinde.
Neighbour Ape, and my Goship eke beside,
(Both two sure bands in friendship to be tide,)
To whom may I more trustely complaine
The evill plight, that doth me sore constraine,
And hope thereof to finde due remedie?
Heare then my paine and inward agonie.
Thus manie yeares I now have spent and worne,
In meane regard, and basest fortunes scorne, 60
Dooing my Countrey service as I might,
No lesse I dare saie than the prowdest wight;
And still I hoped to be up advaunced,
For my good parts; but still it hath mischaunced.
Now therefore that no lenger hope I see,
But froward fortune still to follow mee,
And losels lifted up on high, where I did looke,
I meane to turne the next leafe of the booke.

Yet ere that anie way I doo betake,
I meane my Gossip privie first to make. 70
Ah my deare Gossip, (answer'd then the Ape,)
Deeply doo your sad words my wits awhape,
Both for because your griefe doth great appeare,
And eke because my selfe am touched neare:
For I likewise have wasted much good time,
Still wayting to preferment up to clime,
Whilest others alwayes have before me stept,
And from my beard the fat away have swept;
That now unto despaire I gin to growe
And meane for better winde about to throwe. 80
Therefore to me, my trustie friend, aread
Thy councell: two is better than one head.
Certes (said he) I meane me to disguize
In some straunge habit, after uncouth wize,
Or like a Pilgrime, or a Lymiter,
Or like a *Gipsen*, or a Juggeler,
And so to wander to the worlds ende,
To seeke my fortune, where I may it mend:
For worse than that I have, I cannot meete.
Wide is the world I wote, and everie streete 90
Is full of fortunes, and adventures straunge,
Continuallie subject unto chaunge.
Say my faire brother now, if this device
Doth like you, or may you to like entice.
Surely (said th' Ape) it likes me wondrous well;
And would ye not poore fellowship expell,
My selfe would offer you t' accompanie
In this adventures chauncefull jeopardie.
For to wexe olde at home in idlenesse,
Is disadventrous, and quite fortunelesse: 100
Abroad where change is, good may gotten bee.
The Foxe was glad, and quickly did agree:
So both resolv'd, the morrow next ensuing,
So soone as day appeard to peoples vewing,
On their intended journey to proceede;
And over night, whatso theretoo did neede,
Each did prepare, in readines to bee.

The morrow next, so soone as one might see
Light out of heavens windowes forth to looke,
Both their habiliments unto them tooke, 110
And put themselves (a Gods name) on their way.
Whenas the Ape beginning well to wey
This hard adventure, thus began t' advise;
Now read Sir Reynold, as ye be right wise,
What course ye weene is best for us to take,
That for our selves we may a living make.
Whether shall we professe some trade or skill?
Or shall we varie our device at will,
Even as new occasion appeares?
Or shall we tie our selves for certaine yeares 120
To anie service, or to anie place?
For it behoves ere that into the race
We enter, to resolve first hereupon.
Now surely brother (said the Foxe anon)
Ye have this matter motioned in season:
For everie thing that is begun with reason
Will come by readie meanes unto his end;
But things miscounselled must needs miswend.
Thus therefore I advize upon the case,
That not to anie certaine trade or place, 130
Nor anie man we should our selves applie;
For why should he that is at libertie
Make himselfe bond? sith then we are free borne,
Let us all servile base subjection scorne;
And as we bee sonnes of the world so wide,
Let us our fathers heritage divide,
And chalenge to our selves our portions dew
Of all the patrimonie, which a few
Now hold in hugger mugger in their hand,
And all the rest doo rob of good and land. 140
For now a few have all and all have nought,
Yet all be brethren ylike dearly bought:
There is no right in this partition,
Ne was it so by institution
Ordained first, ne by the law of Nature,
But that she gave like blessing to each creture

As well of worldly livelode as of life,
That there might be no difference nor strife,
Nor ought cald mine or thine: thrice happie then
Was the condition of mortall men. 150
That was the golden age of *Saturne* old,
But this might better be the world of gold:
For without golde now nothing wilbe got.
Therefore (if please you) this shalbe our plot,
We will not be of anie occupation,
Let such vile vassalls borne to base vocation
Drudge in the world, and for their living droyle
Which have no wit to live withouten toyle.
But we will walke about the world at pleasure
Like two free men, and make our ease a treasure. 160
Free men some beggers call, but they be free,
And they which call them so more beggers bee:
For they doo swinke and sweate to feed the other,
Who live like Lords of that which they doo gather,
And yet doo never thanke them for the same,
But as their due by Nature doo it clame.
Such will we fashion both our selves to bee,
Lords of the world, and so will wander free
Where so us listeth, uncontrol'd of anie.
Hard is our hap, if we (emongst so manie) 170
Light not on some that may our state amend;
Sildome but some good commeth ere the end.
Well seemd the Ape to like this ordinaunce:
Yet well considering of the circumstaunce,
As pausing in great doubt awhile he staid,
And afterwards with grave advizement said;
I cannot my lief brother like but well
The purpose of the complot which ye tell:
For well I wot (compar'd to all the rest
Of each degree) that Beggers life is best: 180
And they that thinke themselves the best of all,
Oft-times to begging are content to fall.
But this I wot withall that we shall ronne
Into great daunger like to bee undonne,

Thus wildly to wander in the worlds eye,
Without pasport or good warrantye,
For feare least we like rogues should be reputed,
And for eare marked beasts abroad be bruted:
Therefore I read, that we our counsells call,
How to prevent this mischiefe ere it fall, 190
And how we may with most securitie,
Beg amongst those that beggers doo defie.
Right well deere Gossip ye advized have,
(Said then the Foxe) but I this doubt will save:
For ere we farther passe, I will devise
A pasport for us both in fittest wize,
And by the names of Souldiers us protect;
That now is thought a civile begging sect.
Be you the Souldier, for you likest are
For manly semblance, and small skill in warre: 200
I will but wayte on you, and as occasion
Falls out, my selfe fit for the same will fashion.
The Pasport ended, both they forward went,
The Ape clad Souldierlike, fit for th' intent,
In a blew jacket with a crosse of redd
And manie slits, as if that he had shedd
Much blood throgh many wounds therein receaved,
Which had the use of his right arme bereaved;
Upon his head an old Scotch cap he wore,
With a plume feather all to peeces tore: 210
His breeches were made after the new cut,
Al Portugese, loose like an emptie gut;
And his hose broken high above the heeling,
And his shooes beaten out with traveling.
But neither sword nor dagger he did beare,
Seemes that no foes revengement he did feare;
In stead of them a handsome bat he held,
On which he leaned, as one farre in elde.
Shame light on him, that through so false illusion,
Doth turne the name of Souldiers to abusion, 220
And that, which is the noblest mysterie,
Brings to reproach and common infamie.
Long they thus travailed, yet never met

Adventure, which might them a working set:
Yet manie waies they sought, and manie tryed;
Yet for their purposes none fit espyed.
At last they chaunst to meete upon the way
A simple husbandman in garments gray;
Yet though his vesture were but meane and bace,
A good yeoman he was of honest place, 230
And more for thrift did care than for gay clothing:
Gay without good, is good hearts greatest loathing.
The Foxe him spying, bad the Ape him dight
To play his part, for loe he was in sight,
That (if he er'd not) should them entertaine,
And yeeld them timely profite for their paine.
Eftsoones the Ape himselfe gan up to reare,
And on his shoulders high his bat to beare,
As if good service he were fit to doo;
But little thrift for him he did it too: 240
And stoutly forward he his steps did straine,
That like a handsome swaine it him became:
When as they nigh approached, that good man
Seeing them wander loosly, first began
T' enquire of custome, what and whence they were?
To whom the Ape, I am a Souldiere,
That late in warres have spent my deerest blood,
And in long service lost both limbs and good,
And now constrain'd that trade to overgive,
I driven am to seeke some means to live: 250
Which might it you in pitie please t' afford,
I would be readie both in deed and word,
To doo you faithfull service all my dayes.
This yron world (that same he weeping sayes)
Brings downe the stowtest hearts to lowest state:
For miserie doth bravest mindes abate,
And make them seeke for that they wont to scorne,
Of fortune and of hope at once forlorne.
The honest man, that heard him thus complaine,
Was griev'd, as he had felt part of his paine; 260
And well disposd' him some reliefe to showe,
Askt if in husbandrie he ought did knowe,

To plough, to plant, to reap, to rake, to sowe,
To hedge, to ditch, to thrash, to thetch, to mowe;
Or to what labour els he was prepar'd?
For husbands life is labourous and hard.
Whenas the Ape him hard so much to talke
Of labour, that did from his liking balke,
He would have slipt the coller handsomly,
And to him said; good Sir, full glad am I, 270
To take what paines may anie living wight:
But my late maymed limbs lack wonted might
To doo their kindly services, as needeth:
Scarce this right hand the mouth with diet feedeth,
So that it may no painfull worke endure,
Ne to strong labour can it selfe enure.
But if that anie other place you have,
Which askes small paines, but thriftines to save,
Or care to overlooke, or trust to gather,
Ye may me trust as your owne ghostly father. 280
With that the husbandman gan him avize,
That it for him were fittest exercise
Cattell to keep, or grounds to oversee;
And asked him, if he could willing bee
To keep his sheep, or to attend his swyne,
Or watch his mares, or take his charge of kyne?
Gladly (said he) what ever such like paine
Ye put on me, I will the same sustaine:
But gladliest I of your fleecie sheepe
(Might it you please) would take on me the keep. 290
For ere that unto armes I me betooke,
Unto my fathers sheepe I used to looke,
That yet the skill thereof I have not loste:
Thereto right well this Curdog by my coste
(Meaning the Foxe) will serve, my sheepe to gather,
And drive to follow after their Belwether.
The Husbandman was meanly well content,
Triall to make of his endevourment,
And home him leading, lent to him the charge
Of all his flocke, with libertie full large, 300

Giving accompt of th' annuall increace
Both of their lambes, and of their woolly fleece.
Thus is this Ape become a shepheard swaine,
And the false Foxe his dog. (God give them paine)
For ere the yeare have halfe his course out-run,
And doo returne from whence he first begun,
They shall him make an ill accompt of thrift.
Now whenas Time flying with winges swift,
Expired had the terme, that these two javels
Should render up a reckning of their travels 310
Unto their master, which it of them sought,
Exceedingly they troubled were in thought,
Ne wist what answere unto him to frame,
Ne how to scape great punishment, or shame,
For their false treason and vile theeverie.
For not a lambe of all their flockes supply
Had they to shew: but ever as they bred,
They slue them, and upon their fleshes fed:
For that disguised Dog lov'd blood to spill,
And drew the wicked Shepheard to his will. 320
So twixt them both they not a lambkin left,
And when lambes fail'd, the old sheepes lives they reft;
That how t' acquite themselves unto their Lord,
They were in doubt, and flatly set abord.
The Foxe then counsel'd th' Ape, for to require
Respite till morrow, t' answere his desire:
For times delay new hope of helpe still breeds.
The goodman granted, doubting nought their deeds,
And bad, next day that all should readie be.
But they more subtill meaning had than he: 330
For the next morrowes meed they closely ment,
For feare of afterclaps for to prevent.
And that same evening, when all shrowded were
In careles sleep, they without care or feare,
Cruelly fell upon their flocke in folde,
And of them slew at pleasure what they wolde:
Of which whenas they feasted had their fill,
For a full complement of all their ill,

They stole away, and tooke their hastie flight,
Carried in clowdes of all-concealing night. 340
So was the husbandman left to his losse,
And they unto their fortunes change to tosse.
After which sort they wandered long while,
Abusing manie through their cloaked guile;
That at the last they gan to be descryed
Of everie one, and all their sleights espyed.
So as their begging now them failed quyte;
For none would give, but all men would them wyte:
Yet would they take no paines to get their living,
But seeke some other way to gaine by giving, 350
Much like to begging but much better named;
For manie beg, which are thereof ashamed.
And now the Foxe had gotten him a gowne,
And th' Ape a cassocke sidelong hanging downe;
For they their occupation meant to change,
And now in other state abroad to range:
For since their souldiers pas no better spedd,
They forg'd another, as for Clerkes booke-redd.
Who passing foorth, as their adventures fell,
Through manie haps, which needs not here to tell; 360
At length chaunst with a formall Priest to meete,
Whom they in civill manner first did greete,
And after askt an almes for Gods deare love.
The man straight way his choler up did move,
And with reproachfull tearmes gan them revile,
For following that trade so base and vile;
And askt what license, or what Pas they had?
Ah (said the Ape as sighing wondrous sad)
Its an hard case, when men of good deserving
Must either driven be perforce to sterving, 370
Or asked for their pas by everie squib,
That list at will them to revile or snib:
And yet (God wote) small oddes I often see
Twixt them that aske, and them that asked bee.
Natheles because you shall not us misdeeme,
But that we are as honest as we seeme,

Yee shall our pasport at your pleasure see,
And then ye will (I hope) well mooved bee.
Which when the Priest beheld, he vew'd it nere,
As if therein some text he studying were, 380
But little els (God wote) could thereof skill:
For read he could not evidence, nor will,
Ne tell a written word, ne write a letter,
Ne make one title worse, ne make one better:
Of such deep learning little had he neede,
Ne yet of Latine, ne of Greeke, that breede
Doubts mongst Divines, and difference of texts,
From whence arise diversitie of sects,
And hatefull heresies, of God abhor'd:
But this good Sir did follow the plaine word, 390
Ne medled with their controversies vaine.
All his care was, his service well to saine,
And to read Homelies upon holidayes:
When that was done, he might attend his playes;
An easie life, and fit high God to please.
He having overlookt their pas at ease,
Gan at the length them to rebuke againe,
That no good trade of life did entertaine,
But lost their time in wandring loose abroad,
Seeing the world, in which they bootles boad, 400
Had wayes enough for all therein to live;
Such grace did God unto his creatures give.
Said then the Foxe; who hath the world not tride,
From the right way full eath may wander wide.
We are but Novices, new come abroad,
We have not yet the tract of anie troad,
Nor on us taken anie state of life,
But readie are of anie to make preife.
Therefore might please you, which the world have
proved,
Us to advise, which forth but lately moved, 410
Of some good course, that we might undertake;
Ye shall for ever us your bondmen make.
The Priest gan wexe halfe proud to be so praide,
And thereby willing to affoord them aide;

It seemes (said he) right well that ye be Clerks,
Both by your wittie words, and by your werks.
Is not that name enough to make a living
To him that hath a whit of Natures giving ?
How manie honest men see ye arize
Daylie thereby, and grow to goodly prize ? 420
To Deanes, to Archdeacons, to Commissaries,
To Lords, to Principalls, to Prebendaries ;
All jolly Prelates, worthie rule to beare,
Who ever them envie : yet spite bites neare.
Why should ye doubt then, but that ye likewise
Might unto some of those in time arise ?
In the meane time to live in good estate,
Loving that love, and hating those that hate ;
Being some honest Curate, or some Vicker
Content with little in condition sicker. 430
Ah but (said th' Ape) the charge is wondrous great,
To feed mens soules, and hath an heavie threat.
To feede mens soules (quoth he) is not in man :
For they must feed themselves, doo what we can.
We are but charg'd to lay the meate before :
Eate they that list, we need to doo no more.
But God it is that feedes them with his grace,
The bread of life powr'd downe from heavenly place.
Therefore said he, that with the budding rod
Did rule the Jewes, *All shalbe taught of God.* 440
That same hath Jesus Christ now to him raught,
By whom the flock is rightly fed, and taught :
He is the Shepheard, and the Priest is hee ;
We but his shepheard swaines ordain'd to bee.
Therefore herewith doo not your selfe dismay ;
Ne is the paines so great, but beare ye may ;
For not so great as it was wont of yore,
It's now a dayes, ne halfe so streight and sore :
They whilome used duly everie day
Their service and their holie things to say, 450
At morne and even, besides their Anthemes sweete,
Their penie Masses, and their Complynes meete,

Their Dirges, their Trentals, and their shrifts,
Their memories, their singings, and their gifts.
Now all those needlesse works are laid away;
Now once a weeke upon the Sabbath day,
It is enough to doo our small devotion,
And then to follow any merrie motion.
Ne are we tyde to fast, but when we list,
Ne to weare garments base of wollen twist, 460
But with the finest silkes us to aray,
That before God we may appeare more gay,
Resembling *Aarons* glorie in his place:
For farre unfit it is, that person bace
Should with vile cloaths approach Gods majestie,
Whom no uncleannes may approachen nie:
Or that all men, which anie master serve,
Good garments for their service should deserve;
But he that serves the Lord of hoasts most high,
And that in highest place, t' approach him nigh, 470
And all the peoples prayers to present
Before his throne, as on ambassage sent
Both too and fro, should not deserve to weare
A garment better, than of wooll or heare.
Beside we may have lying by our sides
Our lovely Lasses, or bright shining Brides:
We be not tyde to wilfull chastitie,
But have the Gospell of free libertie.
By that he ended had his ghostly sermon,
The Foxe was well induc'd to be a Parson; 480
And of the Priest eftsoones gan to enquire,
How to a Benefice he might aspire.
Marie there (said the Priest) is arte indeed.
Much good deep learning one thereout may reed,
For that the ground-worke is, and end of all,
How to obtaine a Beneficiall.
First therefore, when ye have in handsome wise
Your selfe attyred, as you can devise,
Then to some Noble man your selfe applye,
Or other great one in the worldes eye, 490

That hath a zealous disposition
To God, and so to his religion :
There must thou fashion eke a godly zeale,
Such as no carpers may contrayre reveale :
For each thing fained, ought more warie bee.
There thou must walke in sober gravitee,
And seeme as Saintlike as Saint *Radegund* :
Fast much, pray oft, looke lowly on the ground,
And unto everie one doo curtesie meeke :
These lookes (nought saying) doo a benefice seeke, 500
And be thou sure one not to lacke or long.
But if thee list unto the Court to throng,
And there to hunt after the hoped pray,
Then must thou thee dispose another way :
For there thou needs must learne, to laugh, to lie,
To face, to forge, to scoffe, to companie,
To crouche, to please, to be a beetle stock
Of thy great Masters will, to scorne, or mock :
So maist thou chaunce mock out a Benefice,
Unlesse thou canst one conjure by device, 510
Or cast a figure for a Bishoprick :
And if one could, it were but a schoole-trick.
These be the wayes, by which without reward
Livings in Court be gotten, though full hard.
For nothing there is done without a fee :
The Courtier needes must recompenced bee
With a Benevolence, or have in gage
The *Primitias* of your Parsonage :
Scarse can a Bishoprick forpas them by,
But that it must be gelt in privitie. 520
Doo not thou therefore seeke a living there,
But of more private persons seeke elswhere,
Whereas thou maist compound a better penie,
Ne let thy learning question'd be of anie.
For some good Gentleman that hath the right
Unto his Church for to present a wight,
Will cope with thee in reasonable wise ;
That if the living yerely doo arise

To fortie pound, that then his yongest sonne
Shall twentie have, and twentie thou hast
wonne: 530
Thou hast it wonne, for it is of franke gift,
And he will care for all the rest to shift;
Both that the Bishop may admit of thee,
And that therein thou maist maintained bee.
This is the way for one that is unlern'd
Living to get, and not to be discern'd.
But they that are great Clerkes, have nearer wayes,
For learning sake to living them to raise:
Yet manie eke of them (God wote) are driven,
T' accept a Benefice in peeces riven. 540
How saist thou (friend) have I not well discourst
Upon this Common place (though plaine, not
wourst)?
Better a short tale, than a bad long shriving.
Needes anie more to learne to get a living?
Now sure and by my hallidome (quoth he)
Ye a great master are in your degree:
Great thankes I yeeld you for your discipline,
And doo not doubt, but duly to encline
My wits theretoo, as ye shall shortly heare.
The Priest him wisht good speed, and well to
fare. 550
So parted they, as eithers way them led.
But th' Ape and Foxe ere long so well them sped,
Through the Priests holesome counsell lately tought,
And throgh their owne faire handling wisely wroght,
That they a Benefice twixt them obtained;
And craftie Reynold was a Priest ordained;
And th' Ape his Parish Clarke procur'd to bee.
Then made they revell route and goodly glee.
But ere long time had passed, they so ill
Did order their affaires, that th' evill will 560
Of all their Parishners they had constraind;
Who to the Ordinarie of them complain'd,
How fowlie they their offices abusd'
And them of crimes and heresies accusd';

That Pursivants he often for them sent :
But they neglected his commaundement.
So long persisted obstinate and bolde,
Till at the length he published to holde
A Visitation, and them cyted thether :
Then was high time their wits about to
geather ; 570
What did they then, but made a composition
With their next neighbor Priest for light condition,
To whom their living they resigned quight
For a few pence, and ran away by night.
So passing through the Countrey in disguize,
They fled farre off, where none might them surprize,
And after that long straied here and there,
Through everie field and forrest farre and nere ;
Yet never found occasion for their tourne,
But almost sterv'd, did much lament and
mourne 580
At last they chaunst to meete upon the way
The Mule, all deckt in goodly rich aray,
With bells and bosses, that full lowdly rung,
And costly trappings, that to ground downe hung.
Lowly they him saluted in meeke wise,
But he through pride and fatnes gan despise
Their meanesse ; scarce vouchsafte them to requite.
Whereat the Foxe deep groning in his sprite,
Said, Ah sir Mule, now blessed be the day,
That I see you so goodly and so gay 590
In your attyres, and eke your silken hyde
Fil'd with round flesh, that everie bone doth hide.
Seemes that in fruitfull pastures ye doo live,
Or fortune doth you secret favour give.
Foolish Foxe (said the Mule) thy wretched need
Praiseth the thing that doth thy sorrow breed.
For well I weene, thou canst not but envie
My wealth, compar'd to thine owne miserie,
That art so leane and meagre waxen late,
That scarse thy legs uphold thy feeble gate. 600
Ay me (said then the Foxe) whom evill hap

Unworthy in such wretchednes doth wrap,
And makes the scorne of other beasts to bee:
But read (faire Sir, of grace) from whence come yee?
Or what of tidings you abroad doo heare?
Newes may perhaps some good unweeting beare.
From royall Court I lately came (said he)
Where all the braverie that eye may see,
And all the happinesse that heart desire,
Is to be found; he nothing can admire, 610
That hath not seene that heavens portracture:
But tidings there is none I you assure,
Save that which common is, and knowne to all,
That Courtiers as the tide doo rise and fall.
But tell us (said the Ape) we doo you pray,
Who now in Court doth beare the greatest sway.
That if such fortune doo to us befall,
We may seeke favour of the best of all.
Marie (said he) the highest now in grace,
Be the wilde beasts, that swiftest are in chase; 620
For in their speedie course and nimble flight
The Lyon now doth take the most delight:
But chieflie, joyes on foote them to beholde,
Enchaste with chaine and circulet of golde:
So wilde a beast so tame ytaught to bee,
And buxome to his bands is joy to see.
So well his golden Circlet him beseemeth:
But his late chayne his Liege unmeete esteemeth;
For so brave beasts she loveth best to see,
In the wilde forrest raunging fresh and free. 630
Therefore if fortune thee in Court to live,
In case thou ever there wilt hope to thrive,
To some of these thou must thy selfe apply:
Els as a thistle-downe in th' ayre doth flie,
So vainly shalt thou too and fro be tost,
And loose thy labour and thy fruitles cost.
And yet full few, which follow them I see,
For vertues bare regard advaunced bee,
But either for some gainfull benefit,
Or that they may for their owne turnes be fit. 640

Nath'les perhaps ye things may handle soe,
That ye may better thrive than thousands moe.
But (said the Ape) how shall we first come in,
That after we may favour seeke to win ?
How els (said he) but with a good bold face,
And with big words, and with a stately pace,
That men may thinke of you in generall,
That to be in you, which is not at all :
For not by that which is, the world now deemeth,
(As it was wont) but by that same that seemeth. 650
Ne do I doubt, but that ye well can fashion
Your selves theretoo, according to occasion :
So fare ye well, good Courtiers may ye bee ;
So proudlie neighing from them parted hee.
Then gan this craftie couple to devize,
How for the Court themselves they might aguize :
For thither they themselves meant to addresse,
In hope to finde there happier successe.
So well they shifted, that the Ape anon
Himselfe had cloathed like a Gentleman, 660
And the slie Foxe, as like to be his groome,
That to the Court in seemly sort they come.
Where the fond Ape himselfe uprearing hy
Upon his tiptoes, stalketh stately by,
As if he were some great *Magnifico*,
And boldlie doth amongst the boldest go.
And his man Reynold with fine counterfesaunce
Supports his credite and his countenaunce.
Then gan the Courtiers gaze on everie side,
And stare on him, with big lookes basen wide, 670
Wondring what mister wight he was, and whence :
For he was clad in strange accoustrements,
Fashion'd with queint devises never seene
In Court before, yet there all fashions beene :
Yet he them in newfanglenesse did pas :
But his behaviour altogether was
Alla Turchesca, much the more admyr'd,
And his lookes loftie, as if he aspyr'd

To dignitie, and sdeign'd the low degree;
That all which did such strangenesse in him
see, 680
By secrete meanes gan of his state enquire,
And privily his servant thereto hire:
Who throughly arm'd against such coverture,
Reported unto all, that he was sure
A noble Gentleman of high regard,
Which through the world had with long travel far'd,
And seene the manners of all beasts on ground;
Now here arriv'd, to see if like he found.
Thus did the Ape at first him credit gaine,
Which afterwards he wisely did maintaine 690
With gallant showe, and daylie more augment
Through his fine feates and Courtly complement;
For he could play, and daunce, and vaute, and
spring,
And all that els pertaines to reveling,
Onely through kindly aptnes of his joynts.
Besides he could doo manie other poynts,
The which in Court him served to good stead:
For he mongst Ladies could their fortunes read
Out of their hands, and merie leasings tell,
And juggle finely, that became him well: 700
But he so light was at legier demaine,
That what he toucht, came not to light againe;
Yet would he laugh it out, and proudly looke,
And tell them, that they greatly him mistooke.
So would he scoffe them out with mockerie,
For he therein had great felicitie;
And with sharp quips joy'd others to deface,
Thinking that their disgracing did him grace:
So whilst that other like vaine wits he pleased,
And made to laugh, his heart was greatly
eased. 710
But the right gentle minde would bite his lip,
To heare the Javell so good men to nip:
For though the vulgar yeeld an open eare,
And common Courtiers love to gybe and fleare

At everie thing, which they heare spoken ill,
And the best speaches with ill meaning spill;
Yet the brave Courtier, in whose beauteous thought
Regard of honour harbours more than ought,
Doth loath such base condition, to backbite
Anies good name for envie or despite: 720
He stands on tearmes of honourable minde,
Ne will be carried with the common winde
Of Courts inconstant mutabilitie,
Ne after everie tattling fable flie;
But heares, and sees the follies of the rest,
And thereof gathers for himselfe the best:
He will not creepe, nor crouche with fained face,
But walkes upright with comely stedfast pace,
And unto all doth yeeld due curtesie;
But not with kissed hand belowe the knee, 730
As that same Apish crue is wont to doo:
For he disdaines himselfe t' embase theretoo,
He hates fowle leasings, and vile flatterie,
Two filthie blots in noble Gentrie;
And lothefull idlenes he doth detest,
The canker worme of everie gentle brest;
The which to banish with faire exercise
Of knightly feates, he daylie doth devise:
Now menaging the mouthes of stubborne steedes,
Now practising the proofe of warlike deedes, 740
Now his bright armes assaying, now his speare,
Now the nigh aymed ring away to beare;
At other times he casts to sew the chace
Of swift wilde beasts, or runne on foote a race,
T' enlarge his breath (large breath in armes most
needfull)
Or els by wrestling to wex strong and heedfull,
Or his stiffe armes to stretch with Eughen bowe,
And manly legs, still passing too and fro,
Without a gowned beast him fast beside;
A vaine ensample of the *Persian* pride, 750
Who after he had wonne th' *Assyrian* foe,
Did ever after scorne on foote to goe.

Thus when this Courtly Gentleman with toyle
Himselfe hath wearied, he doth recoyle
Unto his rest, and there with sweete delight
Of Musicks skill revives his toyled spright,
Or els with Loves, and Ladies gentle sports,
The joy of youth, himselfe he recomforts;
Or lastly, when the bodie list to pause,
His minde unto the Muses he withdrawes; 760
Sweete Ladie Muses, Ladies of delight,
Delights of life, and ornaments of light:
With whom he close confers with wise discourse,
Of Natures workes, of heavens continuall course,
Of forreine lands, of people different,
Of kingdomes change, of divers government,
Of dreadfull battailes of renowmed Knights;
With which he kindleth his ambitious sprights
To like desire and praise of noble fame,
The onely upshot whereto he doth ayme: 770
For all his minde on honour fixed is,
To which he levels all his purposis,
And in his Princes service spends his dayes,
Not so much for to gaine, or for to raise
Himselfe to high degree, as for his grace,
And in his liking to winne worthie place;
Through due deserts and comely carriage,
In whatso please employ his personage,
That may be matter meete to gaine him praise;
For he is fit to use in all assayes, 780
Whether for Armes and warlike amenaunce,
Or else for wise and civill governaunce.
For he is practiz'd well in policie,
And thereto doth his Courting most applie:
To learne the enterdeale of Princes strange,
To marke th' intent of Counsells, and the change
Of states, and eke of private men somewhile,
Supplanted by fine falshood and faire guile;
Of all the which he gathereth, what is fit
T' enrich the storehouse of his powerfull wit, 790

Which through wise speaches, and grave conference
He daylie eekes, and brings to excellence.
Such is the rightfull Courtier in his kinde:
But unto such the Ape lent not his minde;
Such were for him no fit companions,
Such would descrie his lewd conditions:
But the yong lustie gallants he did chose
To follow, meete to whom he might disclose
His witlesse pleasance, and ill pleasing vaine.
A thousand wayes he them could entertaine, 800
With all the thriftles games, that may be found
With mumming and with masking all around,
With dice, with cards, with balliards farre unfit,
With shuttelcocks, misseeming manlie wit,
With courtizans, and costly riotize,
Whereof still somewhat to his share did rize:
Ne, them to pleasure, would he sometimes scorne
A Pandares coate (so basely was he borne);
Thereto he could fine loving verses frame,
And play the Poet oft. But ah, for shame 810
Let not sweete Poets praise, whose onely pride
Is vertue to advance, and vice deride,
Be with the worke of losels wit defamed,
Ne let such verses Poetrie be named:
Yet he the name on him would rashly take,
Maugre the sacred Muses, and it make
A servant to the vile affection
Of such, as he depended most upon,
And with the sugrie sweete thereof allure
Chast Ladies eares to fantasies impure. 820
To such delights the noble wits he led
Which him reliev'd, and their vaine humours fed
With fruitles follies, and unsound delights.
But if perhaps into their noble sprights
Desire of honor, or brave thought of armes
Did ever creepe, then with his wicked charmes
And strong conceipts he would it drive away,
Ne suffer it to house there halfe a day.
And whenso love of letters did inspire

Their gentle wits, and kindly wise desire, 830
That chieflie doth each noble minde adorne,
Then he would scoffe at learning, and eke scorne
The Sectaries thereof, as people base
And simple men, which never came in place
Of worlds affaires, but in darke corners mewd,
Muttred of matters, as their bookes them shewd,
Ne other knowledge ever did attaine,
But with their gownes their gravitie maintaine.
From them he would his impudent lewde speach
Against Gods holie Ministers oft reach, 840
And mocke Divines and their profession:
What else then did he by progression,
But mocke high God himselfe, whom they professe?
But what car'd he for God, or godlinesse?
All his care was himselfe how to advaunce,
And to uphold his courtly countenaunce
By all the cunning meanes he could devise;
Were it by honest wayes, or otherwise,
He made small choyce: yet sure his honestie
Got him small gaines, but shameles flatterie, 850
And filthie brocage, and unseemly shifts,
And borowe base, and some good Ladies gifts:
But the best helpe, which chiefly him sustain'd,
Was his man Raynolds purchase which he gain'd.
For he was school'd by kinde in all the skill
Of close conveyance, and each practise ill
Of coosinage and cleanly knaverie,
Which oft maintain'd his masters braverie.
Besides he usde another slipprie slight,
In taking on himselfe in common sight, 860
False personages fit for everie sted,
With which he thousands cleanly coosined:
Now like a Merchant, Merchants to deceave,
With whom his credite he did often leave
In gage, for his gay Masters hopeless dette:
Now like a Lawyer, when he land would lett,
Or sell fee-simples in his Masters name,
Which he had never, nor ought like the same:

Then would he be a Broker, and draw in
Both wares and money, by exchange to win: 870
Then would he seeme a Farmer, that would sell
Bargaines of woods, which he did lately fell,
Or corne, or cattle, or such other ware,
Thereby to coosin men not well aware;
Of all the which there came a secret fee
To th' Ape, that he his countenaunce might bee.
Besides all this, he usd' oft to beguile
Poore suters, that in Court did haunt some while:
For he would learne their busines secretly,
And then informe his Master hastely, 880
That he by meanes might cast them to prevent,
And beg the sute, the which the other ment.
Or otherwise false Reynold would abuse
The simple Suter, and wish him to chuse
His Master, being one of great regard
In Court, to compas anie sute not hard,
In case his paines were recompenst with reason:
So would he worke the silly man by treason
To buy his Masters frivolous good will,
That had not power to doo him good or ill. 890
So pitifull a thing is Suters state.
Most miserable man, whom wicked fate
Hath brought to Court, to sue for had ywist,
That few have found, and manie one hath mist;
Full little knowest thou that hast not tride,
What hell it is, in suing long to bide:
To loose good dayes, that might be better spent;
To wast long nights in pensive discontent;
To speed to day, to be put back to morrow;
To feed on hope, to pine with feare and sorrow; 900
To have thy Princes grace, yet want her Peeres;
To have thy asking, yet waite manie yeeres;
To fret thy soule with crosses and with cares;
To eate thy heart through comfortlesse dispaires;
To fawne, to crowche, to waite, to ride, to ronne,
To spend, to give, to want, to be undonne.
Unhappie wight, borne to desastrous end,

That doth his life in so long tendance spend.
Who ever leaves sweete home, where meane estate
In safe assurance, without strife or hate, 910
Findes all things needfull for contentment meeke;
And will to Court for shadowes vaine to seeke,
Or hope to gaine, himselfe will a daw trie:
That curse God send unto mine enemie.
For none but such as this bold Ape unblest,
Can ever thrive in that unluckie quest;
Or such as hath a Reynold to his man,
That by his shifts his Master furnish can.
But yet this Foxe could not so closely hide
His craftie feates, but that they were descride 920
At length, by such as sate in justice seate,
Who for the same him fowlie did entreate;
And having worthily him punished,
Out of the Court for ever banished.
And now the Ape wanting his huckster man,
That wont provide his necessaries, gan
To growe into great lacke, ne could upholde
His countenaunce in those his garments olde;
Ne new ones could he easily provide,
Though all men him uncased gan deride, 930
Like as a Puppit placed in a play,
Whose part once past all men bid take away:
So that he driven was to great distresse,
And shortly brought to hopelesse wretchednesse.
Then closely as he might he cast to leave
The Court, not asking any passe or leave;
But ran away in his rent rags by night,
Ne ever stayd in place, ne spake to wight,
Till that the Foxe his copesmate he had found,
To whome complayning his unhappy stound, 940
At last againe with him in travell joynd,
And with him far'd some better chaunce to fynde.
So in the world long time they wandered,
And mickle want and hardnesse suffered;
That them repented much so foolishly
To come so farre to seeke for misery,

And leave the sweetnes of contented home,
Though eating hipps, and drinking watry fome.
Thus as they them complayned too and fro,
Whilst through the forest rechlesse they did goe, 950
Lo where they spide, how in a gloomy glade,
The Lyon sleeping lay in secret shade,
His Crowne and Scepter lying him beside,
And having doft for heate his dreadfull hide:
Which when they sawe, the Ape was sore afrayde,
And would have fled with terror all dismayde.
But him the Foxe with hardy words did stay,
And bad him put all cowardize away:
For now was time (if ever they would hope)
To ayme their counsels to the fairest scope, 960
And them for ever highly to advaunce,
In case the good which their owne happie chaunce
Them freely offred, they would wisely take.
Scarse could the Ape yet speake, so did he quake,
Yet as he could, he askt how good might growe,
Where nought but dread & death do seeme in show.
Now (sayd he) whiles the Lyon sleepeth sound,
May we his Crowne and Mace take from the ground,
And eke his skinne the terror of the wood,
Wherewith we may our selves (if we thinke good) 970
Make Kings of Beasts, and Lords of forests all,
Subject unto that powre imperiall.
Ah but (sayd the Ape) who is so bold a wretch,
That dare his hardy hand to those outstretch:
When as he knowes his meede, if he be spide,
To be a thousand deathes, and shame beside?
Fond Ape (sayd then the Foxe) into whose brest
Never crept thought of honor, nor brave gest,
Who will not venture life a King to be,
And rather rule and raigne in soveraign see, 980
Than dwell in dust inglorious and bace,
Where none shall name the number of his place?
One joyous houre in blisfull happines,

I chose before a life of wretchednes.
Be therefore counselled herein by me,
And shake off this vile harted cowardree.
If he awake, yet is not death the next,
For we may coulor it with some pretext
Of this, or that, that may excuse the cryme:
Else we may flye; thou to a tree mayst clyme, 990
And I creepe under ground; both from his reach:
Therefore be rul'd to doo as I doo teach.
The Ape, that earst did nought but chill and quake,
Now gan some courage unto him to take,
And was content to attempt that enterprise,
Tickled with glorie and rash covetise.
But first gan question, whither should assay
Those royall ornaments to steale away?
Marie that shall your selfe (quoth he theretoo)
For ye be fine and nimble it to doo; 1000
Of all the beasts which in the forrests bee,
Is not a fitter for this turne than yee:
Therefore, mine owne deare brother take good hart,
And ever thinke a Kingdome is your part.
Loath was the Ape, though praised, to adventer,
Yet faintly gan into his worke to enter,
Afraid of everie leafe, that stir'd him by,
And everie stick, that underneath did ly;
Upon his tiptoes nicely he up went,
For making noyse, and still his eare he lent 1010
To everie sound, that under heaven blew;
Now went, now stept, now crept, now backward drew,
That it good sport had been him to have eyde:
Yet at the last (so well he him applyde,)
Through his fine handling, and cleanly play,
He all those royall signes had stolne away,
And with the Foxes helpe them borne aside,
Into a secret corner unespide.
Whether whenas they came, they fell at words,
Whether of them should be the Lord of Lords: 1020

For th' Ape was stryfull, and ambicious;
And the Foxe guilefull, and most covetous,
That neither pleased was, to have the rayne
Twixt them divided into even twaine,
But either (algates) would be Lords alone:
For Love and Lordship bide no paragone.
I am most worthie (said the Ape) sith I
For it did put my life in jeopardie:
Thereto I am in person, and in stature
Most like a man, the Lord of everie creature, 1030
So that it seemeth I was made to raigne,
And borne to be a Kingly soveraigne.
Nay (said the Foxe) Sir Ape you are astray:
For though to steale the Diademe away
Were the worke of your nimble hand, yet I
Did first devise the plot by pollicie;
So that it wholly springeth from my wit:
For which also I claime my selfe more fit
Than you, to rule: for government of state
Will without wisedome soone be ruinate. 1040
And where ye claime your selfe for outward shape
Most like a man, Man is not like an Ape
In his chiefe parts, that is, in wit and spirite;
But I therein most like to him doo merite
For my slie wyles and subtill craftinesse,
The title of the Kingdome to possesse.
Nath'les (my brother) since we passed are
Unto this point, we will appease our jarre,
And I with reason meete will rest content,
That ye shall have both crowne and government, 1050
Upon condition, that ye ruled bee
In all affaires, and counselled by mee;
And that ye let none other ever drawe
Your minde from me, but keepe this as a lawe:
And hereupon an oath unto me plight.
The Ape was glad to end the strife so light,
And thereto swore: for who would not oft sweare,
And oft unsweare a Diademe to beare?

Then freely up those royall spoyles he tooke,
Yet at the Lyons skin he inly quooke; 1060
But it dissembled, and upon his head
The Crowne, and on his backe the skin he did,
And the false Foxe him helped to array.
Then when he was all dight he tooke his way
Into the forest, that he might be seene
Of the wilde beasts in his new glory sheene.
There the two first, whome he encountred, were
The Sheepe and th' Asse, who striken both with feare
At sight of him, gan fast away to flye,
But unto them the Foxe alowd did cry, 1070
And in the Kings name bad them both to stay,
Upon the payne that thereof follow may.
Hardly naythles were they restrayned so,
Till that the Foxe forth toward them did goe,
And there disswaded them from needlesse feare,
For that the King did favour to them beare;
And therefore dreadles bad them come to Corte:
For no wild beasts should do them any torte
There or abroad, ne would his majestye
Use them but well, with gracious clemencye, 1080
As whome he knewe to him both fast and true;
So he perswaded them, with homage due
Themselves to humble to the Ape prostrate,
Who gently to them bowing in his gate,
Receyved them with chearefull entertayne.
Thenceforth proceeding with his princely trayne,
He shortly met the Tygre, and the Bore,
Which with the simple Camell raged sore
In bitter words, seeking to take occasion,
Upon his fleshly corpse to make invasion: 1090
But soone as they this mock-King did espy,
Their troublous strife they stinted by and by,
Thinking indeed that it the Lyon was:
He then to prove, whether his powre would pas
As currant, sent the Foxe to them streight way,
Commaunding them their cause of strife bewray;

And if that wrong on eyther side there were,
That he should warne the wronger to appeare
The morrow next at Court, it to defend;
In the meane time upon the King t' attend. 1100
The subtile Foxe so well his message sayd,
That the proud beasts him readily obayd:
Whereby the Ape in wondrous stomack woxe,
Strongly encorag'd by the crafty Foxe;
That King indeed himselfe he shortly thought,
And all the Beasts him feared as they ought:
And followed unto his palaice hye,
Where taking Conge, each one by and by
Departed to his home in dreadfull awe,
Full of the feared sight, which late they sawe. 1110
The Ape thus seized of the Regall throne,
Eftsones by counsell of the Foxe alone,
Gan to provide for all things in assurance,
That so his rule might lenger have endurance.
First to his Gate he pointed a strong gard,
That none might enter but with issue hard:
Then for the safegard of his personage,
He did appoint a warlike equipage
Of forreine beasts, not in the forest bred,
But part by land, and part by water fed; 1120
For tyrannie is with strange ayde supported.
Then unto him all monstrous beasts resorted
Bred of two kindes, as Griffons, Minotaures,
Crocodiles, Dragons, Beavers, and Centaures:
With those himselfe he strengthned mightelie,
That feare he neede no force of enemie.
Then gan he rule and tyrannize at will,
Like as the Foxe did guide his graceles skill,
And all wylde beasts made vassals of his pleasures,
And with their spoyles enlarg'd his private
treasures. 1130
No care of justice, nor no rule of reason,
No temperance, nor no regard of season
Did thenceforth ever enter in his minde,
But crueltie, the signe of currish kinde,

And sdeignfull pride, and wilfull arrogaunce;
Such followes those whom fortune doth advaunce.
But the false Foxe most kindly plaid his part:
For whatsoever mother wit, or arte
Could worke, he put in proofe: no practise slie,
No counterpoint of cunning policie, 1140
No reach, no breach, that might him profit bring,
But he the same did to his purpose wring.
Nought suffered he the Ape to give or graunt,
But through his hand must passe the Fiaunt.
All offices, all leases by him lept,
And of them all whatso he likte, he kept.
Justice he solde injustice for to buy,
And for to purchase for his progeny.
Ill might it prosper, that ill gotten was,
But so he got it, little did he pas. 1150
He fed his cubs with fat of all the soyle,
And with the sweete of others sweating toyle,
He crammed them with crumbs of Benefices,
And fild their mouthes with meeds of malefices,
He cloathed them with all colours save white,
And loded them with lordships and with might,
So much as they were able well to beare,
That with the weight their backs nigh broken were;
He chaffred Chayres in which Churchmen were
set,
And breach of lawes to privie ferme did let; 1160
No statute so established might bee,
Nor ordinaunce so needfull, but that hee
Would violate, though not with violence,
Yet under colour of the confidence
The which the Ape reposd' in him alone,
And reckned him the kingdomes corner stone.
And ever when he ought would bring to pas,
His long experience the platforme was:
And when he ought not pleasing would put by,
The cloke was care of thrift, and husbandry, 1170
For to encrease the common treasures store;
But his owne treasure he encreased more

And lifted up his loftie towres thereby,
That they began to threat the neighbour sky;
The whiles the Princes pallaces fell fast
To ruine: (for what thing can ever last?)
And whilest the other Peeres, for povertie
Were forst their auncient houses to let lie,
And their olde Castles to the ground to fall,
Which their forefathers famous over all 1180
Had founded for the Kingdomes ornament,
And for their memories long moniment.
But he no count made of Nobilitie,
Nor the wilde beasts whom armes did glorifie,
The Realmes chiefe strength & girlond of the crowne.
All these through fained crimes he thrust adowne,
Or made them dwell in darknes of disgrace:
For none, but whom he list might come in place.
Of men of armes he had but small regard,
But kept them lowe, and streigned verie hard. 1190
For men of learning little he esteemed;
His wisedome he above their learning deemed.
As for the rascall Commons least he cared;
For not so common was his bountie shared;
Let God (said he) if please, care for the manie,
I for my selfe must care before els anie:
So did he good to none, to manie ill,
So did he all the kingdome rob and pill,
Yet none durst speake, ne none durst of him plaine;
So great he was in grace, and rich through gaine. 1200
Ne would he anie let to have accesse
Unto the Prince, but by his owne addresse:
For all that els did come, were sure to faile,
Yet would he further none but for availe.
For on a time the Sheepe, to whom of yore
The Foxe had promised of friendship store,
What time the Ape the kingdome first did gaine,
Came to the Court, her case there to complaine,
How that the Wolfe her mortall enemie

Hath sithence slaine her Lambe most cruellie; 1210
And therefore crav'd to come unto the King,
To let him knowe the order of the thing.
Soft Gooddie Sheepe (then said the Foxe) not soe:
Unto the King so rash ye may not goe,
He is with greater matter busied,
Than a Lambe, or the Lambes owne mothers hed.
Ne certes may I take it well in part,
That ye my cousin Wolfe so fowly thwart,
And seeke with slaunder his good name to blot:
For there was cause, els doo it he would not. 1220
Therefore surcease good Dame, and hence depart.
So went the Sheepe away with heavie hart.
So manie moe, so everie one was used,
That to give largely to the boxe refused.
Now when high *Jove*, in whose almightie hand
The care of Kings, and power of Empires stand,
Sitting one day within his turret hye,
From whence he vewes with his blacklidded eye,
Whatso the heaven in his wide vawte containes,
And all that in the deepest earth remaines, 1230
The troubled kingdome of wilde beasts behelde,
Whom not their kindly Sovereigne did welde,
But an usurping Ape with guile suborn'd,
Had all subverst, he sdeignfully it scorn'd
In his great heart, and hardly did refraine,
But that with thunder bolts he had him slaine,
And driven downe to hell, his dewest meed:
But him avizing, he that dreadfull deed
Forbore, and rather chose with scornfull shame
Him to avenge, and blot his brutish name 1240
Unto the world, that never after anie
Should of his race be voyd of infamie:
And his false counsellor, the cause of all,
To damne to death, or dole perpetuall,
From whence he never should be quit, nor stal'd.
Forthwith he *Mercurie* unto him cal'd,
And bad him flie with never resting speed
Unto the forrest, where wilde beasts doo breed,

And there enquiring privily, to learne,
What did of late chaunce to the Lyon stearne, 1250
That he rul'd not the Empire, as he ought;
And whence were all those plaints unto him brought
Of wronges and spoyles, by salvage beasts committed;
Which done, he bad the Lyon be remitted
Into his seate, and those same treachours vile
Be punished for their presumptuous guile.
The Sonne of *Maia* soone as he receiv'd
That word, streight with his azure wings he cleav'd
The liquid clowdes, and lucid firmament;
Ne staid, till that he came with steep descent 1260
Unto the place, where his prescript did showe.
There stouping like an arrowe from a bowe,
He soft arrived on the grassie plaine,
And fairly paced forth with easie paine,
Till that unto the Pallace nigh he came.
Then gan he to himselfe new shape to frame,
And that faire face, and that Ambrosiall hew,
Which wonts to decke the Gods immortall crew,
And beautefie the shinie firmament,
He doft, unfit for that rude rabblement. 1270
So standing by the gates in strange disguize,
He gan enquire of some in secret wize,
Both of the King, and of his government,
And of the Foxe, and his false blandishment:
And evermore he heard each one complaine
Of foule abuses both in realme and raine.
Which yet to prove more true, he meant to see,
And an ey-witnes of each thing to bee.
Tho on his head his dreadfull hat he dight,
Which maketh him invisible in sight, 1280
And mocketh th' eyes of all the lookers on,
Making them thinke it but a vision.
Through power of that, he runnes through enemies swerds;
Through power of that, he passeth through the herds

Of ravenous wilde beasts, and doth beguile
Their greedie mouthes of the expected spoyle;
Through power of that, his cunning theeveries
He wonts to worke, that none the same espies;
And through the power of that, he putteth on,
What shape he list in apparition. 1290
That on his head he wore, and in his hand
He tooke *Caduceus* his snakie wand,
With which the damned ghosts he governeth,
And furies rules, and Tartare tempereth.
With that he causeth sleep to seize the eyes,
And feare the hearts of all his enemyes;
And when him list, an universall night
Throughout the world he makes on everie wight;
As when his Syre with *Alcumena* lay.
Thus dight, into the Court he tooke his way, 1300
Both through the gard, which never him descride,
And through the watchmen, who him never spide:
Thenceforth he past into each secrete part,
Whereas he saw, that sorely griev'd his hart;
Each place abounding with fowle injuries,
And fild with treasure rackt with robberies:
Each place defilde with blood of guiltles beasts,
Which had been slaine, to serve the Apes beheasts;
Gluttonie, malice, pride, and covetize,
And lawlesnes raigning with riotize; 1310
Besides the infinite extortions,
Done through the Foxes great oppressions,
That the complaints thereof could not be tolde.
Which when he did with lothfull eyes beholde,
He would no more endure, but came his way,
And cast to seeke the Lion, where he may,
That he might worke the avengement for this shame,
On those two caytives, which had bred him blame.
And seeking all the forrest busily,
At last he found, where sleeping he did ly: 1320
The wicked weed, which there the Foxe did lay,
From underneath his head he tooke away,
And then him waking, forced up to rize.

The Lion looking up gan him avize,
As one late in a traunce, what had of long
Become of him : for fantasie is strong.
Arise (said *Mercurie*) thou sluggish beast,
That here liest senseles, like the corpse deceast,
The whilste thy kingdome from thy head is rent,
And thy throne royall with dishonour blent : 1330
Arise, and doo thy selfe redeeme from shame,
And be aveng'd on those that breed thy blame.
Thereat enraged, soone he gan upstart,
Grinding his teeth, and grating his great hart,
And rouzing up himselfe, for his rough hide
He gan to reach ; but no where it espide.
Therewith he gan full terribly to rore,
And chafte at that indignitie right sore.
But when his Crowne and scepter both he wanted,
Lord how he fum'd, and sweld, and rag'd, and
panted ; 1340
And threatned death, & thousand deadly dolours
To them that had purloyn'd his Princely honours.
With that in hast, disroabed as he was,
He toward his owne Pallace forth did pas ;
And all the way he roared as he went,
That all the forrest with astonishment
Thereof did tremble, and the beasts therein
Fled fast away from that so dreadfull din.
At last he came unto his mansion,
Where all the gates he found fast lockt anon, 1350
And manie warders round about them stood :
With that he roar'd alowd, as he were wood,
That all the Pallace quaked at the stound,
As if it quite were riven from the ground,
And all within were dead and hartles left ;
And th' Ape himselfe, as one whose wits were reft,
Fled here and there, and everie corner sought,
To hide himselfe from his owne feared thought.
But the false Foxe when he the Lion heard,
Fled closely forth, streightway of death afeard, 1360
And to the Lion came, full lowly creeping,

With fained face, and watrie eyne halfe weeping,
T' excuse his former treason and abusion,
And turning all unto the Apes confusion:
Nath'les the royall Beast forbore beleeving,
But bad him stay at ease till further preeving.
Then when he saw no entraunce to him graunted,
Roaring yet lowder that all harts it daunted,
Upon those gates with force he fiercely flewe,
And rending them in pieces, felly slewe 1370
Those warders strange, and all that els he met.
But th' Ape still flying, he no where might get:
From rowme to rowme, from beame to beame he fled
All breathles, and for feare now almost ded:
Yet him at last the Lyon spide, and caught,
And forth with shame unto his judgement brought.
Then all the beasts he causd' assembled bee,
To heare their doome, and sad ensample see:
The Foxe, first Author of that treacherie,
He did uncase, and then away let flie. 1380
But th' Apes long taile (which then he had) he quight
Cut off, and both eares pared of their hight;
Since which, all Apes but halfe their eares have left,
And of their tailes are utterlie bereft.
So Mother *Hubberd* her discourse did end:
Which pardon me, if I amisse have pend,
For weake was my remembrance it to hold,
And bad her tongue that it so bluntly tolde.

FINIS.

RUINES OF ROME.

RUINES OF ROME: *by* Bellay

I

Ye heavenly spirites, whose ashie cinders lie
Under deep ruines, with huge walls opprest,
But not your praise, the which shall never die
Through your faire verses, ne in ashes rest;
  If so be shrilling voyce of wight alive
May reach from hence to depth of darkest hell,
Then let those deep Abysses open rive,
That ye may understand my shreiking yell.
  Thrice having seene under the heavens veale
Your toombs devoted compasse over all,
Thrice unto you with lowd voyce I appeale,
And for your antique furie here doo call,
  The whiles that I with sacred horror sing
  Your glorie, fairest of all earthly thing.

2

  Great *Babylon* her haughtie walls will praise,
And sharped steeples high shot up in ayre;
Greece will the olde *Ephesian* buildings blaze;
And *Nylus* nurslings their Pyramides faire;
  The same yet vaunting *Greece* will tell the storie
Of *Joves* great Image in *Olympus* placed,
Mausolus worke will be the *Carians* glorie;
And *Crete* will boast the Labyrinth, now raced.
  The antique *Rhodian* will likewise set forth
The great Colosse, erect to Memorie;
And what els in the world is of like worth,
Some greater learned wit will magnifie.
  But I will sing above all moniments
  Seven *Romane* Hils, the worlds 7. wonderments.

3

Thou stranger, which for *Rome* in *Rome* here seekest,
And nought of *Rome* in *Rome* perceiv'st at all,
These same olde walls, olde arches, which thou seest,
Olde Palaces, is that, which *Rome* men call.
Beholde what wreake, what ruine, and what wast,
And how that she, which with her mightie powre
Tam'd all the world, hath tam'd herselfe at last,
The pray of time, which all things doth devowre.
Rome now of *Rome* is th' onely funerall,
And onely *Rome* of *Rome* hath victorie;
Ne ought save *Tyber* hastning to his fall
Remaines of all: O worlds inconstancie.
That which is firme doth flit and fall away,
And that is flitting, doth abide and stay.

4

She, whose high top above the starres did sore,
One foote on *Thetis*, th' other on the Morning,
One hand on *Scythia*, th' other on the *More*,
Both heaven and earth in roundnesse compassing,
Jove fearing, least if she should greater growe,
The old Giants should once againe uprise,
Her whelm'd with hills, these 7. hils, which be nowe
Tombes of her greatnes, which did threate the skies:
Upon her head he heapt Mount *Saturnal*,
Upon her bellie th' antique *Palatine*,
Upon her stomacke laid Mount *Quirinal*,
On her left hand the noysome *Esquiline*,
And *Cælian* on the right; but both her feete
Mount *Viminal* and *Aventine* doo meete.

5

Who lists to see, what ever nature, arte,
And heaven could doo, O *Rome*, thee let him see,
In case thy greatnes he can gesse in harte,
By that which but the picture is of thee.
Rome is no more: but if the shade of *Rome*

May of the bodie yeeld a seeming sight,
It's like a corse drawne forth out of the tombe
By Magicke skill out of eternall night:
The corpes of *Rome* in ashes is entombed,
And her great spirite rejoyned to the spirite
Of this great masse, is in the same enwombed;
But her brave writings, which her famous merite
In spight of time, out of the dust doth reare,
Doo make her Idole through the world appeare.

6

Such as the *Berecynthian* Goddesse bright
In her swifte charret with high turrets crownde,
Proud that so manie Gods she brought to light;
Such was this Citie in her good daies fownd:
This Citie, more than that great *Phrygian* mother
Renowm'd for fruite of famous progenie,
Whose greatnes by the greatnes of none other,
But by her selfe her equall match could see:
Rome onely might to *Rome* compared bee,
And onely *Rome* could make great *Rome* to tremble:
So did the Gods by heavenly doome decree,
That other earthlie power should not resemble
Her that did match the whole earths puissaunce,
And did her courage to the heavens advaunce.

7

Ye sacred ruines, and ye tragick sights,
Which onely doo the name of *Rome* retaine,
Olde moniments, which of so famous sprights
The honour yet in ashes doo maintaine:
Triumphant Arcks, spyres neighbours to the skie,
That you to see doth th' heaven it selfe appall,
Alas, by little ye to nothing flie,
The peoples fable, and the spoyle of all:
And though your frames do for a time make warre
Gainst time, yet time in time shall ruinate
Your workes and names, and your last reliques marre.
My sad desires, rest therefore moderate:

For if that time make ende of things so sure,
It als will end the paine, which I endure.

8

Through armes & vassals *Rome* the world subdu'd,
That one would weene, that one sole Cities strength
Both land and sea in roundnes had survew'd,
To be the measure of her bredth and length :
This peoples vertue yet so fruitfull was
Of vertuous nephewes, that posteritie
Striving in power their grandfathers to passe,
The lowest earth, join'd to the heaven hie ;
To th' end that having all parts in their power,
Nought from the Romane Empire might be quight,
And that though time doth Commonwealths devowre,
Yet no time should so low embase their hight,
That her head earth'd in her foundations deep,
Should not her name and endles honour keep.

9

Ye cruell starres, and eke ye Gods unkinde,
Heaven envious, and bitter stepdame Nature,
Be it by fortune, or by course of kinde
That ye doo weld th' aflaires of earthlie creature ;
Why have your hands long sithence traveiled
To frame this world, that doth endure so long ?
Or why were not these Romane palaces
Made of some matter no lesse firme and strong ?
I say not, as the common voyce doth say,
That all things which beneath the Moone have being
Are temporall, and subject to decay :
But I say rather, though not all agreeing
With some, that weene the contrarie in thought ;
That all this whole shall one day come to nought.

10

As that brave sonne of *Aeson*, which by charmes

Atcheiv'd the golden Fleece in *Colchid* land,
Out of the earth engendred men of armes
Of Dragons teeth, sowne in the sacred sand;
  So this brave Towne, that in her youthlie daies
An *Hydra* was of warriours glorious,
Did fill with her renowmed nourslings praise
The firie sunnes both one and other hous:
  But they at last, there being then not living
An *Hercules*, so ranke seed to represse;
Emongst themselves with cruell furie striving,
Mow'd downe themselves with slaughter mercilesse;
  Renewing in themselves that rage unkinde,
Which whilom did those earthborn brethren blinde.

11

  Mars shaming to have given so great head
To his off-spring, that mortall puissaunce
Puft up with pride of Romane hardiehead,
Seem'd above heavens powre it selfe to advaunce;
  Cooling againe his former kindled heate,
With which he had those Romane spirits fild;
Did blowe new fire, and with enflamed breath,
Into the Gothicke colde hot rage instil'd:
  Then gan that Nation, th' earths new Giant brood,
To dart abroad the thunder bolts of warre,
And beating downe these walls with furious mood
Into her mothers bosome, all did marre;
  To th' end that none, all were it *Jove* his sire
  Should boast himselfe of the Romane Empire.

12

  Like as whilome the children of the earth
Heapt hils on hils, to scale the starrie skie,
And fight against the Gods of heavenly berth,
Whiles *Jove* at them his thunderbolts let flie;
  All suddenly with lightning overthrowne,
The furious squadrons downe to ground did fall,
That th' earth under her childrens weight did grone,
And th' heavens in glorie triumpht over all:

So did that haughtie front which heaped was
On these seven Romane hils, it selfe upreare
Over the world, and lift her loftie face
Against the heaven, that gan her force to feare.
But now these scorned fields bemone her fall,
And Gods secure feare not her force at all.

13

Nor the swift furie of the flames aspiring,
Nor the deep wounds of victours raging blade,
Nor ruthlesse spoyle of souldiers blood-desiring,
The which so oft thee (*Rome*) their conquest made;
Ne stroke on stroke of fortune variable,
Ne rust of age hating continuance,
Nor wrath of Gods, nor spight of men unstable,
Nor thou opposd' against thine owne puissance;
Nor th' horrible uprore of windes high blowing,
Nor swelling streames of that God snakie-paced,
Which hath so often with his overflowing
Thee drenched, have thy pride so much abaced;
But that this nothing, which they have thee left,
Makes the world wonder, what they from thee reft.

14

As men in Summer fearles passe the foord,
Which is in Winter lord of all the plaine,
And with his tumbling streames doth beare aboord
The ploughmans hope, and shepheards labour vaine:
And as the coward beasts use to despise
The noble Lion after his lives end,
Whetting their teeth, and with vaine foolhardise
Daring the foe, that cannot him defend:
And as at *Troy* most dastards of the Greekes
Did brave about the corpes of *Hector* colde;
So those which whilome wont with pallid cheekes
The Romane triumphs glorie to behold,
Now on these ashie tombes shew boldnesse vaine,
And conquer'd dare the Conquerour disdaine.

15

Ye pallid spirits, and ye ashie ghoasts,
Which joying in the brightnes of your day,
Brought foorth those signes of your presumptuous boasts
Which now their dusty reliques do bewray;
Tell me ye spirits (sith the darksome river
Of *Styx*, not passable to soules returning,
Enclosing you in thrice three wards for ever,
Doo not restraine your images still mourning)
Tell me then (for perhaps some one of you
Yet here above him secretly doth hide)
Doo ye not feele your torments to accrewe,
When ye sometimes behold the ruin'd pride
Of these old *Romane* works built with your hands,
Now to become nought els, but heaped sands?

16

Like as ye see the wrathfull Sea from farre,
In a great mountaine heap't with hideous noyse,
Eftsoones of thousand billowes shouldred narre,
Against a Rocke to breake with dreadfull poyse:
Like as ye see fell *Boreas* with sharpe blast,
Tossing huge tempests through the troubled skie,
Eftsoones having his wide wings spent in wast,
To stop his wearie cariere suddenly:
And as ye see huge flames spred diverslie,
Gathered in one up to the heavens to spyre,
Eftsoones consum'd to fall downe feebily:
So whilom did this Monarchie aspyre
As waves, as winde, as fire spred over all,
Till it by fatall doome adowne did fall.

17

So long as *Joves* great Bird did make his flight,
Bearing the fire with which heaven doth us fray,
Heaven had not feare of that presumptuous might,
With which the Giaunts did the Gods assay.
But all so soone, as scortching Sunne had brent

His wings, which wont the earth to overspredd,
The earth out of her massie wombe forth sent
That antique horror, which made heaven adredd.
Then was the Germane Raven in disguise
That Romane Eagle seene to cleave asunder,
And towards heaven freshly to arise
Out of these mountaines, now consum'd to pouder.
In which the foule that serves to beare the lightning,
Is now no more seen flying, nor alighting.

18

These heapes of stones, these old wals which ye see,
Were first enclosures but of salvage soyle;
And these brave Pallaces which maystred bee
Of time, were shepheards cottages somewhile.
Then tooke the shepheards Kingly ornaments
And the stout hynde arm'd his right hand with steele:
Eftsoones their rule of yearely Presidents
Grew great, and sixe months greater a great deele;
Which made perpetuall, rose to so great might,
That thence th' Imperiall Eagle rooting tooke,
Till th' heaven it selfe opposing gainst her might,
Her power to *Peters* successor betooke;
Who sheaprdlike, (as fates the same foreseeing)
Doth shew, that all things turne to their first being.

19

All that is perfect, which th' heaven beautefies;
All that's imperfect, borne belowe the Moone;
All that doth feede our spirits and our eies;
And all that doth consume our pleasures soone;
All the mishap, the which our daies outweares,
All the good hap of th' oldest times afore,
Rome in the time of her great ancesters,
Like a *Pandora*, locked long in store.
But destinie this huge *Chaos* turmoyling,

In which all good and evill was enclosed,
Their heavenly vertues from these woes assoyling,
Caried to heaven, from sinfull bondage losed:
  But their great sinnes, the causers of their paine,
  Under these antique ruines yet remaine.

20

  No otherwise than raynie cloud, first fed
With earthly vapours gathered in the ayre,
Eftsoones in compas arch't, to steepe his hed,
Doth plonge himselfe in *Tethys* bosome faire;
  And mounting up againe, from whence he came,
With his great bellie spreds the dimmed world,
Till at the last dissolving his moist frame,
In raine, or snowe, or haile he forth is horld;
  This Citie, which was first but shepheards shade,
Uprising by degrees, grewe to such height,
That Queene of land and sea her selfe she made.
At last not able to beare so great weight,
  Her power disperst, through all the world did
    vade;
  To shew that all in th' end to nought shall fade.

21

  The same which *Pyrrhus*, and the puissaunce
Of *Afrike* could not tame, that same brave Citie,
Which with stout courage arm'd against mischaunce,
Sustein'd the shocke of common enmitie;
  Long as her ship tost with so many freakes,
Had all the world in armes against her bent,
Was never seene, that anie fortunes wreakes
Could breake her course begun with brave intent.
  But when the object of her vertue failed,
Her power it selfe against it selfe did arme;
As he that having long in tempest sailed,
Faine would arive, but cannot for the storme,
  If too great winde against the port him drive,
  Doth in the port it selfe his vessell rive.

22

When that brave honour of the Latine name,
Which mear'd her rule with *Africa*, and *Byze*,
With *Thames* inhabitants of noble fame,
And they which see the dawning day arize;
Her nourslings did with mutinous uprore
Harten against her selfe, her conquer'd spoile,
Which she had wonne from all the world afore,
Of all the world was spoyl'd within a while.
So when the compast course of the universe
In sixe and thirtie thousand yeares is ronne,
The bands of th' elements shall backe reverse
To their first discord, and be quite undonne:
The seedes, of which all things at first were bred,
Shall in great *Chaos* wombe againe be hid.

23

O warie wisedome of the man, that would
That *Carthage* towres from spoile should be forborne,
To th' end that his victorious people should
With cancring laisure not be overworne;
He well foresaw, how that the Romane courage,
Impatient of pleasures faint desires,
Through idlenes would turne to civill rage,
And be her selfe the matter of her fires.
For in a people given all to ease,
Ambition is engendred easily;
As in a vicious bodie, grose disease
Soone growes through humours superfluitie.
That came to passe, when swolne with plenties pride,
Nor prince, nor peere, nor kin they would abide.

24

If the blinde furie, which warres breedeth oft,
Wonts not t' enrage the hearts of equall beasts,
Whether they fare on foote, or flie aloft,
Or armed be with clawes, or scalie creasts;
What fell *Erynnis* with hot burning tongs,

Did grype your hearts, with noysome rage imbew'd,
That each to other working cruell wrongs,
Your blades in your owne bowels you embrew'd?
  Was this (ye *Romanes*) your hard destinie?
Or some old sinne, whose unappeased guilt
Powr'd vengeance forth on you eternallie?
Or brothers blood, the which at first was spilt
  Upon your walls, that God might not endure,
  Upon the same to set foundation sure?

25

  O that I had the *Thracian* Poets harpe,
For to awake out of th' infernall shade
Those antique *Cæsars*, sleeping long in darke,
The which this auncient Citie whilome made:
  Or that I had *Amphions* instrument,
To quicken with his vitall notes accord,
The stonie joynts of these old walls now rent,
By which th' *Ausonian* light might be restor'd:
  Or that at least I could with pencill fine,
Fashion the pourtraicts of these Palacis,
By paterne of great *Virgils* spirit divine;
I would assay with that which in me is,
  To builde with levell of my loftie style,
  That which no hands can evermore compyle.

26

  Who list the Romane greatnes forth to figure,
Him needeth not to seeke for usage right
Of line, or lead, or rule, or squaire, to measure
Her length, her breadth, her deepnes, or her hight,
  But him behooves to vew in compasse round
All that the Ocean graspes in his long armes;
Be it where the yerely starre doth scortch the ground,
Or where colde *Boreas* blowes his bitter stormes.
  Rome was th' whole world, & al the world was
    Rome,
And if things nam'd their names doo equalize,
When land and sea ye name, then name ye *Rome*;

And naming *Rome* ye land and sea comprize :
For th' auncient Plot of *Rome* displayed plaine,
The map of all the wide world doth containe.

27

Thou that at *Rome* astonisht dost behold
The antique pride, which menaced the skie,
These haughtie heapes, these palaces of olde,
These wals, these arcks, these baths, these temples hie ;
Judge by these ample ruines vew, the rest
The which injurious time hath quite outworne,
Since of all workmen helde in reckning best,
Yet these olde fragments are for paternes borne :
Then also marke, how *Rome* from day to day,
Repayring her decayed fashion,
Renewes herselfe with buildings rich and gay ;
That one would judge, that the *Romaine Dæmon*
Doth yet himselfe with fatall hand enforce,
Againe on foote to reare her pouldred corse.

28

He that hath seene a great Oke drie and dead,
Yet clad with reliques of some Trophees olde,
Lifting to heaven her aged hoarie head,
Whose foote in ground hath left but feeble holde ;
But halfe disbowel'd lies above the ground,
Shewing her wreathed rootes, and naked armes,
And on her trunke all rotten and unsound
Onely supports herselfe for meate of wormes ;
And though she owe her fall to the first winde,
Yet of the devout people is ador'd,
And manie yong plants spring out of her rinde ;
Who such an Oke hath seene, let him record
That such this Cities honour was of yore,
And mongst all Cities florished much more.

29

All that which *Aegypt* whilome did devise,

All that which *Greece* their temples to embrave,
After th' Ionicke, Atticke, Doricke guise,
Or *Corinth* skil'd in curious workes to grave;
  All that *Lysippus* practike arte could forme,
Apelles wit, or *Phidias* his skill,
Was wont this auncient Citie to adorne,
And the heaven it selfe with her wide wonders fill;
  All that which *Athens* ever brought forth wise,
All that which *Afrike* ever brought forth strange,
All that which *Asie* ever had of prise,
Was here to see. O mervelous great change:
  Rome living, was the worlds sole ornament,
  And dead, is now the worlds sole moniment.

30

  Like as the seeded field greene grasse first showes,
Then from greene grasse into a stalke doth spring,
And from a stalke into an eare forth-growes,
Which eare the frutefull graine doth shortly bring;
  And as in season due the husband mowes
The waving lockes of those faire yeallow heares,
Which bound in sheaves, and layd in comely rowes,
Upon the naked fields in stalkes he reares:
  So grew the Romane Empire by degree,
Till that Barbarian hands it quite did spill,
And left of it but these olde markes to see,
Of which all passers by doo somewhat pill:
  As they which gleane, the reliques use to gather,
  Which th' husbandman behind him chanst to
    scater.

31

  That same is now nought but a champian wide,
Where all this worlds pride once was situate.
No blame to thee, whosoever dost abide
By *Nyle*, or *Gange*, or *Tygre*, or *Euphrate*,
  Ne *Afrike* thereof guiltie is, nor *Spaine*,
Nor the bolde people by the *Thamis* brincks,
Nor the brave warlicke brood of *Alemaine*,

Nor the borne Souldier which *Rhine* running drinks:
Thou onely cause, ô Civill furie, art
Which sowing in th' *Aemathian* fields thy spight,
Didst arme thy hand against thy proper hart;
To th' end that when thou wast in greatest hight
To greatnes growne, through long prosperitie,
Thou then adowne might'st fall more horriblie.

32

Hope ye my verses that posteritie
Of age ensuing shall you ever read?
Hope ye that ever immortalitie
So meane Harpes worke may chalenge for her meed?
If under heaven anie endurance were,
These moniments, which not in paper writ,
But in Porphyre and Marble doo appeare,
Might well have hop'd to have obtained it.
Nath'les my Lute, whom *Phœbus* deignd to give,
Cease not to sound these olde antiquities:
For if that time doo let thy glory live,
Well maist thou boast, how ever base thou bee,
That thou art first, which of thy Nation song
Th' olde honour of the people gowned long.

L' Envoy.

Bellay, first garland of free Poësie
That *France* brought forth, though fruitfull of brave wits,
Well worthie thou of immortalitie,
That long hast traveld by thy learned writs,
Olde *Rome* out of her ashes to revive,
And give a second life to dead decayes:
Needes must he all eternitie survive,
That can to other give eternall dayes.
Thy dayes therefore are endles, and thy prayse
Excelling all, that ever went before;
And after thee, gins *Bartas* hie to rayse

His heavenly Muse, th' Almightie to adore.
Live happie spirits, th' honour of your name,
And fill the world with never dying fame.

FINIS.

MUIOPOTMOS:
OR
THE FATE OF THE BUTTERFLIE.

MUIOPOTMOS:
OR
THE FATE OF THE BUTTERFLIE.

BY ED. SP.

DEDICATED TO THE MOST FAIRE AND VERTUOUS LADIE: THE LADIE CAREY.

TO THE RIGHT WORTHY AND VERTUOUS LADIE:

THE LA: CAREY.

MOST brave and bountifull La: for so excellent favours as I have received at your sweet handes, to offer these fewe leaves as in recompence, should be as to offer flowers to the Gods for their divine benefites. Therefore I have determined to give my selfe wholy to you, as quite abandoned from my selfe, and absolutely vowed to your services: which in all right is ever held for full recompence of debt or damage to have the person yeelded. My person I wot wel how little worth it is. But the faithfull minde & humble zeale which I beare unto your La: may perhaps be more of price, as may please you to account and use the poore service thereof; which taketh glory to advance your excellent partes and noble vertues, and to spend it selfe in honouring you: not so much for your great bounty to my self, which yet may not be unminded; nor for name or kindreds sake by you vouchsafed, beeing also regardable; as for that honorable name, which yee have by your brave deserts purchast to your self, & spred in the mouths of al men: with which I have also presumed to grace my verses, & under your name to commend to the world this smal Poëme, the which beseeching your La: to take in worth, and of all things therein according to your wonted graciousnes to make a milde construction, I humbly pray for your happines.

Your La: ever humbly;
E. S.

MUIOPOTMOS:

OR

THE FATE OF THE BUTTERFLIE.

I SING of deadly dolorous debate,
Stir'd up through wrathfull *Nemesis* despight,
Betwixt two mightie ones of great estate,
Drawne into armes, and proofe of mortall fight,
Through prowd ambition, and hartswelling hate,
Whilest neither could the others greater might
And sdeignfull scorne endure; that from small jarre
Their wraths at length broke into open warre.

The roote whereof and tragicall effect,
Vouchsafe, O thou the mournfulst Muse of nyne, 10
That wontst the tragick stage for to direct,
In funerall complaints and waylfull tyne,
Reveale to me, and all the meanes detect,
Through which sad *Clarion* did at last declyne
To lowest wretchednes; And is there then
Such rancour in the harts of mightie men?

Of all the race of silver-winged Flies
Which doo possesse the Empire of the aire,
Betwixt the centred earth, and azure skies,
Was none more favourable, nor more faire, 20
Whilst heaven did favour his felicities,
Then *Clarion*, the eldest sonne and haire
Of *Muscaroll*, and in his fathers sight
Of all alive did seeme the fairest wight.

With fruitfull hope his aged breast he fed
Of future good, which his yong toward yeares,
Full of brave courage and bold hardyhed,

Above th' ensample of his equall peares,
Did largely promise, and to him forered
(Whilst oft his heart did melt in tender teares) 30
That he in time would sure prove such an one,
As should be worthie of his fathers throne.

The fresh yong flie, in whom the kindly fire
Of lustfull yongth began to kindle fast,
Did much disdaine to subject his desire
To loathsome sloth, or houres in ease to wast,
But joy'd to range abroad in fresh attire;
Through the wide compas of the ayrie coast,
And with unwearied wings each part t' inquire
Of the wide rule of his renowmed sire. 40

For he so swift and nimble was of flight,
That from this lower tract he dar'd to stie
Up to the clowdes, and thence with pineons light,
To mount aloft unto the Christall skie,
To vew the workmanship of heavens hight:
Whence downe descending he along would flie
Upon the streaming rivers, sport to finde;
And oft would dare to tempt the troublous winde.

So on a Summers day, when season milde
With gentle calme the world had quieted, 50
And high in heaven *Hyperions* fierie childe
Ascending, did his beames abroad dispred,
Whiles all the heavens on lower creatures smilde;
Yong *Clarion* with vauntfull lustie head,
After his guize did cast abroad to fare;
And theretoo gan his furnitures prepare.

His breastplate first, that was of substance pure,
Before his noble heart he firmely bound,
That mought his life from yron death assure,
And ward his gentle corpes from cruell wound: 60
For it by arte was framed, to endure
The bit of balefull steele and bitter stownd,

No lesse then that, which *Vulcane* made to sheild
Achilles life from fate of *Troyan* field.

And then about his shoulders broad he threw
An hairie hide of some wilde beast, whom hee
In salvage forrest by adventure slew,
And reft the spoyle his ornament to bee:
Which spredding all his backe with dreadfull vew,
Made all that him so horrible did see, 70
Thinke him *Alcides* with the Lyons skin,
When the *Næmean* Conquest he did win.

Upon his head his glistering Burganet,
The which was wrought by wonderous device,
And curiously engraven, he did set:
The mettall was of rare and passing price;
Not *Bilbo* steele, nor brasse from *Corinth* fet,
Nor costly *Oricalche* from strange *Phœnice*;
But such as could both *Phœbus* arrowes ward,
And th' hayling darts of heaven beating hard. 80

Therein two deadly weapons fixt he bore,
Strongly outlaunced towards either side,
Like two sharpe speares, his enemies to gore:
Like as a warlike Brigandine, applyde
To fight, layes forth her threatfull pikes afore,
The engines which in them sad death doo hyde:
So did this flie outstretch his fearefull hornes,
Yet so as him their terrour more adornes.

Lastly his shinie wings as silver bright,
Painted with thousand colours, passing farre 90
All Painters skill, he did about him dight:
Not halfe so manie sundrie colours arre
In *Iris* bowe, ne heaven doth shine so bright,
Distinguished with manie a twinckling starre,
Nor *Junoes* Bird in her ey-spotted traine
So manie goodly colours doth containe.

Ne (may it be withouten perill spoken)
The Archer God, the Sonne of *Cytheree*,
That joyes on wretched lovers to be wroken,
And heaped spoyles of bleeding harts to see, 100
Beares in his wings so manie a changefull token.
Ah my liege Lord, forgive it unto mee,
If ought against thine honour I have tolde;
Yet sure those wings were fairer manifolde.

Full manie a Ladie faire, in Court full oft
Beholding them, him secretly envide,
And wisht that two such fannes, so silken soft,
And golden faire, her Love would her provide;
Or that when them the gorgeous Flie had doft,
Some one that would with grace be gratifide, 110
From him would steale them privily away,
And bring to her so precious a pray.

Report is that dame *Venus* on a day,
In spring when flowres doo clothe the fruitful ground,
Walking abroad with all her Nymphes to play,
Bad her faire damzels flocking her arownd,
To gather flowres, her forhead to array:
Emongst the rest a gentle Nymph was found,
Hight *Astery*, excelling all the crewe
In curteous usage, and unstained hewe. 120

Who being nimbler joynted than the rest,
And more industrious, gathered more store
Of the fields honour, than the others best;
Which they in secret harts envying sore,
Tolde *Venus*, when her as the worthiest
She praisd', that *Cupide* (as they heard before)
Did lend her secret aide, in gathering
Into her lap the children of the spring.

Whereof the Goddesse gathering jealous feare,
Not yet unmindfull, how not long agoe 130

Her sonne to *Psyche* secrete love did beare,
And long it close conceal'd, till mickle woe
Thereof arose, and manie a rufull teare;
Reason with sudden rage did overgoe,
And giving hastie credit to th' accuser,
Was led away of them that did abuse her.

Eftsoones that Damzel by her heavenly might,
She turn'd into a winged Butterflie,
In the wide aire to make her wandring flight;
And all those flowres, with which so plenteous-
lie 140
Her lap she filled had, that bred her spight,
She placed in her wings, for memorie
Of her pretended crime, though crime none were:
Since which that flie them in her wings doth beare.

Thus the fresh *Clarion* being readie dight,
Unto his journey did himselfe addresse,
And with good speed began to take his flight:
Over the fields in his franke lustinesse,
And all the champion he soared light,
And all the countrey wide he did possesse, 150
Feeding upon their pleasures bounteouslie,
That none gainsaid, nor none did him envie.

The woods, the rivers, and the medowes green,
With his aire-cutting wings he measured wide,
Ne did he leave the mountaines bare unseene,
Nor the ranke grassie fennes delights untride.
But none of these, how ever sweete they beene,
Mote please his fancie, nor him cause t' abide:
His choicefull sense with everie change doth flit.
No common things may please a wavering wit. 160

To the gay gardins his unstaid desire
Him wholly caried, to refresh his sprights:
There lavish Nature in her best attire,
Powres forth sweete odors, and alluring sights;

And Arte with her contending, doth aspire
T' excell the naturall, with made delights :
And all that faire or pleasant may be found,
In riotous excesse doth there abound.

There he arriving, round about doth flie,
From bed to bed, from one to other border, 170
And takes survey with curious busie eye,
Of everie flowre and herbe there set in order ;
Now this, now that he tasteth tenderly,
Yet none of them he rudely doth disorder,
Ne with his feete their silken leaves deface ;
But pastures on the pleasures of each place.

And evermore with most varietie,
And change of sweetnesse (for all change is sweete)
He casts his glutton sense to satisfie,
Now sucking of the sap of herbe most meete, 180
Or of the deaw, which yet on them does lie,
Now in the same bathing his tender feete :
And then he pearcheth on some braunch thereby,
To weather him, and his moyst wings to dry.

And then againe he turneth to his play,
To spoyle the pleasures of that Paradise :
The wholsome Saulge, and Lavender still gray,
Ranke smelling Rue, and Cummin good for eyes,
The Roses raigning in the pride of May,
Sharpe Isope, good for greene wounds remedies, 190
Faire Marigoldes, and Bees alluring Thime,
Sweet Marjoram, and Daysies decking prime.

Coole Violets, and Orpine growing still,
Embathed Balme, and chearfull Galingale,
Fresh Costmarie, and breathfull Camomill,
Dull Poppie, and drink-quickning Setuale,
Veyne-healing Verven, and hed-purging Dill,
Sound Savorie, and Bazil hartie-hale,
Fat Colworts, and comforting Perseline,
Colde Lettuce, and refreshing Rosmarine. 200

And whatso else of vertue good or ill
Grewe in this Gardin, fetcht from farre away,
Of everie one he takes, and tastes at will,
And on their pleasures greedily doth pray.
Then when he hath both plaid, and fed his fill,
In the warme Sunne he doth himselfe embay,
And there him rests in riotous suffisaunce
Of all his gladfulnes, and kingly joyaunce.

What more felicitie can fall to creature
Than to enjoy delight with libertie, 210
And to be Lord of all the workes of Nature,
To raine in th' aire from earth to highest skie,
To feed on flowres, and weeds of glorious feature,
To take what ever thing doth please the eie?
Who rests not pleased with such happines,
Well worthie he to taste of wretchednes.

But what on earth can long abide in state?
Or who can him assure of happie day;
Sith morning faire may bring fowle evening late,
And least mishap the most blisse alter may? 220
For thousand perills lie in close awaite
About us daylie, to worke our decay;
That none, except a God, or God him guide,
May them avoyde, or remedie provide.

And whatso heavens in their secret doome
Ordained have, how can fraile fleshly wight
Forecast, but it must needs to issue come?
The sea, the aire, the fire, the day, the night,
And th' armies of their creatures all and some
Do serve to them, and with importune might 230
Warre against us the vassals of their will.
Who then can save, what they dispose to spill?

Not thou, O *Clarion*, though fairest thou
Of all thy kinde, unhappie happie Flie,
Whose cruell fate is woven even now

Of *Joves* owne hand, to worke thy miserie:
Ne may thee helpe the manie hartie vow,
Which thy olde Sire with sacred pietie
Hath powred forth for thee, and th' altars sprent:
Nought may thee save from heavens avengement. 240

It fortuned (as heavens had behight)
That in this gardin, where yong *Clarion*
Was wont to solace him, a wicked wight
The foe of faire things, th' author of confusion,
The shame of Nature, the bondslave of spight,
Had lately built his hatefull mansion,
And lurking closely, in awayte now lay,
How he might anie in his trap betray.

But when he spide the joyous Butterflie
In this faire plot dispacing too and fro, 250
Fearles of foes and hidden jeopardie,
Lord how he gan for to bestirre him tho,
And to his wicked worke each part applie:
His hearte did earne against his hated foe,
And bowels so with ranckling poyson swelde,
That scarce the skin the strong contagion helde.

The cause why he this Flie so maliced,
Was (as in stories it is written found)
For that his mother which him bore and bred,
The most fine-fingred workwoman on ground, 260
Arachne, by his meanes was vanquished
Of *Pallas*, and in her owne skill confound,
When she with her for excellence contended,
That wrought her shame, and sorrow never ended.

For the *Tritonian* Goddesse having hard
Her blazed fame, which all the world had fil'd,
Came downe to prove the truth, and due reward
For her prais worthie workmanship to yeild
But the presumptuous Damzel rashly dar'd

The Goddesse selfe to chalenge to the field, 270
And to compare with her in curious skill
Of workes with loome, with needle, and with quill.

Minerva did the chalenge not refuse,
But deign'd with her the paragon to make :
So to their worke they sit, and each doth chuse
What storie she will for her tapet take.
Arachne figur'd how *Jove* did abuse
Europa like a Bull, and on his backe
Her through the sea did beare ; so lively seene,
That it true Sea, and true Bull ye would weene. 280

Shee seem'd still backe unto the land to looke,
And her play-fellowes aide to call, and feare
The dashing of the waves, that up she tooke
Her daintie feet, and garments gathered neare :
But (Lord) how she in everie member shooke,
When as the land she saw no more appeare,
But a wilde wildernes of waters deepe :
Then gan she greatly to lament and weepe.

Before the Bull she pictur'd winged Love,
With his yong brother Sport, light fluttering 290
Upon the waves, as each had been a Dove ;
The one his bowe and shafts, the other Spring
A burning Teade about his head did move,
As in their Syres new love both triumphing :
And manie Nymphes about them flocking round,
And manie *Tritons*, which their hornes did sound.

And round about, her worke she did empale
With a faire border wrought of sundrie flowres,
Enwoven with an Yvie winding trayle :
A goodly worke, full fit for Kingly bowres, 300
Such as Dame *Pallas*, such as Envie pale,
That al good things with venemous tooth devowres,
Could not accuse. Then gan the Goddesse bright
Her selfe likewise unto her worke to dight.

She made the storie of the olde debate,
Which she with *Neptune* did for *Athens* trie:
Twelve Gods doo sit around in royall state,
And *Jove* in midst with awfull Majestie,
To judge the strife betweene them stirred late:
Each of the Gods by his like visnomie 310
Eathe to be knowen; but *Jove* above them all,
By his great lookes and power Imperiall.

Before them stands the God of Seas in place,
Clayming that sea-coast Citie as his right,
And strikes the rockes with his three-forked mace;
Whenceforth issues a warlike steed in sight,
The signe by which he chalengeth the place,
That all the Gods, which saw his wondrous might
Did surely deeme the victorie his due:
But seldome seene, forejudgement proveth true. 320

Then to her selfe she gives her *Aegide* shield,
And steelhed speare, and morion on her hedd,
Such as she oft is seene in warlicke field:
Then sets she forth, how with her weapon dredd
She smote the ground, the which streight foorth did yield
A fruitfull Olyve tree, with berries spredd,
That all the Gods admir'd; then, all the storie
She compast with a wreathe of Olyves hoarie.

Emongst those leaves she made a Butterflie,
With excellent device and wondrous sight, 330
Fluttring among the Olives wantonly,
That seem'd to live, so like it was in sight:
The velvet nap which on his wings doth lie,
The silken downe with which his backe is dight,
His broad outstretched hornes, his hayrie thies,
His glorious colours, and his glistering eies.

Which when *Arachne* saw, as overlaid,
And mastered with workmanship so rare,

She stood astonied long, ne ought gainesaid,
And with fast fixed eyes on her did stare, 340
And by her silence, signe of one dismaid,
The victorie did yeeld her as her share:
Yet did she inly fret, and felly burne,
And all her blood to poysonous rancor turne:

That shortly from the shape of womanhed
Such as she was, when *Pallas* she attempted,
She grew to hideous shape of dryrihed,
Pined with griefe of folly late repented:
Eftsoones her white streight legs were altered
To crooked crawling shankes, of marrowe
empted, 350
And her faire face to fowle and loathsome hewe,
And her fine corpes to a bag of venim grewe.

This cursed creature, mindfull of that olde
Enfestred grudge, the which his mother felt,
So soone as *Clarion* he did beholde,
His heart with vengefull malice inly swelt;
And weaving straight a net with manie a folde
About the cave, in which he lurking dwelt,
With fine small cords about it stretched wide,
So finely sponne, that scarce they could be
spide. 360

Not anie damzell, which her vaunteth most
In skilfull knitting of soft silken twyne;
Nor anie weaver, which his worke doth boast
In dieper, in damaske, or in lyne;
Nor anie skil'd in workmanship embost;
Nor anie skil'd in loupes of fingring fine,
Might in their divers cunning ever dare,
With this so curious networke to compare.

Ne doo I thinke, that that same subtil gin,
The which the *Lemnian* God framde craftilie, 370
Mars sleeping with his wife to compasse in,

That all the Gods with common mockerie
Might laugh at them, and scorne their shamefull sin,
Was like to this. This same he did applie,
For to entrap the careles *Clarion*,
That rang'd each where without suspition.

Suspition of friend, nor feare of foe,
That hazarded his health, had he at all,
But walkt at will, and wandred too and fro,
In the pride of his freedome principall : 380
Litle wist he his fatall future woe,
But was secure, the liker he to fall.
He likest is to fall into mischaunce,
That is regardles of his governaunce.

Yet still *Aragnoll* (so his foe was hight)
Lay lurking covertly him to surprise,
And all his gins that him entangle might,
Drest in good order as he could devise.
At length the foolish Flie without foresight,
As he that did all daunger quite despise, 390
Toward those parts came flying careleslie,
Where hidden was his hatefull enemie.

Who seeing him, with secrete joy therefore
Did tickle inwardly in everie vaine,
And his false hart fraught with all treasons store,
Was fil'd with hope, his purpose to obtaine :
Himselfe he close upgathered more and more
Into his den, that his deceiptfull traine
By his there being might not be bewraid,
Ne anie noyse, ne anie motion made. 400

Like as a wily Foxe, that having spide,
Where on a sunnie banke the Lambes doo play,
Full closely creeping by the hinder side,
Lyes in ambushment of his hoped pray,
Ne stirreth limbe, till seeing readie tide,
He rusheth forth, and snatcheth quite away

One of the litle yonglings unawares:
So to his worke *Aragnoll* him prepares.

Who now shall give unto my heavie eyes
A well of teares, that all may overflow? 410
Or where shall I finde lamentable cryes,
And mournfull tunes enough my griefe to show?
Helpe O thou Tragick Muse, me to devise
Notes sad enough, t' expresse this bitter throw:
For loe, the drerie stownd is now arrived,
That of all happines hath us deprived.

The luckles *Clarion*, whether cruell Fate,
Or wicked Fortune faultles him misled,
Or some ungracious blast out of the gate
Of *Aeoles* raine perforce him drove on hed, 420
Was (O sad hap and howre unfortunate)
With violent swift flight forth caried
Into the cursed cobweb, which his foe
Had framed for his finall overthroe.

There the fond Flie entangled, strugled long,
Himselfe to free thereout; but all in vaine.
For striving more, the more in laces strong
Himselfe he tide, and wrapt his winges twaine
In lymie snares the subtill loupes among;
That in the ende he breathelesse did remaine, 430
And all his yougthly forces idly spent,
Him to the mercie of th' avenger lent.

Which when the greisly tyrant did espie,
Like a grimme Lyon rushing with fierce might
Out of his den, he seized greedelie
On the resistles pray, and with fell spight,
Under the left wing stroke his weapon slie
Into his heart, that his deepe groning spright
In bloodie streames foorth fled into the aire,
His bodie left the spectacle of care. 440

FINIS.

VISIONS OF THE WORLDS VANITIE

1.

One day, whiles that my daylie cares did sleepe,
My spirit, shaking off her earthly prison,
Began to enter into meditation deepe
Of things exceeding reach of common reason;
  Such as this age, in which all good is geason,
And all that humble is and meane debaced,
Hath brought forth in her last declining season,
Griefe of good mindes, to see goodnesse disgraced.
  On which when as my thought was throghly
    placed,
Unto my eyes strange showes presented were,
Picturing that, which I in minde embraced,
That yet those sights empassion me full nere.
  Such as they were (faire Ladie) take in worth,
  That when time serves, may bring things better
    forth.

2.

  In Summers day, when *Phœbus* fairly shone,
I saw a Bull as white as driven snowe,
With gilden hornes embowed like the Moone,
In a fresh flowring meadow lying lowe:
  Up to his eares the verdant grasse did growe,
And the gay floures did offer to be eaten;
But he with fatnes so did overflowe,
That he all wallowed in the weedes downe beaten,
  Ne car'd with them his daintie lips to sweeten:
Till that a Brize, a scorned little creature,
Through his faire hide his angrie sting did threaten,
And vext so sore, that all his goodly feature,
  And all his plenteous pasture nought him pleased:
  So by the small the great is oft diseased.

3.

Beside the fruitfull shore of muddie *Nile*,
Upon a sunnie banke outstretched lay
In monstrous length, a mightie Crocodile,
That cram'd with guiltles blood, and greedie pray
Of wretched people travailing that way,
Thought all things lesse than his disdainfull pride.
I saw a little Bird, cal'd *Tedula*,
The least of thousands which on earth abide,
That forst this hideous beast to open wide
The greisly gates of his devouring hell,
And let him feede, as Nature doth provide,
Upon his jawes, that with blacke venime swell.
Why then should greatest things the least disdaine,
Sith that so small so mightie can constraine ?

4.

The kingly Bird, that beares *Joves* thunder-clap,
One day did scorne the simple Scarabee,
Proud of his highest service, and good hap,
That made all other Foules his thralls to bee :
The silly Flie, that no redresse did see,
Spide where the Eagle built his towring nest,
And kindling fire within the hollow tree,
Burnt up his yong ones, and himselfe distrest ;
Ne suffred him in anie place to rest,
But drove in *Joves* owne lap his egs to lay ;
Where gathering also filth him to infest,
Forst with the filth his egs to fling away :
For which when as the Foule was wroth, said *Jove*,
Lo how the least the greatest may reprove.

5.

Toward the sea turning my troubled eye,
I saw the fish (if fish I may it cleepe)
That makes the sea before his face to flye,
And with his flaggie finnes doth seeme to sweepe
The fomie waves out of the dreadfull deep,
The huge *Leviathan*, dame Natures wonder,

Making his sport, that manie makes to weep :
A sword-fish small him from the rest did sunder,
That in his throat him pricking softly under,
His wide Abysse him forced forth to spewe,
That all the sea did roare like heavens thunder,
And all the waves were stain'd with filthie hewe.
Hereby I learned have, not to despise,
What ever thing seemes small in common eyes.

6.

An hideous Dragon, dreadfull to behold,
Whose backe was arm'd against the dint of speare
With shields of brasse, that shone like burnisht golde,
And forkhed sting, that death in it did beare,
Strove with a Spider his unequall peare :
And bad defiance to his enemie.
The subtill vermin creeping closely neare,
Did in his drinke shed poyson privilie ;
Which through his entrailes spredding diversly,
Made him to swell, that nigh his bowells brust,
And him enforst to yeeld the victorie,
That did so much in his owne greatnesse trust.
O how great vainnesse is it then to scorne
The weake, that hath the strong so oft forlorne.

7.

High on a hill a goodly Cedar grewe,
Of wondrous length, and streight proportion,
That farre abroad her daintie odours threwe ;
Mongst all the daughters of proud *Libanon*,
Her match in beautie was not anie one.
Shortly within her inmost pith there bred
A litle wicked worme, perceiv'd of none,
That on her sap and vitall moysture fed :
Thenceforth her garland so much honoured
Began to die, (O great ruth for the same)
And her faire lockes fell from her loftie head,
That shortly balde, and bared she became.

I, which this sight beheld, was much dismayed,
To see so goodly thing so soone decayed.

8.

Soone after this I saw an Elephant,
Adorn'd with bells and bosses gorgeouslie,
That on his backe did beare (as batteilant)
A gilden towre, which shone exceedinglie;
That he himselfe through foolish vanitie,
Both for his rich attire, and goodly forme,
Was puffed up with passing surquedrie,
And shortly gan all other beasts to scorne.
Till that a little Ant, a silly worme,
Into his nosthrils creeping, so him pained,
That casting down his towres, he did deforme
Both borrowed pride, and native beautie stained.
Let therefore nought that great is, therein glorie,
Sith so small thing his happines may varie.

9.

Looking far foorth into the Ocean wide,
A goodly ship with banners bravely dight,
And flag in her top-gallant I espide,
Through the maine sea making her merry flight:
Faire blew the winde into her bosome right;
And th' heavens looked lovely all the while,
That she did seeme to daunce, as in delight,
And at her owne felicitie did smile.
All sodainely there clove unto her keele
A little fish, that men call *Remora*,
Which stopt her course, and held her by the heele,
That winde nor tide could move her thence away.
Straunge thing me seemeth, that so small a thing
Should able be so great an one to wring.

10.

A mighty Lyon, Lord of all the wood,
Having his hunger throughly satisfide,

With pray of beasts, and spoyle of living blood,
Safe in his dreadles den him thought to hide:
  His sternesse was his prayse, his strength his pride,
And all his glory in his cruell clawes.
I saw a wasp, that fiercely him defide,
And bad him battaile even to his jawes;
  Sore he him stong, that it the blood forth drawes,
And his proude heart is fild with fretting ire;
In vaine he threats his teeth, his tayle, his pawes,
And from his bloodie eyes doth sparkle fire;
  That dead himselfe he wisheth for despight.
  So weakest may anoy the most of might.

11.

  What time the Romaine Empire bore the raine
Of all the world, and florisht most in might,
The nations gan their soveraigntie disdaine,
And cast to quitt them from their bondage quight:
  So when all shrouded were in silent night,
The *Galles* were, by corrupting of a mayde,
Possest nigh of the Capitol through slight,
Had not a Goose the treachery bewrayde.
  If then a Goose great *Rome* from ruine stayde,
And *Jove* himselfe, the patron of the place,
Preservd from being to his foes betrayde,
Why do vaine men mean things so much deface,
  And in their might repose their most assurance,
  Sith nought on earth can chalenge long endurance?

12.

  When these sad sights were overpast and gone,
My spright was greatly moved in her rest,
With inward ruth and deare affection,
To see so great things by so small distrest:
  Thenceforth I gan in my engrieved brest
To scorne all difference of great and small,
Sith that the greatest often are opprest,
And unawares doe into daunger fall.
  And ye, that read these ruines tragicall

Learne by their losse to love the low degree,
And if that fortune chaunce you up to call
To honours seat, forget not what you be :
  For he that of himselfe is most secure,
  Shall finde his state most fickle and unsure.

FINIS.

THE VISIONS OF BELLAY.

I.

It was the time, when rest soft sliding downe
From heavens hight into mens heavy eyes,
In the forgetfulnes of sleepe doth drowne
The carefull thoughts of mortall miseries:
  Then did a Ghost before mine eyes appeare,
On that great rivers banck, that runnes by *Rome*,
Which calling me by name, bad me to reare
My lookes to heaven whence all good gifts do come,
  And crying lowd, loe now beholde (quoth hee)
What under this great temple placed is:
Lo all is nought but flying vanitee.
So I that know this worlds inconstancies,
  Sith onely God surmounts all times decay,
  In God alone my confidence do stay

2.

On high hills top I saw a stately frame,
An hundred cubits high by just assize,
With hundreth pillours fronting faire the same,
All wrought with Diamond after Dorick wize:
  Nor brick, nor marble was the wall in view,
But shining Christall, which from top to base
Out of her womb a thousand rayons threw,
On hundred steps of *Afrike* golds enchase:
  Golde was the parget, and the seeling bright
Did shine all scaly with great plates of golde;
The floore of *Jasp* and *Emeraude* was dight.
O worlds vainesse. Whiles thus I did behold,
An earthquake shooke the hill from lowest seat,
And overthrew this frame with ruine great.

3.

Then did a sharped spyre of Diamond bright,
Ten feete each way in square, appeare to mee,
Justly proportion'd up unto his hight,
So far as Archer might his level see:
The top thereof a pot did seeme to beare,
Made of the mettall, which we most do honour,
And in this golden vessell couched weare
The ashes of a mightie Emperour:
Upon foure corners of the base were pight,
To beare the frame, foure great Lyons of gold;
A worthy tombe for such a worthy wight.
Alas this world doth nought but grievance hold.
I saw a tempest from the heaven descend,
Which this brave monument with flash did rend.

4.

I saw raysde up on yvorie pilloures tall,
Whose bases were of richest mettalls warke,
The chapters Alablaster, the fryses christall,
The double front of a triumphall Arke:
On each side purtraid was a Victorie,
Clad like a Nimph, that wings of silver weares,
And in triumphant chayre was set on hie,
The auncient glory of the Romaine Peares.
No worke it seem'd of earthly craftsmans wit,
But rather wrought by his owne industry,
That thunder-dartes for *Jove* his syre doth fit.
Let me no more see faire thing under sky,
Sith that mine eyes have seene so faire a sight
With sodain fall to dust consumed quight.

5.

Then was the faire *Dodonian* tree far seene,
Upon seaven hills to spread his gladsome gleame,
And conquerours bedecked with his greene,
Along the bancks of the *Ausonian* streame:
There many an auncient Trophee was addrest,
And many a spoyle, and many a goodly show,

Which that brave races greatnes did attest,
That whilome from the *Troyan* blood did flow.
  Ravisht I was so rare a thing to vew,
When lo a barbarous troupe of clownish fone
The honour of these noble boughs down threw,
Under the wedge I heard the tronck to grone;
  And since I saw the roote in great disdaine
  A twinne of forked trees send forth againe.

6.

  I saw a Wolfe under a rockie cave
Noursing two whelpes; I saw her litle ones
In wanton dalliance the teate to crave,
While she her neck wreath'd from them for the nones:
  I saw her raunge abroad to seeke her food,
And roming through the field with greedie rage
T' embrew her teeth & clawes with lukewarm blood
Of the small heards, her thirst for to asswage.
  I saw a thousand huntsmen, which descended
Downe from the mountaines bordring *Lombardie*,
That with an hundred speares her flank wide rended.
I saw her on the plaine outstretched lie,
  Throwing out thousand throbs in her owne soyle:
  Soone on a tree uphang'd I saw her spoyle.

7.

  I saw the Bird that can the Sun endure
With feeble wings assay to mount on hight,
By more and more she gan her wings t' assure,
Following th' ensample of her mothers sight:
  I saw her rise, and with a larger flight
To pierce the cloudes, and with wide pinneons
To measure the most haughtie mountaines hight,
Untill she raught the Gods owne mansions:
  There was she lost, when suddaine I behelde,
Where tumbling through the ayre in firie fold,
All flaming downe she on the plaine was felde;
And soone her bodie turn'd to ashes colde.

I saw the foule that doth the light dispise,
Out of her dust like to a worme arise.

8.

I saw a river swift, whose fomy billowes
Did wash the ground work of an old great wall;
I saw it cover'd all with griesly shadowes,
That with black horror did the ayre appall:
Thereout a strange beast with seven heads arose,
That townes and castles under her brest did coure,
And seem'd both milder beasts and fiercer foes
Alike with equall ravine to devoure.
Much was I mazde, to see this monsters kinde
In hundred formes to change his fearefull hew,
When as at length I saw the wrathfull winde,
Which blows cold storms, burst out of *Scithian* mew
That sperst these cloudes, and in so short as thought,
This dreadfull shape was vanished to nought.

9.

Then all astonied with this nightly ghoast,
An hideous bodie big and strong I sawe,
With side long beard, and locks down hanging loast,
Sterne face, and front full of Saturnlike awe;
Who leaning on the belly of a pot,
Pourd foorth a water, whose out gushing flood
Ran bathing all the creakie shore aflot,
Whereon the *Troyan* prince spilt *Turnus* blood;
And at his feete a bitch wolfe suck did yeeld
To two young babes: his left the *Palme* tree stout,
His right hand did the peacefull *Olive* wield,
And head with Lawrell garnisht was about.
Sudden both *Palme* and *Olive* fell away,
And faire greene Lawrell branch did quite decay.

10.

Hard by a rivers side a virgin faire,
Folding her armes to heaven with thousand throbs,

And outraging her cheekes and golden haire,
To falling rivers sound thus tun'd her sobs.
 Where is (quoth she) this whilom honoured face?
Where the great glorie and the auncient praise,
In which all worlds felicitie had place,
When Gods and men my honour up did raise?
 Suffisd' it not that civill warres me made
The whole worlds spoile, but that this Hydra new,
Of hundred *Hercules* to be assaide,
With seven heads, budding monstrous crimes anew,
 So many *Neroes* and *Caligulaes*
 Out of these crooked shores must dayly rayse.

11.

 Upon an hill a bright flame I did see,
Waving aloft with triple point to skie,
Which like incense of precious Cedar tree,
With balmie odours fil'd th' ayre farre and nie.
 A Bird all white, well feathered on each wing,
Hereout up to the throne of Gods did flie,
And all the way most pleasant notes did sing,
Whilst in the smoake she unto heaven did stie.
 Of this faire fire the scattered rayes forth threw
On everie side a thousand shining beames:
When sudden dropping of a silver dew
(O grievous chance) gan quench those precious flames;
 That it which earst so pleasant sent did yeld,
 Of nothing now but noyous sulphure smeld.

12.

 I saw a spring out of a rocke forth rayle,
 As cleare as Christall gainst the Sunnie beames,
 The bottome yeallow, like the golden grayle
That bright *Pactolus* washeth with his streames;
 It seem'd that Art and Nature had assembled
All pleasure there, for which mans hart could long;
And there a noyse alluring sleepe soft trembled,
Of manie accords more sweete than Mermaids song:

The seates and benches shone as yvorie,
And hundred Nymphes sate side by side about;
When from nigh hills with hideous outcrie,
A troupe of Satyres in the place did rout,
Which with their villeine feete the streame did ray,
Threw down the seats, & drove the Nymphs away.

13.

Much richer then that vessell seem'd to bee,
Which did to that sad *Florentine* appeare,
Casting mine eyes farre off, I chaunst to see,
Upon the *Latine* Coast herselfe to reare:
But suddenly arose a tempest great,
Bearing close envie to these riches rare,
Which gan assaile this ship with dreadfull threat,
This ship, to which none other might compare.
And finally the storme impetuous
Sunke up these riches, second unto none,
Within the gulfe of greedie *Nereus*.
I saw both ship and mariners each one,
And all that treasure drowned in the maine:
But I the ship saw after raisd' againe.

14.

Long having deeply gron'd these visions sad,
I saw a Citie like unto that same,
Which saw the messenger of tidings glad;
But that on sand was built the goodly frame:
It seem'd her top the firmament did rayse,
And no lesse rich than faire, right worthie sure
(If ought here worthie) of immortall dayes,
Or if ought under heaven might firme endure.
Much wondred I to see so faire a wall:
When from the Northerne coast a storme arose,
Which breathing furie from his inward gall
On all, which did against his course oppose,
Into a clowde of dust sperst in the aire
The weake foundations of this Citie faire.

15.

At length, even at the time, when *Morpheus*
Most trulie doth unto our eyes appeare,
Wearie to see the heavens still wavering thus,
I saw *Typhœus* sister comming neare;
Whose head full bravely with a morion hidd,
Did seeme to match the Gods in Majestie.
She by a rivers bancke that swift downe slidd,
Over all the world did raise a Trophee hie;
An hundred vanquisht Kings under her lay,
With armes bound at their backs in shamefull wize;
Whilst I thus mazed was with great affray,
I saw the heavens in warre against her rize:
Then downe she stricken fell with clap of thonder,
That with great noyse I wakte in sudden wonder.

FINIS.

THE VISIONS OF PETRARCH.

FORMERLY TRANSLATED.

I.

BEING one day at my window all alone,
So manie strange things happened me to see,
As much it grieveth me to thinke thereon.
At my right hand a Hynde appear'd to mee,
  So faire as mote the greatest God delite;
Two eager dogs did her pursue in chace,
Of which the one was blacke, the other white:
With deadly force so in their cruell race
  They pincht the haunches of that gentle beast,
That at the last, and in short time I spide,
Under a Rocke where she alas opprest,
Fell to the ground, and there untimely dide.
  Cruell death vanquishing so noble beautie,
  Oft makes me wayle so hard a destenie.

2.

  After at sea a tall ship did appeare,
Made all of Heben and white Yvorie,
The sailes of golde, of silke the tackle were,
Milde was the winde, calme seem'd the sea to bee,
  The skie eachwhere did show full bright and faire;
With rich treasures this gay ship fraighted was:
But sudden storme did so turmoyle the aire,
And tumbled up the sea, that she (alas)
  Strake on a rock, that under water lay,
And perished past all recoverie.
O how great ruth and sorrowfull assay,
Doth vex my spirite with perplexitie,
  Thus in a moment to see lost and drown'd,
  So great riches, as like cannot be found.

3.

The heavenly branches did I see arise
Out of the fresh and lustie Lawrell tree,
Amidst the yong greene wood: of Paradise
Some noble plant I thought my selfe to see:
Such store of birds therein yshrowded were,
Chaunting in shade their sundrie melodie,
That with their sweetnes I was ravish't nere.
While on this Lawrell fixed was mine eie,
The skie gan everie where to overcast,
And darkned was the welkin all about,
When sudden flash of heavens fire out brast,
And rent this royall tree quite by the roote,
Which makes me much and ever to complaine:
For no such shadow shalbe had againe.

4.

Within this wood, out of a rocke did rise
A spring of water, mildly rumbling downe,
Whereto approched not in anie wise
The homely shepheard, nor the ruder clowne;
But manie Muses, and the Nymphes withall,
That sweetly in accord did tune their voyce
To the soft sounding of the waters fall,
That my glad hart thereat did much rejoyce.
But while herein I tooke my chiefe delight,
I saw (alas) the gaping earth devoure
The spring, the place, and all cleane out of sight.
Which yet aggreeves my hart even to this houre,
And wounds my soule with rufull memorie,
To see such pleasures gon so suddenly.

5.

I saw a Phœnix in the wood alone,
With purple wings, and crest of golden hewe;
Strange bird he was, whereby I thought anone,
That of some heavenly wight I had the vewe;
Untill he came unto the broken tree,

And to the spring, that late devoured was.
What say I more? each thing at last we see
Doth passe away: the Phœnix there alas
  Spying the tree destroid, the water dride,
Himselfe smote with his beake, as in disdaine,
And so foorthwith in great despight he dide:
That yet my heart burnes in exceeding paine,
  For ruth and pitie of so haples plight.
  O let mine eyes no more see such a sight.

6.

  At last so faire a Ladie did I spie,
That thinking yet on her I burne and quake;
On hearbs and flowres she walked pensively,
Milde, but yet love she proudly did forsake:
  White seem'd her robes, yet woven so they were,
As snow and golde together had been wrought.
Above the wast a darke clowde shrouded her,
A stinging Serpent by the heele her caught;
  Wherewith she languisht as the gathered floure,
And well assur'd she mounted up to joy.
Alas, on earth so nothing doth endure,
But bitter griefe and sorrowfull annoy:
  Which make this life wretched and miserable,
  Tossed with stormes of fortune variable.

  When I beheld this tickle trustles state
Of vaine worlds glorie, flitting too and fro,
And mortall men tossed by troublous fate
In restles seas of wretchednes and woe,
  I wish I might this wearie life forgoe,
And shortly turne unto my happie rest,
Where my free spirite might not any moe
Be vext with sights, that doo her peace molest.
  And ye faire Ladie, in whose bounteous brest
All heavenly grace and vertue shrined is,
When ye these rythmes doo read, and vew the rest,
Loath this base world, and thinke of heavens blis:

And though ye be the fairest of Gods creatures,
Yet thinke, that death shall spoyle your goodly
features.

FINIS.

APPENDIX:

EPIGRAMS AND SONNETS FROM

A Theatre for Voluptuous Worldlings, 1569.

APPENDIX.

EPIGRAMS.

Being one day at my window all alone,
So many strange things hapned me to see,
As much it grieveth me to thinke thereon.
At my right hande, a Hinde appearde to me,
So faire as mought the greatest God delite:
Two egre Dogs dyd hir pursue in chace,
Of which the one was black, the other white.
With deadly force, so in their cruell race
They pinchte the haunches of this gentle beast,
That at the last, and in shorte time, I spied,
Under a rocke, where she (alas) opprest,
Fell to the grounde, and there untimely dide.
Cruell death vanquishing so noble beautie,
Oft makes me waile so harde a destinie.

After at Sea a tall Ship dyd appere,
Made all of Heben and white Ivorie,
The sailes of Golde, of Silke the tackle were:
Milde was the winde, calme seemed the sea to be:
The Skie eche where did shew full bright and faire.
With riche treasures this gay ship fraighted was.
But sodaine storme did so turmoyle the aire,
And tombled up the sea, that she, alas,
Strake on a rocke that under water lay.
O great misfortune, O great griefe, I say,
Thus in one moment to see lost and drownde
So great riches, as lyke can not be founde.

Then heavenly branches did I see arise,
Out of a fresh and lusty Laurell tree
Amidde the yong grene wood. Of Paradise
Some noble plant I thought my selfe to see,
Such store of birdes therein yshrouded were,
Chaunting in shade their sundry melodie.
My sprites were ravisht with these pleasures there.
While on this Laurell fixed was mine eye,

The Skie gan every where to overcast,
And darkned was the welkin all aboute,
When sodaine flash of heavens fire outbrast,
And rent this royall tree quite by the roote.
Which makes me much and ever to complaine,
For no such shadow shall be had againe.

Within this wood, out of the rocke did rise
A Spring of water mildely romblyng downe,
Whereto approched not in any wise
The homely Shepherde, nor the ruder cloune,
But many Muses, and the Nymphes withall,
That sweetely in accorde did tune their voice
Unto the gentle sounding of the waters fall.
The sight wherof dyd make my heart rejoyce.
But while I toke herein my chiefe delight,
I sawe (alas) the gaping earth devoure
The Spring, the place, and all cleane out of sight.
Whiche yet agreves my heart even to this houre.

I saw a Phœnix in the wood alone,
With purple wings and crest of golden hew,
Straunge birde he was, wherby I thought anone,
That of some heavenly wight I had the vew:
Untill he came unto the broken tree
And to the spring that late devoured was.
What say I more? Eche thing at length we see
Doth passe away: the Phœnix there, alas,
Spying the tree destroyde, the water dride,
Himselfe smote with his beake, as in disdaine,
And so forthwith in great despite he dide.
For pity and love my heart yet burnes in paine.

At last so faire a Ladie did I spie,
That in thinking on hir I burne and quake,
On herbes and floures she walked pensively.
Milde, but yet love she proudely did forsake.
White seemed hir robes, yet woven so they were,
As snowe and golde together had bene wrought.
Above the waste a darke cloude shrouded hir,
A stinging Serpent by the heele hir caught,
Wherewith she languisht as the gathered floure:
And well assurde she mounted up to joy.
Alas in earth so nothing doth endure
But bitter griefe that dothe our hearts anoy.

My Song thus now in thy Conclusions,
Say boldly that these same six visions
Do yelde unto thy lorde a sweete request,
Ere it be long within the earth to rest.

SONETS.

It was the time when rest the gift of Gods
Sweetely sliding into the eyes of men,
Doth drowne in the forgetfulnesse of slepe,
The carefull travailes of the painefull day :
Then did a ghost appeare before mine eyes
On that great rivers bank that runnes by Rome,
And calling me then by my propre name,
He bade me upwarde unto heaven looke.
He cride to me, and loe (quod he) beholde,
What under this great Temple is containde,
Loe all is nought but flying vanitie.
So I knowing the worldes unstedfastnesse,
Sith onely God surmountes the force of tyme,
In God alone do stay my confidence.

On hill, a frame an hundred cubites hie
I sawe, an hundred pillers eke about,
All of fine Diamant decking the front,
And fashiond were they all in Dorike wise.
Of bricke, ne yet of marble was the wall,
But shining Christall, which from top to base
Out of deepe vaute threw forth a thousand rayes
Upon an hundred steps of purest golde.
Golde was the parget : and the sielyng eke
Did shine all scaly with fine golden plates.
The floore was Jaspis, and of Emeraude.
O worldes vainenesse. A sodein earthquake loe,
Shaking the hill even from the bottome deepe,
Threwe downe this building to the lowest stone.

Then did appeare to me a sharped spire
Of diamant, ten feete eche way in square,
Justly proportionde up unto his height,
So hie as mought an Archer reache with sight.
Upon the top thereof was set a pot
Made of the mettall that we honour most.
And in this golden vessell couched were

The ashes of a mightie Emperour.
Upon foure corners of the base there lay
To beare the frame, foure great Lions of golde.
A worthie tombe for such a worthie corps.
Alas, nought in this worlde but griefe endures.
A sodaine tempest from the heaven, I saw,
With flushe stroke downe this noble monument.

I SAW raisde up on pillers of Ivorie,
Whereof the bases were of richest golde,
The chapters Alabaster, Christall frises,
The double front of a triumphall arke.
On eche side portraide was a victorie.
With golden wings in habite of a Nymph.
And set on hie upon triumphing chaire,
The auncient glorie of the Romane lordes.
The worke did shew it selfe not wrought by man
But rather made by his owne skilfull hande
That forgeth thunder dartes for Jove his sire.
Let me no more see faire thing under heaven,
Sith I have seene so faire a thing as this,
With sodaine falling broken all to dust.

THEN I behelde the faire Dodonian tree,
Upon seven hilles throw forth his gladsome shade.
And Conquerers bedecked with his leaves
Along the bankes of the Italian streame.
There many auncient Trophees were erect,
Many a spoile, and many goodly signes,
To shewe the greatnesse of the stately race,
That erst descended from the Trojan bloud.
Ravisht I was to see so rare a thing,
When barbarous villaines in disordred heape,
Outraged the honour of these noble bowes.
I heard the tronke to grone under the wedge.
And since I saw the roote in hie disdaine
Sende forth againe a twinne of forked trees.

I SAW the birde that dares beholde the Sunne,
With feeble flight venture to mount to heaven,
By more and more she gan to trust hir wings,
Still folowing th' example of hir damme:
I saw hir rise, and with a larger flight
Surmount the toppes even of the hiest hilles,
And pierce the cloudes, and with hir wings to reache

The place where is the temple of the Gods,
There was she lost, and sodenly I saw
Where tombling through the aire in lompe of fire,
All flaming downe she fell upon the plaine.
I saw hir bodie turned all to dust,
And saw the foule that shunnes the cherefull light
Out of hir ashes as a worme arise.

THEN all astonned with this nightly ghost,
I saw an hideous body big and strong,
Long was his beard, and side did hang his hair,
A grisly forehed and Saturnelike face.
Leaning against the belly of a pot
He shed a water, whose outgushing streame
Ran flowing all along the creekie shoare
Where once the Troyan Duke with Turnus fought.
And at his feete a bitch Wolfe did give sucke
To two yong babes. In his right hand he bare
The tree of peace, in left the conquering Palme,
His head was garnisht with the Laurel bow.
Then sodenly the Palme and Olive fell,
And faire greene Laurel witherd up and dide.

HARD by a rivers side, a wailing Nimphe,
Folding hir armes with thousand sighs to heaven,
Did tune her plaint to falling rivers sound,
Renting hir faire visage and golden haire,
Where is (quod she) this whilome honored face?
Where is thy glory and the auncient praise,
Where all worldes hap was reposed,
When erst of Gods and man I worshipt was?
Alas, suffisde it not that civile bate
Made me the spoile and bootie of the world,
But this new Hydra mete to be assailde
Even by an hundred such as Hercules,
With seven springing heds of monstrous crimes,
So many Neroes and Caligulaes
Must still bring forth to rule this croked shore.

UPON a hill I saw a kindled flame,
Mounting like waves with triple point to heaven,
Which of incense of precious Ceder tree
With Balmelike odor did perfume the aire.
A bird all white, well fetherd on hir winges
Hereout did flie up to the throne of Gods,

And singing with most plesant melodie
She climbed up to heaven in the smoke.
Of this faire fire the faire dispersed rayes
Threw forth abrode a thousand shining leames,
When sodain dropping of a golden shoure
Gan quench the glystering flame. O grevous chaunge !
That which erstwhile so pleasaunt scent did yelde,
Of Sulphure now did breathe corrupted smel.

I SAW a fresh spring rise out of a rocke,
Clere as Christall against the Sunny beames,
The bottome yellow like the shining land,
That golden Pactol drives upon the plaine.
It seemed that arte and nature strived to joyne
There in one place all pleasures of the eye.
There was to heare a noise alluring slepe
Of many accordes more swete than Mermaids song,
The seates and benches shone as Ivorie,
An hundred Nymphes sate side by side about,
When from nie hilles a naked rout of Faunes
With hideous cry assembled on the place,
Which with their feete uncleane the water fouled,
Threw down the seats, & drove the Nimphs to flight.

AT length, even at the time when Morpheus
Most truely doth appeare unto our eyes,
Wearie to see th' inconstance of the heavens :
I saw the great Typhæus sister come,
Hir head full bravely with a morian armed ;
In majestie she seemde to matche the Gods.
And on the shore, harde by a violent streame,
She raisde a Trophee over all the worlde.
An hundred vanquisht kings gronde at hir feete,
Their armes in shamefull wise bounde at their backes.
While I was with so dreadfull sight afrayde,
I saw the heavens warre against hir tho,
And seing hir striken fall with clap of thunder,
With so great noyse I start in sodaine wonder.

I SAW an ugly beast come from the sea,
That seven heads, ten crounes, ten hornes did beare,
Having theron the vile blaspheming name.
The cruell Leopard she resembled much :
Feete of a beare, a Lions throte she had.
The mightie Dragon gave to hir his power.

One of hir heads yet there I did espie,
Still freshly bleeding of a grievous wounde.
One cride aloude. What one is like (quod he)
This honoured Dragon, or may him withstande?
And then came from the sea a savage beast,
With Dragons speche, and shewde his force by fire,
With wondrous signes to make all wights adore
The beast, in setting of hir image up.

I SAW a Woman sitting on a beast
Before mine eyes, of Orenge colour hew:
Horrour and dreadfull name of blasphemie
Filde hir with pride. And seven heads I saw,
Ten hornes also the stately beast did beare.
She seemde with glorie of the scarlet faire,
And with fine perle and golde puft up in heart.
The wine of hooredome in a cup she bare.
The name of Mysterie writ in her face.
The bloud of Martyrs dere were hir delite.
Most fierce and fell this woman seemde to me.
An Angell then descending downe from Heaven,
With thondring voice cride out aloude, and sayd,
Now for a truth great Babylon is fallen.

THEN might I see upon a white horse set
The faithfull man with flaming countenaunce,
His head did shine with crounes set therupon.
The worde of God made him a noble name.
His precious robe I saw embrued with bloud.
Then saw I from the heaven on horses white,
A puissant armie come the selfe same way.
Then cried a shining Angell as me thought,
That birdes from aire descending downe on earth
Should warre upon the kings, and eate their flesh.
Then did I see the beast and Kings also
Joinyng their force to slea the faithfull man.
But this fierce hatefull beast and all hir traine,
Is pitilesse throwne downe in pit of fire.

I SAW new Earth, new Heaven, sayde Saint John.
And loe, the sea (quod he) is now no more.
The holy Citie of the Lorde, from hye
Descendeth garnisht as a loved spouse.
A voice then sayde, beholde the bright abode
Of God and men. For he shall be their God,

And all their teares he shall wipe cleane away.
Hir brightnesse greater was than can be founde.
Square was this Citie, and twelve gates it had.
Eche gate was of an orient perfect pearle,
The houses golde, the pavement precious stone.
A lively streame, more cleere than Christall is,
Ranne through the mid, sprong from triumphant seat.
There growes lifes fruite unto the Churches good.

COMMENTARY.

COMMENTARY.

It is not on these *Complaints* that Spenser's poetic reputation rests. None of his greatest things are here. There are many good passages, and pretty pieces which none but he could have written, and innumerable scholarly ingenuities which he obviously enjoyed devising, but only one capital poem, only one whose loss would alter our conception of Spenser—*Mother Hubberds Tale.*

The minor works of great poets, however, like the drawings of great painters, sometimes disclose even more of the personality, the interests, and the habits of their authors than do the elaborate masterpieces. There is a certain parti pris in *The Faerie Queene*, *Paradise Lost*, *Hyperion.* Spenser, Milton, Keats fold their singing robes somewhat consciously about them, somewhat deliberately assume the laurel, laying aside some part of the man to soar as The Poet. It is an enlargement but also an abstraction of the Self—the self we find more easily, since it is nearer our own level, in *Mother Hubberds Tale*, in *Muiopotmos*, in *Lycidas*, in *I stood Tiptoe.* Even where that Self is projected into the theme, the very scale of it removes it from us. The Milton of *Samson Agonistes* affects us by a more awful majesty than any one man's physical disabilities and political disappointments have any right to give him in this sublunary world; the Colin Clout of the Sixth Book of *The Faerie Queene* glows Giorgionesque in a rapturous vision of poetry: and having gazed and wondered, having trembled, having envied, we turn to the lesser works to meet the man in his less godlike moments, to watch him experimenting, to hear his opinions, to share his amusements, his personal attachments, his tastes and his grievances.

The bookseller Ponsonby states quite explicitly the motive for this publication. The First Part of *The Faerie Queene* was a success, Spenser's position as the best poet of his time was definitely established, and—like Harrison, who brought out the third edition of *The Shepheardes Calender* at the same time—poet and publisher were taking the tide of fortune. Ponsonby assumes all the responsibility for the collection and publication of these poems, but it is difficult to believe that Spenser was not concerned. He was in England at the time, and he had too keen a sense of his own dignity and of the value of his work to leave the collection and arrangement even of minor poems to chance and the taste of his publisher. The position of both Spenser and Ponsonby precludes any idea of unauthorised publication. The book itself is fair evidence against the suggestion of a casual gleaning, for one or two of the corrections which cause variation between copies look like author's corrections, and the volume is carefully arranged to open with a poem of general contemporary interest and to divide the remainder between the three ladies to whom they are dedicated, even separating *The Visions of Bellay* from *The Ruines of Rome* (which should go together) in order to make the shares of original work and translation approximately equal. If, lastly, this was merely a print of such poems of Spenser as Ponsonby could scrape together, it is a strange coincidence that they should so uniformly " containe like matter of argument." Ponsonby's preface is best understood as but another example of the common deprecatory preface made fashionable by the lingering aristocratic prejudice against publishing the fruits of a gentleman's leisure.

Spenser and Ponsonby, then, made up this volume of minor poems, selecting them by subject and not by date. The first poem in the book is the most recent, *The Ruines of Time*, which, since it alludes to the death of Walsingham, cannot be dated—in its present form, at least—earlier than April, 1590. Only a small part of it could be written before 1586. Of the other poems which can be dated, *Virgils Gnat* belongs to the period of Spenser's relations with Leicester, that is, to 1580 or thereabout, and so does *Mother Hubberds Tale*, since it contains what all commentators are agreed is an allusion to Queen Elizabeth's anger at Leicester's marriage to the Countess of Essex, of which she became aware in 1579. None of the other poems contain any detail by which the date of composition can be deduced conclusively, and the attempt to assign them to particular years within the decade 1580-1590 is fraught with difficulty. The translations from du Bellay and Petrarch, for instance, might be supposed to be early work, since they are revisions of versions published anonymously as early as 1569, but the poem most closely related to them is the latest of all, *The*

Ruines of Time. Similarly, that extremely skilful poem *Muiopotmos* seems "mature," and may be comparatively late work, but it is strongly influenced by the early *Virgils Gnat*, and any placing of it within the decade is entirely conjectural.

Nor is style a sure criterion in dating the work of so self-conscious a craftsman as Spenser. His verse and language are always those of a master, of one who can do with verse and language what he wants to do; his very roughnesses are wilful. We cannot trace development from clumsiness to skill, nor development through a series of discipleships, for on one hand Spenser remained faithful to the same gods throughout his working life, and on the other, no English poet has left on all his work, early and late, so original an impress of accent and idiom. Craik, indeed, refuses to believe that *The Teares of the Muses* could be early work, on the ground that the style is closer to that of *The Faerie Queene* than to that of *The Shepheardes Calender*: but Gabriel Harvey had seen part of *The Faerie Queene* in 1580, and in any case it would have been an impossible breach of Decorum to have made the Muses talk like the shepherds.* Arguments from style are apt to be based on individual feeling, even when they seem most scientific. On this understanding I may state my own impression that the violent, noisy style of this poem betrays lack of experience. But leaving that aside, a comparison of *The Teares of the Muses* and *The Shepheardes Calender* reveals certain resemblances in the matter.

The date of *The Teares of the Muses* may receive further consideration here, because personal allusions are involved —allusions, like so many of Spenser's, obscure and controversial. It is improbable that Spenser wrote this poem in Ireland, since the subject would surely have moved him to include among his distresses, as in *Colin Clouts Come Home Again*, the barbarity of his surroundings and the disturbances he suffered. It appears to belong, then, either to the years 1578-80 or to 1589-90, when he was again in England. Now the Muses have two main complaints: the small reward of learning, and the low condition of poetry in England. The first is exactly parallelled

* The same neglect of an important critical principle led Professor A. S. Cook to date Sidney's *Defense of Poesy* as late as possible, because the style differs so markedly from that of *Arcadia*—as if Sidney, or anyone else, would write a critical treatise and a chivalric-pastoral romance in the same style.

in *The Returne from Parnassus*, and may be believed to belong to the same painful time of life, the first disillusioning encounter of the young graduate with an unsympathetic world. The second complaint would seem strange if it were uttered by the man who, in the poem which recounted his experiences during this English visit of 1590, praised eleven poets of his acquaintance, and might have praised as many more. On the other hand, if it were uttered about 1580, it merely said in verse what Sidney had said, or was about to say, in prose, and what the group of friends were probably saying often in conversation. We must believe either that Spenser deliberately and unsparingly condemned the work of Lyly, Greene, Peele, Watson, Warner, Marlowe, Daniel, Fraunce, and a dozen others, or else that *The Teares of the Muses* was written before these men began their careers. It is no answer that Spenser knew the value of Sidney and Dyer in 1580, for members of the coterie from which the poem issued would naturally be exempt from criticism. Calliope, again, complains that the degenerate age provides no matter for a heroic poet to sing. Was this written two years after the defeat of the Spanish Armada, or just before Drake reappeared from sailing round the world ? Since nothing that Spenser ever wrote, or that anyone wrote about Spenser, will support a charge of stupidity, jealousy, or discourtesy—and that to the two professions, poetry and arms, which he most held in honour—we are forced to the latter conclusion.

This conclusion, if it be accepted, removes *The Teares of the Muses* in some degree from the too numerous group of poems which commentators describe as attacks on or complaints against Burghley. The well known but late tradition charges Burghley with reducing a pension ordered to Spenser by the Queen. This story, however, must belong to the year 1590, and Spenser's grudge was of older standing. It began in 1579 or 1580 when Spenser became in some fashion a retainer of Leicester, and, a Puritan enrolling himself under the banner of the political leader of the Puritans, definitely joined the opposite camp from that of Burghley. To this partisanship we must ascribe the attacks on Burghley in *Mother Hubberds Tale ;* and Spenser had no legitimate grievance if the Lord Treasurer eyed him askance. A more personal cause of enmity, and one explicitly stated by Spenser himself, was Burghley's indifference and even hostility to poetry. This, I believe with Todd, and perhaps some overt expression of it, weighed most heavily in Spenser's mind, since it is to this, and not to any more definitely personal grievance, that Spenser always recurs in his direct references to Burghley. Our poet had a proper sense of his own importance and of the dignity of his vocation. Thus as political partisan and as a sectary of the outraged Muses he had good cause, even before and apart from the affair of the pension, against this double enemy.

It is a far cry from this, however, to the representation of Spenser as complaining in poem after poem and allegory after allegory of a check to his private advancement. The man who wrote the dignified and independent protests at the opening and close of the Sixth Book of *The Faerie Queene* and in the sonnet attached to the First Part, the poet of *The Faerie Queene* was not that kind of man. He was no querulous minor poet, nor was he obsessed with Burghley, though some of his commentators are. He complains that art and learning are insufficiently appreciated in certain high quarters—a complaint which, like all his complaints, might be echoed with equal justice from that day to this—but it is for art and learning and for all their votaries, not merely for himself, that he pleads. There were readier ways, had Spenser cared to take them, either to conciliate or to annoy the Lord Treasurer.

Men naturally seek for allegory in the works of a professed allegorist, but those who have attempted of late years to unravel the complicated meanings of these poems have more rigidly systematic minds than I believe Spenser had; certainly narrower minds. It is easy to press too closely this one point of personal allusion, to find Burghley and that unlucky pension at every turn, forgetting that there may have been other men in England whom Spenser may have disliked, and forgetting—what is more important—that Spenser was a professed philosopher and moralist. The *Complaints* do contain allusions to persons and events. What poem does not? The fact that accidents of survival enable us to recognise some of them should not make us overrate their importance: in doing so we reverse the error of Wordsworth, who could not understand why persons and events which to him were charged with significance and emotion, were regarded by his critics as trivial and even ludicrous. We must not allow these side-allusions to distract us from the main theme, which is not the enmity of Burghley, but the World's

Vanity—the fleetingness of strength and power and beauty, the theme of *Ecclesiastes* which went before and of the Seventh Book of *The Faerie Queene* which was to come after—the theme of Loys le Roy in a treatise Spenser may have known, *De la Vicissitude des Choses Humaines*.

We are so accustomed to panegyrics on the unsophisticated exuberance of the Elizabethans that we are apt to overlook their moral seriousness. We are so interested in the glimpses our poet affords us of those fascinating people, and so entranced with the brilliance of his fancy, that we miss some of the things he most laboured to impress upon us, and disregard the *grave morall Spenser*, the *sage and serious Spenser* who appealed so strongly to his own generation and the next. In this the verdict of posterity may be just, but the æsthetic judgment should not distort the historical perception. Spenser may have mistaken his true task as poet, but not through inadvertence—and after all he was a greater man than any of his critics, and his opinion should carry weight—nor was he alone in his time. As moral poetry these *Complaints of the Worlds Vanitie* are not isolated phenomena, but part of a great mass of similar writings which includes the Eclogues of Mantuan, the *Zodiacus Vitae* of Marcellus Palingenius (which Spenser must have known), the works of his beloved du Bartas, the Quatrains of Pibrac admired by Montaigne, and, less popular but more ambitious, the philosophical profundities—or obscurities—of Fulke Greville and Sir John Davies. The men of the Renaissance, so far from being merely instinctive and exuberant in animal spirits, were restlessly thoughtful, and enjoyed thinking. We like our morality expressed in the idiom of science; they liked theirs in that of poetry. The poets in general took upon themselves the task of gathering up and expressing for their new generation the wisdom of their ancestors—the task of extending ethical enquiry fell to those whose proper business it is, to the dramatists—and the *Complaints* are but another proof that the uneasy melancholy of the next reign, though more morbid, was no new thing. Even Shirley's moralising on *The glories of our blood and state* is but a magnificent paraphrase from Ronsard.

The poet of the *Complaints*, however, is not inspired by this melancholy mood alone. He was the poet of the antiquarianism of which Archbishop Parker was the leader and Camden the registrar. *The Ruines of Time* testifies to the taste for English antiquities which appears also in

The Faerie Queene, and the same antiquarian interest led him to translate the *Antiquités de Rome* of Joachim du Bellay, another antiquary in whom scientific curiosity was transcended by moral feeling. In *Mother Hubberds Tale* we find our poet expressing intelligent opinions upon contemporary affairs, as he had done, though more covertly, in *The Shepheards Calender*, and was to do in *The Faerie Queene*. And everywhere there is evidence of the two constant passions of his life, the love of books and the love of his craft of poetry. He learns from the practice in translation, exercises himself in the creation of beautiful verse and the design of bright pictures, experiments in the choice and use of words, strives to attain the secret of the significant presentation of material things and the suggestion through material things of spiritual truths and eternally valid ethics. Cicero and Seneca enrich his thought, Virgil and Ovid his style. He imitates the inventions of du Bellay, and imitates also his boldness of diction. In these poems, less subject to the over-ruling Decorum of Pastoral or Romance, Spenser's freedom of language may best be studied, and that peculiar blend of classical and foreign loan-words, and homely dialect, with new-coined forms of his own and with the marrowy phrase of Chaucer.

This artistic fervour provides at least a partial solution of the philosophical preoccupation with time and change. Spenser cannot solve the problem for all men, but he can solve it for himself, and even for his friends. By the eager practice of his art and the memory of his fathers in letters, he is roused from his melancholy to proclaim the triumph of the poets, their victory over death and time. The importance of poetry is not merely that it gives Edmund Spenser the chance of a comfortable living and the favour of the great, but that it gives to the elect among men the hope, even the certainty, of permanent existence. The enemies of learning live in the moment, like beasts; its friends are freed from the reproach of the World's Vanity. The same notion moved Francis Bacon to one of his finest passages of eloquence, at the close of the first Book of *The Advancement of Learning*. It does not seem to us a religious conclusion: they might justify it by the reflexion that wisdom and poetic power are the gifts of God, so that God giveth this victory also. And if the thought be barely divine, it is very human: and it is very true.

If the reader be irked, then, by so many observations of "sources" and "influences" and "parallels" in the commentaries which follow, let him remember our poet's ardent love of letters and the moral comfort it gave him. Some of these observations are but literary gossip, illustrating this bookish trait in Spenser's character. But some are more than that. In all Spenser's work, as in the work of all poets, worldly experience and literary experience combine. Some few poets have been all but unconscious of the debt they owed to others—Shelley is an example—but Spenser, and Renaissance poets in general, were not only conscious of debt, but deliberately incurred it. He believed in learning as a guide to the good life and as a necessity in art. The canons of good craftsmanship, as he would learn them, demanded some display of erudition in idea and phrase. So, like Virgil before him and like Mr. Sturge Moore and Mr. T. S. Eliot in a later day, he dug in the old mines for jewels to set in his new gold, sought the help of his predecessors alike in the search for truth and in the effort after the right ordering and fair setting-out of his matter. Here are memories of things learned at school and University, so that they have become part of the general furniture of his mind. Other things seem to be imitated from memory, others again specially studied or re-studied for the purpose in hand. Some are decorations, some are accepted tricks of the trade; some convey useful moral teaching, or have value as pure erudition or for the memory they call up in the reader's mind of origins whose weight is thus brought in to re-inforce the impression. Since we have fallen out of the habit of noticing such things, and since the content of customary education has changed since Spenser's day, I have tried to remind the reader of them. If they bore him, let him skip them; if he wishes to read Spenser as Spenser expected to be read, he will note the imitations in passing, and as he reads quietly and slowly as Spenser should be read, he will appreciate the value of each in its time and place.

Comme l'on voit, â l'ouvrir de la porte
D'un cabinet Royal, maint beau tableau,
Maint antiquaille, et tout ce que de beau
Le Portugais des Indes nous apporte :

Ainsi deslors que l'homme qui medite
Et est sçavant, commence à s'ouvrir,
Un grand thresor vient à se descouvrir,
Thresor caché au puis de Democrite.

> On dict soudain, voila qui fut de Grece,
> Cecy de Rome, et cela d'un tel lieu,
> Et le dernier est tiré de l'Hebrieu,
> Mais tout en somme est remply de sagesse.
>
> —PIBRAC, *Quatrains* 76-78 (1583).

This trick of imitation is constant in Spenser, and in Spenser's time. But never do his reminiscences supersede the thought or drown the voice of Spenser himself. He is never a slave to his authorities, never hesitates to alter, re-apply, re-interpret. We must see his imitations in relation to the whole design of his art and the whole current of his thought. For emphatically he is the Maker, the man who of his own will and by his own power sets out to make beautiful significant things out of words. What power it is by virtue of which he is able to create, we do not know: nor is it our business here to find out. It is enough to watch him at work, and to admire his handicraft, the tireless energy of his rhymes, the long full flow of his rhythm, the indefinable richness of timbre in which we recognise our Spenser.

THE PRINTER TO THE GENTLE READER.

The implication that Spenser had nothing to do with this collection has already been discussed. The phrase "since his departure over sea" must refer to his leaving for Ireland in 1580, since Spenser dated the dedication of *Daphnaida* from London "this first of January, 1591," by which time the *Complaints* volume was already in being and entered on the Stationers' Register.

None of the poems whose titles Ponsonby quotes have survived. The biblical paraphrases might be taken as indications of Spenser's early Puritanism, but many sixteenth-century poets had done such things. It was, indeed, rather fashionable. The more secular titles suggest the influence of Clement Marot and the last survivals of the mediæval secular allegory of the school of *The Romance of the Rose*, of which Spenser would find enough in Chaucer and in works attributed to Chaucer in contemporary editions. Both strains, the biblical and the *Rose*, may be traced among the many others which contributed to his greater works.

THE RUINES OF TIME.

During his sojourn in England in 1590, Spenser found himself in a circle different from that he had left in 1580. Personal friends indeed remained to welcome him, but the political leaders of his old Puritan allegiance, Leicester and Walsingham, were dead—the former in 1586, the latter in April, 1590—and so was their natural successor, Philip Sidney. Social convention expected some commemoration of his old patrons: one literary circle of the Court in particular awaited from its best poet some mourning remembrance of their former centre and chief exemplar, and Spenser acknowledges explicitly, even naively, the justice of the reproaches he incurred by his delay in fulfilling this well-understood duty of a social laureate.

Critics who, without any evidence, have imagined a warm personal friendship between Spenser and Sidney, have accused the poet of ingratitude and lack of feeling, because of this delay and because the elegies, when they did appear, fail to suggest that depth of sorrow they consider appropriate. For the delay Spenser apologises himself in the Dedication and in the course of the poem; for the supposed coldness it is unnecessary to apologise. Even if the relations of the two men had been intimate, this was a formal occasion. The poet's business, by all the rules and conventions, was to praise Sidney, just as it was Ben Jonson's, in his lines on Shakespeare, to praise the man he admired and loved "on this side idolatry." Neither poet attempted to expose his own inmost feelings or to vent a personal grief. The time for that was not yet, by a century or two. And when one comes to think of it, how many English elegies convince us that they are heartfelt outpourings of warm passion? No one can say that Spenser's lines on Sidney are insincere, or unworthy either of their maker or their subject.

The changes Spenser would observe, moreover, were not confined to his own circle. England itself was different. Certain great problems were solved, for Spain was defeated, Mary Queen of Scots dead, there was no more question of the Queen's marriage, and the Pope's impatience had simplified, while it intensified, the problem of England's relations with Roman Catholicism. Men's minds were oriented towards new problems, looking to new leaders. Thus though the immediate occasion of *The Ruines of Time* was personal and social, the situation, the comparison, was bound to evoke more general reflexions in the sensitive mind of a meditative poet. Even had his emotions been strong enough to sustain a poem of the length and impressiveness the occasion demanded, thought also was required of him, and Spenser's thoughts, in the face of such a contrast, naturally made Leicester, Walsingham, Sidney, symbols of the eternal vicissitude.

For the framing of this poem, Spenser adopted from du Bellay's *Antiquités de Rome* the device of a double structure, a series of direct assertions followed by a series of allegorical restatements of the same motives. Two themes are developed in the poem: the fall of great men, and the immortality conferred on men by poetry. These grow out of meditation upon Leicester, the dead favourite, Sidney, the dead poet, and Walsingham, the dead patron, and are resumed in the "emblems" with which the poem closes. *The Ruines of Time*, however, was not only late in appearing; it was hurried, and its conduct is disjointed. The Genius of Verulam, whose lament over her fall and over that of Leicester occupies the first 238 lines, disappears thereafter, to allow the poet to speak in his own person, and is recovered only at the close, some 220 lines later. It is obvious also that the poem was written in fragments and pieced together in haste. The funeral catalogue of lines 239-280 is lamentably bald, repetitive, and spasmodic; and suspicion is roused when we find a poet who was remarkably skilled in the art of transition making no attempt at a smooth passage to the elegy on Philip Sidney at line 281. Spenser imitated himself so often that we are not surprised at coincidence of the first line of this section with line 361 of *The Teares of the Muses*, but he worked normally in close syntax, not in ejaculations, and here we find a whole stanza without a finite verb.

We must read 175 lines, rather more than a quarter of the poem, before we come to its ostensible subject, and the whole trend of the thought is broken in the last two stanzas of this section (lines 164-175) by an irrelevant compliment to Camden. Here, indeed, is a true conclusion, arranged like the close of *The Teares of the Muses*, and cast in the regular convention of the Commendatory Poem. The moralising strain in which this part is conceived would carry the poet fairly easily across to the subject of Leicester's death. The transition is adroit—though all Spenser's commentators have been somewhat mystified by the lack of connexion between Leicester and Verulam—but the impetus is insufficient to carry him through the family necrology, which is inspired neither by personal feeling nor by the moral impressiveness of a spectacular ruin.

With line 281 a new inspiration begins, that of the memory of Philip Sidney. Now Spenser wrote a later elegy on Sidney, published in 1595 along with others by various hands. Among these was one by his friend Ludovick Bryskett, which had been entered on the Stationers' Register in 1587. Is it not possible that the publication of Bryskett's elegy was delayed by the suggestion of a joint publication, and delayed still further, first by Spenser's failure to produce a contribution and then by his incorporation here of the elegy he had intended for the joint production? This is mere guessing, but it would account for the tardy appearance of the Sidney elegies (headed by *Astrophel*) nine years after his death, and also for the disjointed state of *The Ruines of Time*.

To return to the poem: the favourite theme of poetic immortality, inevitable in an elegy on a poet, carries Spenser on, until he wishes to draw to a conclusion, and so he casts back to his first motive, the antiquarian evocation of the Genius of Verulam. Of the first series of Visions, only the sixth has any personal reference, and the rest might well be a relic of the *Dreames* and *Pageants* mentioned by Spenser and Harvey in their letters. The second series is modelled on the first, and a brief address to the lady to whom the poem is dedicated closes the whole. With all diffidence, I would suggest (as a conjecture merely) that not only was the poem written in fragments, but that some of the fragments were originally intended for other purposes, and that the scheme we have is an afterthought: that the poem is constructed out of a poem commendatory of Camden's *Britannia* (1586-87-90), an elegy on Sidney the place of which was eventually taken by *Astrophel*, and bits of the old *Dreames* or *Pageants*. The structure is ingenious, but the value of *The Ruines of Time*, apart from its historical interest and this ingenious carpentry, lies in the beauty of certain passages. These more than compensate for its weaknesses; we certainly would not wish it away.

THE DEDICATION: Mary, daughter of Sir Henry Sidney and sister of Sir Philip, was born in 1561; married Henry Herbert, second Earl of Pembroke, in 1577, and died in 1621. She was a famous patroness of poets, wrote the second elegy in the *Astrophel* collection, and translated Garnier's *Tragedie of Antonie* (1595), de Mornay's *Discourse of Life and Death* (1592), and perhaps some Psalms. Spenser mentions her in lines 316-322 and at the close of this poem, and as *Urania* in *Colin Clouts Come Home Again*, 486-491.

1-42 : Commentators have found difficulty in connecting Leicester with Verulam, but no connexion is required if we take as Spenser's starting-point the first of *The Visions of Bellay*. The French poet saw the Genius of the fallen city of Rome on the banks of the Tiber; his translator, seeking an English equivalent, saw on the banks of Thames (see below, note on lines 134-154) the Genius of the fallen Roman city, to which Holinshed had devoted a quite disproportionate space in his *Description of England*, II. xiii. The representation of the Genius of Verulam as "a Woman sitting sorrowfully wailing" may owe something to the tenth *Vision of Bellay*, and to *Lamentations*, i, and 2 *Esdras*, ix and x, in which Sion is figured as a woman mourning.

26 : Compare *The Ruines of Rome*, iii, 9 :

Rome now of *Rome* is th' only funerall.

43-77 : Here opens one of the main themes. "Our life shall passe away as the trace of a cloude, and come to nought as the mist that is driven away with the beames of the sunne, and cast downe with the heate thereof. Our name also shall be forgotten in time, and no man shall have our workes in remembrance." *Wisedom of Solomon*, II, 4.

48-49 : Seneca (*Epist*. cii, 26), speaking of the hour of death, says, "Gemis, ploras, et hoc ipsum flere nascentis est." The biblical parallel is obvious.

57-77 : The verses attributed to St. Bernard, the fountainhead of this mediæval commonplace, were still popular in Spenser's time. The first poem in *The Paradise of Dainty Devises* (1576) is a paraphrase of them, and they must have been in Spenser's mind :

Dic ubi Salomon, olim tam nobilis? vel ubi
Samson est, dux invincibilis?
Vel dulcis Jonathas, multum amabilis? vel pulcher
Absolon, vultu mirabilis?
Quo Cæsar abiit, celsus imperio, vel dives splendidus, totus in prandio,
Dic ubi Tullius, clarus eloquio, vel Aristoteles,
summus ingenio?

63 : *meare* : march, boundary. Compare *Ruines of Rome*, xxii, xxvi.

64-70: *The Book of Daniel*, vii, 3-7. In his study of visions Spenser included *Daniel*, and in the Geneva Bible, which he would certainly use (and from which, accordingly, all biblical quotations in this edition are given), he would find these traditional identifications noted in the marginal commentary: the Lion=Assyria; the Bear=Persia; the Leopard=Alexander the Great.

71-77: *seven headded beast:* "That is, the Romane Empire which was a monster and coulde not be compared to any beast, because the nature of none was able to expresse it." (Geneva Commentary). Daniel's beast had not seven heads, but it had ten horns, which naturally leads Spenser to the Beast of *Revelations*, xiii, "having seven heads, and ten horns," also interpreted as signifying the Roman Empire. The Geneva comment on *Revelations*, xiii, 2, returns to the same signification of the Lion, the Bear, and the Leopard.

77: Compare *The Ruines of Rome*, especially sonnet xxvii.

78-154: Spenser's knowledge of Verulam appears to come largely from Holinshed and Camden. Holinshed (*Description of England*, II. xiii) saith: "It should seeme when these ancient cities flourished, that the same towne, which we now call saint Albons, did most of all excell: but cheefelie in the Romans time, and was not onelie nothing inferior to London (*Troynovant*, line 102-3) it selfe, but rather preferred before it. . . . Good notice hereof is also to be taken by Matthew Paris, and others before him, out of whose writings I have thought good to note a few things, whereby the majestie of this ancient citie may appeare unto posteritie, and the former state of Verlamcester not lie altogither (as it hath doone hitherto) raked up in forgetfulnes . . . Eldred . . . found an exceeding number of pillers, peeces of antike worke, thresholds, doore frames, and sundrie other peeces of fine masonrie for windowes and such like. . . . Of these also some were of porphyrite stone, some of divers kinds of marble, touch, and alabaster, besides many curious devises of hard metall. . . . Besides these also he found sundrie pillers of brasse, and sockets of latton, alabaster, and touch. . . . Eadmerus . . . not onelie found infinite other peeces of excellent workemanship, but came at the last to certeine vaults under the ground, in which stood divers idols, and not a few altars, verie superstitiouslie and religiouslie adorned. . . . The images were of sundrie mettals, and some of pure gold, their altars likewise were richlie covered . . ." and so on. Also Camden, *Britannia*, quoted here in Philemon Holland's translation: "From *Hertford* twelve miles westward, stood VEROLAMIUM, a City in times past very much renowned, and as greatly frequented. . . . Neither hath it as yet lost that ancient name, for commonly they call it *Verulam*, although there remaineth nothing of if to bee seene, beside the few remaines of ruined walles, the checkered pavements, and peeces of Roman Coine other whiles digged up there. It was . . . fenced about with passing strong wals, a double Rampire and deepe Trenches toward the South." (p. 408.) "If I were disposed upon the report of the common people to reckon up what great store of Romane peeces of coine, how many cast images of gold and silver, how many vessels, what a sort of modules or Chapiters of pillars, and how many wonderful things of antique worke, have been digged up, my words would not carry credit: The thing is so incredible." (p. 411.)

104: "*Uther* the Britan, sirnamed for his serpentine wisedome *Pendragon*, by a sore seige and a long recovered it." (Camden.) "Thus much for the antiquity and dignity of *Verulam;* now have also with you for an over-deale in the commendation of *Verulam* an *Hexastich* of *Alexander Necham* . . .

The famous towne whilom cal'd Verolame
To Nature ought lesse than to painful art;
When *Arthurs* Syre *Pendragon* gainst it came,
With force of armes to worke her peoples smart;
His seven yeeres seige did never daunt their heart."

(Camden.)

106-112: "In the Raigne of the same *Nero*, when *Bunduica* or *Boadicia* Queene of the *Icenes* in her deepe love for her Country, and conceived bitter hatred against the Romanes, raised bloudy and mortall Warre upon them, it was rased and destroied by the Britans, as *Tacitus* recordeth." (Camden.) Holinshed translates Tacitus (*Annals*, xiv, 33). So Spenser deliberately falsifies history in this stanza. He was trying to work up to a climax, and seems careless of aught but the effect to be produced.

113-119: I can find no authority for this either. Geoffrey of Monmouth says that Uther defeated and slew Octa and Eosa, sons of Hengist, at Verulam, and is followed by the *Flores Historiarum*, Harding, and Holinshed, who calls them Occa and Osca. None of them say anything about a monument. Did Spenser confound—intentionally or through faulty memory—Occa and Offa, the builder and benefactor of St. Edmund's abbey? As it stands it all makes a neat curve from the glory of Verulam to its ruin; but it is queer history.

134-154: Gildas, speaking of the martyrdom of St. Alban at Verulam, says "iter ignotum trans Tamesis nobilis fluvii alveum . . . aperiret." But both Spenser's main authorities deny it. Holinshed says: "Furthermore, whereas manie are not afraid to saie that the Thames came sometimes by this citie, indeed it is nothing so."

Verulam was, says Camden, "Eastward watered with a Brooke, which in old time made a great Meere, or standing Poole." And later, "The name whereof yet remaineth still heere in a certaine street of the towne named *Fish-poole-street*. Neere unto which streete, because certaine ankers were in our remembrance digged up, divers have verily thought (induced thereunto by a corrupt place in *Gildas*) that the river *Tamis* sometimes had his course and chanell this way." Here once more Spenser deliberately departs from his authority. His main concern was to build up an effective image; the Thames parallelled du Bellay's Tiber, and to a lover of rivers like Spenser, nothing could better heighten the picture of desolation.

166-175: William Camden, 1551-1623, head master of Westminster School, Clarenceux King of Arms, and most famous of English antiquaries. He published *Britannia* first in 1586, then with increasing store of additions in 1587, 1590, 1594, and so on. Spenser probably knew the later editions, which contain details he used in this poem; he may have known Camden personally, and could not fail to be interested in his work. It is perhaps worthy of mention that in his Oxfordshire chapter Camden prints part of a Latin Epithalamium of Thame and Isis; and another part in the third edition under Gloucestershire. Spenser had long before devised an Epithalamion of Thames and Medway (letter to Harvey, 1580). Did they talk over their poems when they met? But for the letter to Harvey we might have credited Camden with suggesting *The Faerie Queene*, II. xi.

183-238: This passage commemorates the death of the Earl of Leicester, who is identified by his motto *Droict et Loyal* in line 189. "Robert Dudley, K.G. son to *John* Duke of *Northumberland* . . . made Earl of *Leicester*, and Baron of *Denbigh*, by Queen *Elizabeth*, Anno Dom.

1564. . . . He died at Cornebury-lodge in Oxfordshire, the fourth of September, Anno 1588." (*The Catalogue of Honour*, 1610.)

199: *halfe happie:* compare line 435, and *Mother Hubberds Tale*, 413. This use of *half* to produce a meiosis is not uncommon in Spenser's earlier work.

214-215: Compare *The Ruines of Rome*, xiv, 5-8.

214: The syntax of this compressed line is simpler in Latin than in English, *dead* being in the genitive case agreeing with *his*. I imagine Spenser thought of his grammar often on Latin principles.

215: *Bayd* is used transitively, as in the phrase *to bay the moon.*

216-217: This has been interpreted as a reference to Burghley, now supreme in Council after the death of his rival Leicester. It is highly probable.

220: *glass:* gloss, sun-glint.

225-231: Spenser puts into the mouth of the Genius the reproaches of his friends. See the Dedication.

239: The poet begins to lose sight of the Genius of Verulam, and to open, very baldly, the second theme, poetic immortality, which he develops fully later in the poem.

239-259: The *brother* was Ambrose Dudley, second son of the Earl of Northumberland, elder brother of Robert. He died on 20th February, 1589-90. His widow, here addressed, was Anne, daughter of Francis Russell, 2nd Earl of Bedford.

260: *His sister* cannot be Catherine Dudley, wife of another Puritan leader, the Earl of Huntingdon, since she did not die till 1620. It must therefore be a first reference to Mary Dudley, wife of Sir Henry Sidney—an awkward and unnecessary anticipation of lines 274-280: unless the second reference is an afterthought, designed to introduce the subject of her son, Philip Sidney.

Thy father: Francis, 2nd Earl of Bedford, died in 1585.

266-273: *Sonne* here stands for *grandson*, as line 267 shows. For some reason Spenser ignores the lady's brother Francis Lord Russell, son and heir of the 2nd Earl. He was killed the day before his father's death, and his son Edward succeeded as 3rd Earl. When Spenser addressed him in this stanza the 3rd Earl was eighteen years of age.

274-280: *Thy husbands sister:* The reference to her family shows that Spenser meant Mary Dudley, wife of Sir Henry Sidney, and mother of Sir Philip Sidney, Sir

Robert, who was invested by James I with the old Dudley title of Viscount Lisle, and Mary, who married Henry Herbert, Earl of Pembroke. Lady Sidney died in August, 1586, about three months after her husband. It is strange that Spenser does not mention the excellent Sir Henry: but all this section is hasty and clumsy work, in marked contrast with the flowing ease of the passage which follows it.

291 : *too soone :* Sidney was only 32 years of age when he died, on 17th October, 1586, of wounds received near Zutphen on 22nd September.

296-298 : "I beseech you, therefore, brethren, by the mercies of God, that yee give up your bodies a living sacrifice holy, acceptable unto God, which is your reasonable serving of God."—*Romans*, xii, 1.

316-322 : The reference is, of course, to the Countess of Pembroke. See the note on the dedication.

323-329 : The reference is to Sidney's *Arcadia.*

332-343 : Spenser clearly had in mind here the famous passage of his favourite Sixth Book of the *Æneid*, 637-678; but rested content with an allusion, without complete imitation. Virgil mentions Orpheus and Musæus, Spenser remembers the collocation of Orpheus and Linus in the *Bucolics*, iv, 55-57.

344-455 : Spenser now develops his second theme, the famous theme of the immortality which, even in this transitory world, the poets can achieve and can bestow. This is the banner and ensign of Renaissance poetry everywhere. The chief sources are well known—Horace's *Odes*, III. xxx, IV. viii and ix; Ovid, *Amores*, I. xv, *Metamorphoses* xv, 871; and *Propertius*, III.; Theocritus, *Idyll* xvi; and so on. It would seem unnecessary to exemplify so universal a theme, but some passages which Spenser would know and perhaps had read shortly before writing this, may be added in illustration of so honourable a sentiment, and for comparison.

> En vain certes, en vain les Princes se travaillent
> En vain pour triompher l'un à l'autre bataillent
> Si après cinquante ans fraudez de leur renom
> Le peuple ne sçait point s'ils ont vescu ou non . . .
>
> Les Palais, les citez, l'or, l'argent et le cuivre
> Ne font les puissans Rois sans les Muses revivre . . .

seulement cette gloire
Est de Dieu concedée aux filles que Memoire
Conceut de Jupiter, pour la donner à ceux
Qui attirent par dons les Poetes chez eux.
RONSARD, *Odes*, III. 1.

"Et quelquefois estant pres du Tumbeau d'Achile [cet autre grand Monarque] s'ecria haultement. O bienheureux Adolescent, qui as trouvé un tel Buccinateur de tes louanges ! Et à la verité, sans la divine Muse d' Homere, le mesme Tumbeau qui couvroit le corps d'Achile, eust aussi accablé son Renom. Ce qu'avient a tous ceux qui mettent l'asseurance de leur immortalité au Marbre, au Cuyvre, aux Collosses, aux Pyramides, aux laborieux Edifices, et autres choses non moins subjectes aux injures du Ciel et du Tens, de la Flamme, et du fer, que de frais excessifs, et perpetuelle sollicitude."—Du Bellay, *Deffence et Illustration de la Langue Françoyse*, II. v. Du Bellay's motto was "Cælo Musa beat" (Horace, *Odes* IV. viii, 29.) and the same strain recurs all through his books—see especially his *Discours au Roy sur la poesie.* The Renaissance latinists nearly destroyed the virtue of the notion by vain repetition; but a good poet can refresh a hackneyed idea, especially when it is true.

356: Spenser here adapts the phrase of Isaiah, ii, 22: "Cease you from man whose breath is in his nostrils."

372-392: The Sixth *Æneid* again, 119-123:

Si potuit Maneis arcessere conjugis Orpheus,
Threicia fretus cithara, fidibusque canoris:
Si fratrem Pollux alterna morte redimit,
Itque reditque viam toties. Quid Thesea, magnum
Quid memorem Alciden?

Spenser may also have in mind Seneca's *Hercules Furens*, where the story of Eurydice is told in the Chorus (524-591) which expresses the hope of Hercules' return from Hades: the phrase *golden-girt Alcmena*—an epithet nowhere applied to Alcmena that I can find—may be a reminiscence of the description of Hippolyta in that Chorus, *aurato religans ilia balteo.*

381: Hercules built his pyre on Mount Œta. (Hesiod, *Theogony*, 950-955, and innumerable references in all the Latin poets.)

390: *wayment:* lamentation.

393-399: Compare the close of Seneca's *Hercules Œtæus*, and Horace, *Odes*, IV. viii once more.

395 : *impacable :* implacable—apparently from *impacatus* on the analogy of *implacabilis.* The form is rare, but not confined to Spenser.

400-406 : In this stanza Spenser gave the best expression to the idea of poetic immortality : the most truthful, best in phrase, and finest in melody of verse. The management of the rhythm from the sorrowful opening to the proud, quiet close, makes this a notable thing, one of Spenser's minor triumphs. This is a stanza to learn by heart, as an amulet, and a touchstone for English verse. And the words of the poet are *wise words,* says our Spenser ; and so Seneca, moved by the same thought to the same figures : " Hi dabunt ad æternitatem iter, et te in illum locum ex quo nemo ejiciet, sublevabunt ; hæc una ratio est extendendæ mortalitatis, immo in immortalitatem vertendæ. Honores, monumenta, quidquid aut decretis ambitio jussit aut operibus extruxit, cito subruitur ; nihil non longa demolitur vetustas, et movet ocius quod consecravit. Sapientiæ noceri non potest, nulla delebit ætas, nulla diminuet." (*de Brevitate Vitæ,* xv.)

416 : This is obscure, but may be a vague reminiscence of Plutarch's *Life of Marcellus :* " He thought to consecrate the temple of honor and vertue, which he had built with the spoyles he gotte in the warres of Sicile. But the priests were against it . . . and he did take it for an evil token, besides divers other signes in the element. . . . For there were many temples set a fire with lightening at one time." (North's translation, 1579.)

417 : Spenser may be remembering from Plutarch that Lysippus made statues of Alexander, or may have in mind these lines of Statius, *Silvæ,* I. i, 84 :

> Cedat equus, Latiæ qui contra templa Diones
> Cæsarei stat sede fori. quem traditus ausus
> Pellæo, Lysippe, duci, mox Cæsaris ora
> Mirata cervice tulit . . .
> Non hoc imbriferas hiemes opus aut Jovis ignem
> Tergeminum, Æolii non agmina carceris horret
> Annorumque moras : stabit dum terra polusque
> Dum Romana dies.

In which assertion Statius was wrong : his own verses have survived the Imperial statue.

418 : Camden describes in his *Britannia* the greatness, beauty, and wealth of the abbey of St. Edmund, and added to his later editions : " But as great a peece of worke as this was, so long in building and still encreasing, and as much

riches as they gathered together for so many yeares . . . were by King Henry the Eighth utterly overthrowne. What time as at one clappe hee suppressed all Monasteries; perswaded thereto by such as under a goodly pretense of reforming religion preferred their private and their owne enriching before the honour of Prince and Country, yea and before the glory of God himselfe. And yet there remaineth still lying along the carcasse, as one would say, of that auncient monument, altogether deformed." We need not suspect either Spenser or Camden of leanings to the old faith; the average honest Englishman of their time probably regretted such destruction, as Wordsworth regretted similar destruction two hundred years later. (*Prelude*, ix, 465-478.)

428: Achilles was, of course, dipped by his mother Thetis in *Styx*, not in *Lethe;* but Spenser was never pedantically accurate in mythology, which was to him a poetic inheritance to use as he pleased. The Water of Oblivion was in his mind, and suited his purpose, the impression he wished to create at the moment: the mention of it here is not a solecism.

430: Compare the quotation from du Bellay at line 344 above. The story is told by Plutarch in his *Life of Alexander*, by Amyot in his Preface to Plutarch's *Lives*, and by Cicero in his *pro Archia;* Spenser probably had in mind also Petrarch's reference, sonnet cxxxv *in Vita*, quoted by E.K. in his gloss to *The Shepheards Calender*, *October*, 65:

> Giunto Alessandro alla famosa tomba
> Del fero Achille, sospirando disse:
> Oh fortunato, che si chiara tromba
> Trovasti, e chi di te si alto scrisse!

435-441: Sir Francis Walsingham, Secretary of State, died on April 6th, 1590. His *poet* is Thomas Watson (1557 ?-1592), who published in 1590 his Latin *Melibœus*, with an English version, *An Eglogue upon the death of the Right Honorable Sir Francis Walsingham.* In this poem (line 411 ff. of the Latin, 371 ff. of the English) Watson makes a complimentary reference to Spenser, who returns it here.

440-441: Spenser must have had some reason for regarding Walsingham as a patron both of scholars and of soldiers, since he addressed him in a sonnet attached to

The Faerie Queene as

> the great Mecenas of this age,
> As wel to al that civil arts professe
> As those that are inspired with Martial rage. . . .

which suggests something more definite than the mere contrast with Burghley which follows. The Walsinghams were a literate family; I can give no evidence of special interest in soldiers.

440-445: *Ecclesiasticus*, xxvi, 29: "There bee two thinges that grieve mine heart, and a third maketh me angrie: a man of warre that suffereth povertie: and men of understanding that are not set by."

446-455: The reference is to Burghley, the enemy of Leicester, and no friend to Leicester's protégé Spenser.

456: Here a somewhat abrupt return is made to the Genius of Verulam, to close the poem in accordance with its scheme.

463-468: Compare Seneca, *Troades*, 1-4:

> Quicumque regno fidit et magna potens
> Dominatur aula nec leves metuit deos
> Animumque rebus credulum lætis dedit,
> Me videat et te, Troia. Non umquam tulit
> Documenta fors majora, quam fragili loco
> Starent superbi.

481: *Recording* here probably means *remembering* (from Italian *ricordare*) rather than *inscribing*.

489: Compare *Visions of the Worlds Vanitie*, i, 10:

> Unto mine eyes strange showes presented were.

491-574: Spenser has been meditating upon the disappearance of great and conspicuous figures in his own world; it is not surprising that the Seven Wonders of the ancient world occur to his mind: he is led to them naturally by the mention of two in earlier imitations—the Pyramids and the Mausoleum—and they are quoted in *The Ruines of Rome*, ii. The list of the Wonders provides only the suggestion, and he disguises it, but it gives the line of connexion through the first four Visions that follow.

491-504: *Vision* 1: The point of departure is the statue of Zeus at Olympia. This leads to another famous statue, in the Book of Daniel, iii, and so to chapter ii, 31-33: "There was a great image. . . . This images head was of fine gold . . . and his feete were part of yron, part of clay." The Geneva commentary interprets Nebuchadnezzar's dream as symbolic, once more, of the four Empires which successively ruled the world and were overthrown in turn. (Compare lines 64-77 above.)

505-518: *Vision* 2: The Pharos of Alexandria + *Visions of Bellay*, xiv + St. Matthew, vii, 24-27—the parable of the house built upon sand. Compare Spenser's description of the House of Pride in *The Faerie Queene*, II. iv, 4-5. The confusion of the Tower of Babel and the city of Babylon founded by Ninus occurs in the Geneva Bible, and especially in its Index. Spenser may have distinguished them, but, as is already sufficiently obvious, his method here is a kind of continuous *contaminatio*, and he would not reject this ready-made relationship between sacred and secular history, even if he recognised its uncertainty. He repeats the notion in *The Faerie Queene*, II. ix, 21:

Whereof King Nine whilome built Babel towre.

519-532: *Vision* 3: The Gardens of Semiramis in Babylon + *Visions of Bellay*, xii + an episode apparently designed for *The Faerie Queene*—perhaps an abandoned counterpart to Book III. v, 39-40.

525: *staine*: bedim, outrival. Chaucer, Ballade in *The Legend of Good Women*: "My lady cometh, that al this may disteyne."

533-546: *Vision* 4: The Colossus at Rhodes + the story of David and Goliath.

547-560: *Vision* 5: Trajan's bridge over the Danube, the magnificence and the destruction of which are described by Dio (LXVIII. xiii, 1-2, 5-6), was not one of the Wonders; but another reference to the Mausoleum and the Pyramids would be otiose, and so might one to the Temple of Diana at Ephesus, after the temples of Marcellus and the Abbey of St. Edmund. Spenser's mind is now straying over the great structures of the elder age, and away from the Wonders themselves.

561-574: *Vision* 6: Spenser is now thinking more directly of the persons of his elegy, and finding symbols more directly suggestive of them. The bears may come from the Dudley crest—the Bear and Ragged Staff—and may represent the Earls of Leicester and Warwick.

580-586: Compare *Visions of Bellay*, i.

589-672: Here begins a series of emblems developed, at first, from these poetic symbols which are also constellations, to celebrate the entrance into immortality of the poet Philip Sidney, *Philisides*, *Astrophel*, the Star-lover. This series varies from the former in adding the idea of immortality through poetry to that of the evanescence of human life, thus carrying out in symbol the ideas expressed above in argument.

589-602: *Vision* 1: The swan that sings before his death is a fitting symbol for the poet who died untimely. A hint of why it opens the series is given by the place: the *famous River* is the Thames, and the swans of Thames were famous even outside England. The constellation Cycnus completes the emblem.

603-616: *Vision* 2: The harp of Orpheus + the constellation Lyra: a conjunction already made and requiring only the reference to Sidney. Ovid, *Metamorphoses* xi, 50-52:

> caput Hebre lyramque
> Excipis; et mirum medio dum labitur amne
> Flebile nescio quid queritur lyra.

And Natalis Comes, *Mythologia*, VII. xiv: "Fertur eius caput in Hebrum deiectum cum lyra fluminis in Lesbum delatum fuisse . . . lyram autem inter sidera relatam." The change of the sound made by the harp is more than ingenious.

The constellation Lyra and the Great Bear are both in the Northern Hemisphere. The latter enters here through its coincidence with the Bear of the Dudley crest: Sidney and Leicester are in the heavens together.

603: *adowne the Lee:* In line 135 *Lee* seems to mean *meadow, lea*. Here it may have the same sense, and the phrase may mean *down past the meadow*, as we say *sailing along the shore*. In *The Faerie Queene*, IV. ii, 16, the sea is called *the watry lea*, so that it may mean an expanse of land or water. *Downe along the Lee* occurs again in *The Faerie Queene*, V. ii, 19, and in *Prothalamion*, 38; *adowne the Lee* in *Prothalamion*, 115; in *The Faerie Queene*, IV. xi, 41, *the Liffy rolling downe the lea*. This last supports the interpretation suggested above.

611: *divin'd:* made divine. Compare *Daphnaida*, 214:

> Living on earth like Angell new divinde.

617-630: *Vision* 3: This is more vague, and much more difficult. It has been suggested that the *ebony coffer* is the Black Pinnace, Sidney's official ship as Governor of Flushing, in which his body was brought back to England. But the constellation Argo does not suit *that starre, In which all heavenly treasures locked are*. This *starre* should be the clue, but I cannot identify it. The notion of the river persists in Spenser's mind, and it is possible, in view of his earlier trend of thought, that he had in mind *Psalm* cxliv: "Man is like to vanitie: his dayes are like a shadowe, that vanisheth. . . . Send thine hand from above: deliver me, and take me out of the great waters." But both *coffer* and *starre* have eluded my search.

631-644: *Vision* 4: This again is vague. The order of the constellations in Ptolemy's *Almagest,* is Lyra—Cycnus—Cassiopeia—Perseus; in the *Urania* of Pontanus, Aquila—Cassiopeia—Andromeda—Perseus—Pegasus. So Spenser's mind was probably hovering about Cassiopeia and Andromeda: Cassiopeia in her chair, and Andromeda waiting for Perseus. With this is fused memories of *Revelations,* xxi, 2 and xxii, 7, perhaps *Solomon's Song,* with all the train of religious imagery they have suggested to the preachers. The soul of Sidney turns to God as a bride to her Bridegroom.

In these two Visions Spenser rises above the common pedestrian parallelism of the emblem-writers to a truer poetic suggestiveness. This is more than ingenuity; or rather, through ingenuity he succeeds for the moment in solving his permanent problem of the relation of beauty and truth, of the material and the spiritual, impresses the imagination directly, without interposition of the intellect.

645-658: *Vision* 5: Here he returns to more obvious matter. Pegasus is again an obvious poetic symbol; to that is added the thought of the soldier-poet mortally wounded. Following Hesiod (*Theogony,* 280-286), Natalis Comes says (*Mythologia,* VII, xi): "E sanguine . . . Medusæ de colle defluente natus est . . . Pegasus." Spenser fuses this with the memory of Ariosto's imitation of the Perseus story in *Orlando Furioso,* x, where Ruggiero, mounted on the Hippogriff, rescues Angelica from the sea-monster.

659-672: *Vision* 6: Compare *The Visions of Bellay,* iii and iv. Mercury is brought in as the guide of souls from one life to the next. No constellation seems to be indicated, unless perhaps Ara. There may be here also a vague memory of the end of Seneca's *Hercules Œtæus,* already suggested above, where Alcmena carries the ashes of Hercules in an urn, and mourns for him until he appears in the heavens and proclaims his passage to bliss.

680-687: Spenser now turns to address the Countess of Pembroke, thus repeating the dedication. She is *of heavenlie offspring borne* as being beautiful. See the whole argument in *A Hymne in Honour of Beautie.*

THE TEARES OF THE MUSES.

The date of this poem has already been discussed, and only one point need be added—the coincidence of line 361 with line 281 of *The Ruines of Time*. There is no real evidence by which we can fix the precedence of the two uses of the same phrase; on the balance of probability it seems to lie with the former. The phrase is a fine one, an invention of which a notable phrase-maker might well be fond. Clearly, Spenser had been going over some of these poems just before he wrote *The Ruines of Time*, and might well pick out the best line in *The Teares of the Muses* as naturally as some poorer matter from *The Visions*. It occurs in *The Ruines of Time*, as we have seen, as the first line of a disconnected opening, in such a way as to suggest that Spenser was using it—only half consciously, perhaps—as priming, to get himself started.

On the literary side, *The Teares of the Muses* is simpler than the curious macedoine it follows, but the same methods are visible here as everywhere in Spenser. He had been reading, or re-reading, certain poems of du Bellay (certainly an early taste), perhaps some of Ronsard, perhaps something of Seneca, and, as usual, the Bible, especially the " Wisdom " Books. This last strain links *The Teares of the Muses* with the *Ecclesiastes* mentioned by Ponsonby in his preface, The temper of the poem is reminiscent of the Prophets. and not unlike that of some parts of *Mother Hubberds Tale*.

As for its personal bearing, we have already observed that though it may be read as another attack upon Burghley, that interpretation is not strictly necessary. The argument is directed rather against those general enemies comprised in what Ronsard called *le vulgaire*—that is, all the enemies of the new school of learned poetry inaugurated by the Pleiade in France and the Sidney-Spenser group in England. The poem is, in part at least, a literary manifesto. Even if Burghley is included among those aimed at, it is difficult to ascribe the faults of ignorance and pride of birth to an eminently efficient Lord Treasurer and a devoted son of St. John's College, Cambridge, whose lack of a pedigree was notorious. A better target for the latter arrow would be the Earl of Oxford, whose quarrel with Sidney in 1579 would certainly range him among Spenser's dislikes even if he were not already the patron of a rival school of poets.

Spenser, again, may have thought of his friends at times, as well as of himself. A clue to part of the motive may lurk in the title, which, as many commentators have noted, seems to be borrowed from Gabriel Harvey's *Smithus, vel musarum lachrymæ pro obitu T. Smithi*, 1578. Harvey's friends thought him a poet, as E.K. shows in his Introduction to *The Shepheardes Calender* and his note on *September*, 176. The virtues specially quoted in the poem are not so much beauty and melody as learning and wisdom, qualities which Spenser specially admired in his friend. The Stoic cast of the poem reminds us of Spenser's own description of Harvey:

> Oratore amplo, et generoso pectore, quam non
> Stoica formidet veterum Sapientia vinclis
> Sancire æternis.

If we can date this poem about 1579-80—I have suggested some reasons why we should, and can find none why we should not—we may find cause for it in Harvey's situation as much as in Spenser's, for the brilliant hopes of his early career were now clouding over, and he was writing in one of his law books: "Common Lerning, & ye name of A good scholler, was never so much contemn'd, & abjected of princes, Pragmaticals, & common Gallants, as nowadays; insomuch that it necessarily concernith, & importith ye lernid ether praesently to hate yr books; or actually to insinuate, & inforce themselves, by very special, & singular propertyes of emploiable, & necessary use, in all affaires." (*Marginalia*, ed. G. C. Moore Smith, p. 151.) Harvey had some acquaintance with Burghley, who had tried to be serviceable to him, but to no purpose. *The Teares of the Muses* may well have grown out of something wider than Spenser's own personal grievances.

THE DEDICATION: Alice Spenser, the sixth daughter of Sir John Spenser of Althorp, and one of the three with whom Spenser claimed a kinship which they acknowledged (either by proof of pedigree or, prettily, as a mutual compliment), married Ferdinando Stanley, Lord Strange, who succeeded his father as 5th Earl of Derby in 1593 and died in 1594. This patron of poetry and drama is lamented by Spenser in *Colin Clouts Come Home Again*, 432-443, under the name of *Amyntas*, and his lady there and in lines 536-571 under that of *Amaryllis*. In 1600 she married Thomas Egerton, Lord Ellesmere, the Lord Chancellor; in 1633 the young members of her family performed, in her honour, *Arcades*, by John Milton. Egerton's son and her daughter by their previous marriages were that Earl and Countess of Bridgewater whose children performed *Comus*. She died on January 26th, 1636-7.

2: Why Spenser here (and at lines 57-58) makes the Muses daughters of Apollo instead of Jupiter is known to himself alone. He did not labour after precision in mythology. For one thing, Renaissance scholarship was more genial than exact, and for another, the gods of the ancients, however respectable in literature, were heathen fables. To students of mythology they were dead historical facts; for the poets they still possessed symbolic power, since, in the words of Ronsard, "Les Muses, Apollon, Mercure, Pallas, Venus, et autres telles deitez ne vous representent autre chose que les puissances de Dieu." Thus by grace of the poets the dead gods maintained a sort of deity, and since the poets gave them that measure of existence, the poets could make and remake them as they pleased.

7-12: There is no record of the lamentation of the Muses over Phæthon. Ovid tells how he was mourned by his sisters the Heliades (*Metam.*, ii, 333-366): Spenser, having made the Muses his sisters, transfers the mourning to them.

13-18: This has even less precedent. There is a tale about the *birth* of the Palici, twin sons of Jupiter and the nymph Thalia (Macrobius, *Saturnalia*, V. xix; Servius *in Æneid* ix, 585, and references in Statius and others), but I can find nothing about their *death*. It seems to be another case of *contaminatio* like that above: the coincidence of the names of the Muse Thalia and the nymph Thalia suggested the transference of the Palici to a Muse; Calliope had lamented her son Orpheus, so she is made responsible for the Palici also. Orpheus himself might have been a trifle obvious—scarcely a poem but had some mention of him. Otherwise it is sheer caprice and the pleasure of using fine names in verse.

18-36: Compare *The Shepheardes Calender*, *April*, 100-112; *The Faerie Queene*, II. xii, 70-71; VI. x, 6-12. The "consort" of music and running water is a favourite luxury of Spenser's.

44: *Impatient: unbearable.*

The order in which the Muses appear is that of certain mnemonic verses *de Musarum inventis*, printed in early editions of Virgil and in the *Mythologia* of Natalis Comes. E.K. quotes from them in his gloss to *April*, 100 and *November* 53. Harvey adopts the same order in his *Smithus*.

CLIO : 55-108.

Cleio gesta canens transactis tempora reddit.

Compare with this the *October* Eclogue of *The Shepheardes Calender*, and its original, Mantuan's Eclogue v, *Candidus*.

69-78 : Compare Mantuan, v. 146 :

> Adde quod et nostri curant ita carmina reges
> Ut frondes Aquilo, mare Libs, vineta pruinæ.

79-84 : Compare Castiglione, *Cortegiano*, i, translated by Hoby, 1561 : " Beside goodnesse, the true & principall ornament of the mynde in everye manne (I beeleave) are letters, although the Frenchmen know onelye the noblenesse of armes, and passe for nothing beside.: so that they do not onelye not sett by letters, but they rather abhor them, & all learned men they count verie rascalles, & they think it a great vilany whan any one of them is called a clarke . . . I would do my diligence to show them, how much letters (which undoubtedlye have bene graunted of God unto men for a soveraign gift) are profytable and necessarye for our leif and estimation." See *Mother Hubberds Tale*, 760. Castiglione was of great authority, and even Roger Ascham praised and borrowed from him.

82 : For this figurative use of *forhead*, compare the Introduction to Book IV of *The Faerie Queene*.

91-96 : This, while it is reminiscent of Juvenal's 8th Satire, *Stemmata quid valeant*, may possibly be aimed at the Earl of Oxford, Burghley's son-in-law, and both personal and literary rival of Sidney. Peck proposed to publish (but did not), " A pleasant Conceit of Vere Earl of Oxford, discontented at the Rising of a mean Gentleman in the English Court, circa MDLXXX." (*Desiderata Curiosa*, vi, 50 ; 1732.) Of all Elizabeth's prominent courtiers the 14th Earl of Oxford could most fittingly boast his ancestry, and in 1580 he persecuted Gabriel Harvey for supposed satire upon him. See *Mother Hubberds Tale*.

97-108 : Compare *The Shepheardes Calender*, *October*, 67-72, and Mantuan, v, 157-164 :

> At cessere viri fortes et mascula virtus,
> Dicendum altiloqui nihil invenere poetæ,
> Occidit ingenium vatum, ruit alta poesis.
> At si forte aliquis regum gerit aspera bella
> Et decus armorum venturaque sæcula curat
> Laude suæ gentis satur et præsentibus annis ;
> Barbarus est neque carmen amat vel avarus in auro
> Mergitur atque Midæ curis flagrantibus ardet.

97-106: "An historie is an orderly register of notable things said, done, or happened in times past, to maintaine the continuall remembrance of them, and to serve for the instruction of them to come."—Amyot, Preface to Plutarch's *Lives*, translated by North. See also du Bellay's *Discours au Roy sur la Poesie*, and many historians.

98: The *trump of gold* may be a not unnatural reminiscence of *The Hous of Fame* of our master Chaucer.

MELPOMENE: 115-354.

Melpomene Tragico proclamat mæsta boatu.

115-119: The metaphors are simple enough, but Spenser may have had in mind *Georgics* ii, 43-44, or, more likely, *Æneid* vi, 625-627:

> Non mihi si lingua centum sint oraque centum,
> Ferrea vox, omnes scelerum comprendere formas
> Omnia pœnarum percurrere nomina possim.

and Ovid, *Tristia*, I. iv, 53-54:

> Si vox in fragili mihi pectore firmior ære,
> Pluraque cum linguis pluribus ora forent.

and, as Jortin suggested, *Jeremiah* ix, 1: "O that mine head were full of waters, and mine eyes a fountaine of teares, that I might weepe day and night . . . !"

127-128: "Who so despiseth wisdome, and discipline, is miserable, and their hope is vaine, and their labours are foolish, and their woorkes unprofitable."—*Wisdom*, iii, 11.

129-130: See Seneca *passim* on the text "Summum bonum est animus fortuita dispiciens, virtute lætus," especially in his *De Tranquillitate Animi* and *de Vita Beata*; also Cicero, *de Finibus* IV. vii, "Varietates autem injuriasque fortunæ facile veterum philosophorum præceptis instituta vita superabat," and *Tusculan Disputations*, II; Boethius, *Consolatio Philosophiæ*; and Virgil, *Georgics*, ii, 490-492:

> Felix qui potuit rerum cognoscere causas,
> Atque metus omnes et inexorabile fatum
> Subjecit pedibus.

Much more could be quoted, and little added; but Spenser would certainly know these, and would almost certainly have them in mind as he wrote.

134: *throwes*: in modern spelling, *throes*.

145-146: See *Proverbs*, especially iii, 13-15, and viii;

Wisdom, viii, 5: "If riches be a possession to be desired in this life, what is richer than wisedome?" And so on.

164: Professor de Selincourt (*Spenser's Minor Poems*, Oxford, page 516), says *Persephone* is "a mistake for Tisiphone, as at *Virgils Gnat*, 422"; but that line translates *Culex*, 261, where every edition has *Persephone*. This would bring *The Teares of the Muses* and *Virgils Gnat* nearer together, but need we presume a mistake? Is it not better to name the Goddess and a Fury, rather than two out of the three Furies? It is a matter of taste. *Persephone* is more sonorous than *Tisiphone*, and we have seen enough to understand that Spenser would not let mere exactitude interfere with a well-sounding line.

THALIA: 174-228.

Comica lascivo gaudet sermone Thaleia.

Spenser had some interest in Thalia, for Harvey's correspondence tells us he had himself planned or written a series of comedies: "I am voide of al judgement, if your *Nine Comœdies*, wherunto in imitation of *Herodotus*, you give the names of the *Nine Muses* (and in one mans fansie not unworthily) come not neerer *Ariostoes Comœdies*, eyther for the finenesse of plausible Elocution, or the rarenesse of Poetical Invention, than that *Elvish Queene* doth to his *Orlando Furioso*. . . ." (*Three Letters*, iii.) Harvey encouraged the project, but we know nothing more of the *Nine Comœdies*, which were probably an outcome of Spenser's life in the household of Leicester.

177: James Burbadge built The Theatre in 1576, but whether Spenser had this or any other in mind we cannot tell. The epithet *painted* may be a quite general reference to the gaudiness of dramatic spectacle both public and private.

187-190: Compare lines 250 ff., and comments thereon.

191-204: This need not disturb the fondest lover of Elizabethan drama, if we take it as written about 1578-80 —before Lyly's career as dramatist began. Compare the remarks of Sidney in his *Defense of Poesy*.

205-210: Much conjecture has centred round this stanza, and with it lines 217-222 below. Did Spenser refer to two different men, or are *Willy* and the *gentle Spirit* one? I believe the former, since the phrase *that same* defined by a following clause and not by reference to anything before it, is not uncommon in Spenser, and because in the other case the intervening stanza would be an awkward interruption to the thought. For *Willy* the names of Shakespeare, T. Wilson, Alabaster, and Sidney have been suggested, and a considerable body of opinion holds that *Willy* was Richard Tarlton the comedian, who died in 1588. The first three names may be ruled out because they were alive even in 1590, and if this poem was written by the summer of 1580 Tarlton also is excluded. It is clear that Spenser was thinking of a writer of comedies, not a public clown, nor the writer of a romance, so that neither Tarlton nor Sidney will suit. With grave misgiving I hazard another name. In Harvey's letter quoted above he parallels *The Faerie Queene*, accurately enough, with Ariosto's *Orlando Furioso*: we may then believe—and we might have guessed it even without this or the mention of Bibbiena and Machiavelli in the same context—that Spenser's idea of comedy was the scholarly, witty Italian kind. Might not *Willy* be the translator of Ariosto's *Suppositi*—George Gascoigne, who died in 1577? I cannot tell why he should call Gascoigne *Willy*, but it is by no means the only puzzle of the kind. *Willy* may be some obscure Cambridge acquaintance who attempted academic comedy, perhaps his friend Willie of *August*, whoever he was; certainly I can recall no writer of the kind who died between the death of Gascoigne and 1590.

217-222: Who then is *that same gentle Spirit?* Captain B. M. Ward suggests the Earl of Oxford (*The Seventeenth Earl of Oxford*, App. D), but the identification is mere conjecture. I have given reason to think that Spenser would have personal cause to dislike Oxford in 1579-80. He did indeed address a sonnet to Oxford in *The Faerie Queene*, and one that hints at some interest, but he addressed one also to Burghley. When both Leicester and Sidney were dead Spenser had to be more prudent, and could not afford to neglect influential courtiers. He did not celebrate Oxford (so far as we can tell) among the other poets in *Colin Clouts Come Home Again*. Is it not possible that the *gentle Spirit* is Spenser himself? Thalia speaks, not Spenser, and she praises the *gentle Spirit* no more fulsomely than Hobbinol praises Colin Clout in *April* and *June*, or Willy and Perigot in *August*, or than Piers praises Cuddie in *October*, of *The Shepheardes Calender*. The facts are, that about 1579-80 Spenser complained that a good poet was discouraged from writing learned comedy, and that about 1579-80 Spenser, who considered himself a good poet, was writing comedies after the learned Italian manner, and desisted. It is perhaps too long a shot to suggest that in this poem the Nine Muses are made to bewail his discouragement precisely because they ought to have been introducing the works his discouragement made him abandon : but it is not impossible.

EUTERPE : 234-292.

Dulciloquis calamos Euterpe flatibus urget.

245-246 : *Culvers :* doves. Compare *Amoretti*, lxxxix :

Lyke as the Culver on the bared bough,
Sits mourning for the absence of her mate. . . .

253-264 : Compare *A Theatre for Worldlings*, fol. 91 : " First the divell begot Darknesse. And darknesse begot Ignorance. Ignorance begot error and his brethren." And du Bellay, *La Musagnoeomachie* :

Au milieu d'un val ombreux
Sous une voute ancienne
Gist un Antre tenebreux . . .
La le Sommeil endurcy
Tient l'Ignorance embrassée,
Que la Terre courroussée
D'un estommac verd de fiel,
Avec' Encelade et Cée
Vomit encontre le Ciel . . .
C'est la furieuse armée
Qui saccageant l'univers
Par tant d'alarmes divers
Par fer, par flamme, par mine,
Nostre bonheur extermine,
Sous le Monstre dereglé
Par la vengeance divine
A son malheur aveuglé. . . .

Ronsard, *Ode à Michel de l'Hôpital :*

Tandis l'Ignorance arma
L'aveugle fureur des Princes,
Et le peuple des provinces
Contre les Sœurs (*sc. les Muses*) anima.

Ronsard, *Ode* xii, *a Bouju :*

ou ta Muse luit,
La sourde Ignorance fuit,

Rendant les bouches muetes
De noz malheureux Poetes,
Qui souloient comme pourceaux
Souiller le clair des ruisseaux.

Spenser has not the splendid arrogance of the Pleiade, and is full of fear and despondency; but their enemy is the same Ignorance, and the breed of Ignorance is the same.

265-288: Compare *Visions of Bellay*, xii.

273: Statius, *Silvæ*, V. v, 2, says Jortin:

Castaliæ vocalibus undis.

TERPSICHORE: 301-354.

Terpsichore affectus citharis movet, imperat, auget.

The reader will observe that there is nothing about dancing here. Terpsichore seems to have puzzled the staid scholars of the Renaissance, and she usually appears as in Lilius Gyraldus, *de Musis Syntagma*, not as the Muse of the dance, but as *inventrix humaniorum literarum*. Fulgentius interpreted her name, *delectans instructione*.

301-306: Bœthius, *Consolatio Philosophiæ*, II. iv: "Vera, inquam, commemoras, o virtutum omnium nutrix, nec infitiari possum prosperitatis meæ velocissimum cursum. Sed hoc est quod recolentem vehementius coquit. Nam in omni adversitate fortunæ infelicissimum est genus infortunii fuisse felicem." In Chaucer's translation, "For in alle adversitee of fortune, the most unsely kinde of contrarious fortune is to han ben weleful."

307-336: Mantuan, v. 146, ff.:

Adde quod et nostri curant ita carmina reges
Ut frondes Aquilo, mare Libs, vineta pruinæ.
Ipsi ad delicias reges et ad otia versi
Quod celebrant laudari optant; hinc carmina manant
Perdita de studio Veneris, de scurrilitate,
De ganea, de segnitie, de infamibus actis
Quæ castum capitale nefas celebrare poetam . . .
Est et apud reges rudis, invida, rustica turba,
Mimus, adulator, leno, assentator, adulter,
Histrio, scurra, quibus virtus odiosa; poetas
Mille modis abigunt.

Compare *Mother Hubberds Tale*, 809-838.

339-354: This (and the poem in general) may owe something to Ronsard's *Dialogue entre les Muses Deslogées et Ronsard*, quoted below; but the notion is not very recondite. George Buchanan and others used it for courtly pageantry.

ERATO: 361-420.

Plectra gerens Erato saltat pede, carmine, vultu.

The *Hymnes in Honour of Love and Beauty* are the *locus classicus* for Spenser's philosophy of love, but the same ideas recur wherever the subject does, from *The Shepheardes Calender* (*October*, 91-96) onward. It can better be discussed at length in another place.

379-380: The survival of this old idea that verse serves to regulate the flow of passion may be studied as late as Wordsworth's Preface to *Lyrical Ballads*.

384-396: Compare du Bartas, *Uranie*:

> Je ne puis d'un œil sec voir mes sœurs maquerelles
> Des amoureux François, dont les mignards escrits
> Sont pleins de feints souspirs, de feints pleurs, de feints cris,
> D'impudiques discours, et de veines querelles.

395: *At riot*: a term of venery, used of ill-trained hounds. It is not "decorous" here, but Spenser was fond of hunting and hawking metaphors and terms.

403-406: Compare the picture and interpretation of the Graces in *The Faerie Queene*, VI. x, 15 and 21-24. The interpretation comes from Seneca, *de Beneficiis*, i, 3; from Servius *in Æneid* i, 724; and the mythologists.

409-414: This is du Bellay's complaint also, in *Le Poete Courtisan*, and in *La Deffence et Illustration de la Langue Françoyse*.

CALLIOPE: 421-474.

Carmina Calliope libris heroica mandat.

There is considerable repetition here of the complaint of Clio: Spenser never distinguished clearly between History and Heroic Poetry.

445-450: Spenser may have had in mind Horace, *Odes*, II. iii, 21-28:

> Divesne prisco natus ab Inacho,
> Nil interest, an pauper et infima
> De gente, sub divo moreris
> Victima nil miserantis Orci.

He defeats the melancholy of Horace by the no less Stoic doctrine of the value of good reputation.

451-460 : Compare Amyot, Preface to Plutarch's *Lives :* " The immortal praise and glorie wherwith History rewardeth wel-doers, is a verie lively and sharpe spurre for men of noble courage and gentleman-like nature, to cause them to adventure upon all manner of noble and great things." The reader will remember also his *Lycidas.* Compare also the *Dialogue entre les Muses deslogées et Ronsard :*

> Notre mestier estoit d'honorer les grands Rois,
> De rendre venerable et le peuple et les lois,
> Faire que la vertu du monde fust aimée,
> Et forcer le trepas par longue renommée :
> D'une flamme divine allumer les esprits,
> Avoir d'un cœur hautain le vulgaire à mespris,
> Ne priser que l'honneur et la gloire cherchée,
> Et tousjours dans le ciel avoir l'ame attachée.

And Castiglione : " You knowe in great matters & aventrous in warres the true provocation is glory. . . . And every man maye conceive it to be the true glorye, that is stored up in the holy treasure of letters. . . . What minde is so fainte, so bashful and of so base a courage, that in reading the actes & greatnesse of Cesar, Alexander, Scipio, Hannibal, and so many other, is not incensed with a fervent longing to be like them : & doth not prefer the getting of that perpetuall fame, before this rotten life that lasteth twoo dayes ? Which in despite of death maketh him lyve a great deale more famous then before. But he that savoureth not the sweetnesse of letters, cannot know how much is the greatnesse of glorie, which is a longe whyle preserved by them. . . ." Harvey rallied Spenser on the inveteracy of the commonplace : " What though you and a thousand such nurrishe a stronge imagination amongst yourselves that Alexander, Scipio, Cæsar, and most of ower honorablist and worthyest captaynes had never bene what they were but for pore blinde Homer ? " (*Letter-Book,* Camden Soc., page 65.)

461 : Spenser probably had in mind Horace, *Odes,* I. xii, 21 ff., and *Epistles,* II. i, 5-6 :

> Romulus et Liber pater et cum Castore Pollux
> Post ingentia facta deorum in templa recepti . . .

and at line 10, Diram qui contudit Hydram, etc. He would find the notion also in Macrobius, Natalis Comes, and Cicero. The addition of Charlemagne and Charles's Wain is ingenious.

463-472: Compare the complaints of Clio and Terpsichore, and notes thereon.

URANIA: 481-534.

Uranie cæli motus scrutatur, et astra.

"A cœlo . . . Urania appellata est, quoniam docti ubique gentium noscuntur, seu quoniam viros eruditos ad cœlum usque evehat, seu quod gloria et sapientia animos elevat ad cœlestium contemplationem." (L. Gyraldus, *de Musis Syntagma.*)

This is typical of the mixed origins of Spenser's philosophy, and of the comprehensive welcome extended by sixteenth-century scholars, especially in England, to every system that carried the prestige of learning and the promise of wisdom. The age of Elizabeth was one of transition in thought; for good and evil the needs of government stamped the habits of non-inquiry and suspension of judgment permanently on the English mind. Here Spenser summarises rapidly the content of philosophical studies, forgetting for a moment the Muse of Astronomy in his pleased recollection of the Bible, Cicero, Christian theology, natural philosophy, and ethics.

487-498: No particular text need have been in Spenser's mind, but this passage may be illustrated from the *Book of Wisdom* and *Ecclesiasticus*, and the *de Officiis* of Cicero. "Inter hominem et beluam hoc maxime interest, quod hæc tantum, quantum sensu movetur, ad id solum, quod adest quodque præsens est, se accomodat . . . homo autem, quod rationis est particeps . . . facile totius vitæ cursum videt ad eamque degendam præparat res necessarias." (I, 11.) Wisdom is "the brightness of the everlasting light" (*Wisedome*, vii, 26), and "Learning is unto a wise man a jewell of gold, and like a bracelet upon his right arme." (*Ecclesiasticus*, xxi, 21.) "For there is a golden ornament in her, and her bands are the laces of purple colour" (vi, 30). All the 7th and 8th chapters of *Wisdom* are relevant, and *Proverbs* i, 9; iv, 9.

499-502: Observe the movement from *Gods* (481), to *Wisdom, Nature, the Almighty* (510). Spenser remembers, perhaps, the beginning of Ovid's *Metamorphoses*; as well as the Book of Genesis:

> Ante mare et tellus et, quod tegit omnia, cœlum,
> Unus erat toto Naturæ vultus in orbe,
> Quem dixere Chaos, rudis indigestaque moles . . .
> (I, 5-7.)

503-504: " Sapientia autem est . . . rerum divinarum et humanarum causarumque quibus eæ res continentur, scientia." (*de Officiis*, II, 5.) " Illa autem sapientia . . . rerum est divinarum et humanarum scientia, in qua continetur deorum et hominum communitas et societas inter ipsos." (I, 153.) The threefold division is, of course, a commonplace of the schools.

503-508: Compare *Wisdom*, vii, 17-21 with all this passage, and *Georgics* ii, 475-482.

505-516: Compare with this progression the *Hymne of Heavenly Beauty* and the Platonic method of progression from the physical to the metaphysical. Spenser is not thinking of the " trinal triplicity " of the spiritual powers, but uses his terms quite vaguely, for the Angels are the lowest order.

511-516: This is of another kind of metaphysic—definitely New Testament.

517-522: Compare *Ecclesiasticus*, vi, 20-29: " Howe exceeding sharpe is she unto the unlearned! . . . Put thy feete into her links, and thy necke into her chaine (*through humbled will*, line 522) . . . and that shalbe turned to thy joy."

524-527: Spenser remembers his Muse more clearly, and that the contemplation of the heavens is, for her, *self-delight*.

528-529: Is he thinking of Astræa? (See *Mother Hubberds Tale*, 1-3.)

532: A weak line—*ghostly* (i.e. spiritual) *darkenes* linked with the merely physical, vague *gastlie dread*.

POLYHYMNIA : 541-594.

Loquitur Polymneia gestu.

This complaint is more proper to the Muse of Rhetoric, as a shortened version of the mnemonic more explicitly names Polyhymnia, for here Spenser turns to more technical criticism of contemporary poetry.

547-552: Compare line 395, " But rime at riot."

547-558: Compare E.K., Preface to *The Shepheardes Calender*: " I scorne and spue out the rakehellye route of our ragged rymers (for so themselves use to hunt the letter) which without learning boste, without judgement jangle, without reason rage and fume." And Sidney; in his *Defense of Pœsy* : "Let but most of the verses bee put into Prose, and then aske the meaning, and it will be found that one verse did but beget another, without ordering at the first what should be at the last; which becomes a confused masse of wordes, with a tingling sound of ryme, barely accompanied with reason." (*Elizabethan Critical Essays*, I, 196.) This is an accurate enough description of *A Gorgeous Gallery of Gallant Inventions* and some other popular collections. Spenser may not have objected if men applied it also to *The Paradise of Dainty Devices*; though it is by no means so applicable there, there was probably some feeling between the two schools as between their patrons, and the poets of *The Paradise* were certainly less philosophical in their aims than the Sidney-Spenser group.

559-564: Compare the beginning and end of *The Defense of Poesy*. Minturno, *de Poeta* (1559), page 15: "Quapropter apud priscos illos veteres essent interpretes Deorum, & sacerdotes, qui sapientes, qui eloquentes haberentur . . . omnes Poetæ dicebantur." Side-note: "Poetæ omnes qui vates, aut sacerdotes erant, quique Remp. gubernabant." "Civibus autem ita in unum locum congregatis iura & instituta Poeticis condita numeris fuisse." (Ibid.) "Nullum sane dicunt oraculum ab Appolline editum, quod versibus ille non fudisset." (page 14); "Both the Oracles of *Delphos* and *Sibillas* prophecies were wholly delivered in verses." (Sidney, p. 154.)

566-568: Olney's edition of Sidney's *Defense of Poesy* bore as motto on its title page: "Odi profanum vulgus, et arceo," and though this may not have been authorised, it expresses one aspiration of the New Poets. The similarity of their attitude to that of the Pleiade, and the meaning of *le vulgaire*, have already been noticed.

571-582: The flattery poured out at Queen Elizabeth's feet by our poet and his contemporaries has often been animadverted upon, and often severely; yet it was not wholly undeserved, nor is it out of place here. For Elizabeth was the centre of more than political England: she was a cultural focus, as no monarch has been since. Scholars, musicians, poets, dramatists, all could look to her for cultivated sympathy; England was experiencing a tremendous artistic movement, and her Queen was in it.

583-588: The group of Court poets, obviously; Spenser does not include King James VI, for if this poem was written in 1590 he could scarcely praise the son of Duessa (who indeed was about to complain of him), and if it was written in 1580 it preceded James's *Essayes of a Prentise* by four years. It was five or six years after that James gave du Bartas cause to praise him as poet and patron.

589-591: Compare *Virgils Gnat*, 206-208.

VIRGILS GNAT.

The occasion of this translation remains as Spenser left it, enshrouded in mystery. It would appear that he had been checked by Leicester for some well-meant indiscretion, and it has been suggested that *Mother Hubberds Tale* was the cause of offence; but nobody knows, no Œdipus has read the whole *secrete of this riddle rare*. The only facts we can ascertain from the dedicatory sonnet are that the translation was made before the summer of 1580, since it was sent to Leicester, and that Spenser devised the peculiar rhyme-scheme of the *Amoretti* fairly early in his career. Apart from these we must but content ourselves with noting among the curiosities of literature this attempt by a great poet to deprecate an offended patron's wrath by means of a translation from Latin.

Literary historians have long recognised the value of translation to the development of English prose. English verse also gained by the practice, for verse also lacked style, and could acquire something of it in this exercise, wherein the freedom from the necessity of invention leaves the poet free to concentrate on manner, and the fixed matter forces him to attempt precise expression. The translating of Virgil especially is a constant invitation to construct neat phrases and a standing challenge to the cunning modulation of rhythms. For such a task Spenser had innate gifts, and had the desire, moreover, to excel in just those directions. To measure his success he must be compared with his elder contemporaries, the heavy-handed Googe and Turberville, the flamboyant translators of Seneca's tragedies, the egregious Stanyhurst. Comparison with this last shows with abundant clearness the difference between the real master of language and the inexpert, able indeed to feel what is wanted, but too clumsy and too impatient to attempt it but by brute force.

As for the verse, Spenser wisely rejected the popular fourteener, a metre he seems to have disliked; it is incapable of the subtlety and variety of rhythm for which he was always striving and which, as we have said, is particularly requisite in such translation as this. Theatrical practice had not yet developed blank verse into the wonderful medium it was to become; the verse had to be rhymed. The choice, then, lay between the ten-syllable couplet and a stanza. If this translation were made before *Mother Hubberds Tale*, Spenser had behind him only the practice of the deliberately rough Chaucerian couplets of the February, May and September Eclogues; if it came after *Mother Hubberds Tale*, he may have felt that the harder epigrammatic brilliance of his later couplets was unsuitable to the soft eloquence of the poem he set out to translate. In any case he liked stanza-forms—he never repeated the indubitable success of *Mother Hubberds Tale*—he liked playing with rhymes, and so he adopted this Italian *ottava rima* from his other master Ariosto. The employment of a stanzaic metre involved the breaking up of the continuous metre of the original into short paragraphs, treatment to which the *Culex* lends itself fairly well, and which Spenser applied cleverly. The old test of comparing original and translation by the number of lines they contain does not, of course, favour Spenser. Where the sense breaks the hexameters into passages approximating in length to his stanza, all is well; but where a paragraph is too short he sometimes adds a line or two of his own to fill out the stanza, and, since he wishes to do justice to his author, and since his own temperament is leisurely, he does not attempt to compensate by condensing elsewhere.

Warton called *Virgils Gnat* "a vague and arbitrary paraphrase," but really, as verse translations go, its accuracy is fairly high. As we have said, Spenser was hampered somewhat by his stanza; occasionally he is tempted to extend a mythological reference by a detail not in his original; he mistranslates three or four times, and misunderstands twice or thrice, but these are made up for by many brilliant lines and phrases. Spenser indeed belongs to that other school of translators who try to produce a translation that will read like an original, but the spirit of his version is impeccably just. It is instructive to observe how his unmistakably personal style reproduces the soft glow of Virgil—the mark both of temperamental sympathy and of early training in the humanist school. It is well, however, to warn any reader who may care to test Spenser—and his critics—by comparing *Virgils Gnat* with a modern text of *Culex*, that he will find many discrepancies; so, lest he blame Spenser for aberrations which are really due to the alteration wrought by generations of busy emendators of the Latin, I give the original where their emendations necessarily affect the translation. The modern text collated is that of the Oxford *Appendix Virgiliana*, the older text, that of the Plantin editions of 1564-66-75. This text does not correspond with Spenser's version in two places at least, but I have not found an edition which will correspond at all points, and the two first were cheap and handy editions such as a non-professional scholar might be expected to use. Spenser was surely introduced to textual criticism at some time in his seven years of University life: if so, what more obvious field of exercise than *Culex*?

19-20: *Culex* 14-15: Alma Chimæreo Xanthus perfusa liquore
Seu nemus Asteriæ. . . .

29-32: 21-22: Agrestum bona cura, sequi sit cura tenentis
Æreos nemorum tractus, silvasque virenteis.

30: *Successe:* succession, as elsewhere in Spenser.

33: *Professing thee* may be a mistranslation of *te cultrice*; or Spenser may have reversed the notion, taking it from the side of the worshipper instead of from that of the goddess.

34: *Starrie sky* translates the old reading *astra*. (23)

39-40: The old editions omit the phrase *triste Jovis Rhœtique*, and read:

tibi nanque canit non pagina bellum
Phlegra . . .

51: *As for her power more meet:* viribus apta. (36)

54-56: Et tu sancte puer venerabilis, et tibi certet
Gloria perpetuum lucis . . .

61: Debita feliceis memoretur vita per annos.

72: *Where pasture best befalls:* ad pabula læta. (44-5)

74: *Thickest grass* does not translate the modern epithet *florida*, but seems an avoidance of the difficult reading *lurida*.

77-79: This is one of the places where the Plantin text

does not fit, since the modern order of lines 50-51 are nearer Spenser's version. This, however, may be accidental: the exigencies of his verse may have caused the very slight variation. The sense is not really affected.

84: *stud:* this general term, equivalent to *stem*, or *shoot*, is preferred to *alder* (*alnus*) presumably for the rhyme's sake.

92: et probet illis
Omnia luxuriæ pretiis . . .

98: Si non Assyrio fuerint bis lauta colore

100: *summer beames:* roof-beams supporting the ends of joists—used here for *rafters* generally.

109: Vere notat dulci . . . (71)

111: *from:* far from—invidia . . . ac fraude remota. (73)

114: Vitea pampineo . . . (75)

142: *may . . . lend* translates *locet.* (93)

143-4: This couplet is an addition of Spenser's own, to fill out the stanza and avoid running over a useful sentence-ending of the original.

145: Spenser neatly preserves the alliteration of *o pecudes, o Panes.* (94)

Springs: O gratissima Tempe Fontis Hamadryadum.

149: *Ascrean bard:* Hesiod.

155: *rusticke rime* avoids the difficulty of *solidum carmen.* (100)

170-176: Spenser knew the tale of Agave (Ovid, *Met.*, iii, 511 ff), since he interpolates the explanation *having slaine her sonne*; but he forgot, or did not know, that *Nyctelius* is but a name of Bacchus. He confuses the passage by imagining a Nyctilius king of Thebes, evidently her husband and father of her son Pentheus.

180: The old editions read *Orpheus*, not *Œagrius* (117): it makes no difference to the meaning.

182-184: Quantum te Peneu remorantem dia chorea
Multa tibi læto fundentes gaudia vultu.
(119-120)

201-203: Spenser has misunderstood this couplet—an allusion to Phyllis who was changed into an almond-tree:

Posterius cui Demophoon æterna reliquit
Perfidiam lamentandi mala perfida multis.

The old editions omit the line which follows in modern texts:

Perfide Demophoon, et nunc deflende, puellis.

204-205 : Spenser has missed the allusion to the oracle of Dodona (134) ; his mind is still running on metamorphoses.

211 : An addition of Spenser's own, probably to acquire a rhyme to *Pine*.

213 : Appetit æreis contingere montibus astra. (139)

216 : The old editions read *læta cupressus*.

227 : Quæ levibus placidum rivis sonat orta liquorem. (149)

268 : Spenser seems to take *ingens* as *ingentem*, referring to *ducem gregis* instead of to the serpent, " the monster." The error seems childish ; perhaps Spenser was quite aware of what he was doing, and preferred this.

271 : The old editions read *torvo*. (176)

285 : And *gemmis*.

298-304 : Et validum dextra truncum detraxit ab orno :
Qui casus sociaret opem, numenve Deorum.
Namque illi dederitne viam casusve, Deusve,
Prodere sit dubium : voluit sed vincere taleis. (192 *ff.*)

Alder does not translate *orno* : but what matter ?

310-311 : Nescius, adspiciens, timor obcæcaverat artus :
Hoc minus implicuit dira formidine mentem. (198-9)

313-316 : Iam quatit et bijuges oriens Erebo cit equos nox,
Et piger aurato procedit Vesper ab Œta. (203-4)

323 : *Deaw* is scarcely accurate ; unless it is really an original addition.

329 : Inquit quid meritus . . . (210)

340-341 : viden' ut flagrantia tedis
Lumina collucent infestis omnia templis. (216-7)

343 : verbera pœnæ : (219)

345-346 : Cerberus et diris flagrant latratibus ora.

350 : Sanguineique micant ardorem luminis orbes.

351-352 : Another couplet intruded to complete the stanza.

361 : . . . instantia vidi . . . (227)

368 : . . . modo sit dum grata voluntas . . . (230)

371 : Quem circa tristes densentur in omnia pœnæ. (234)

375 : *Ephialtes tide* seems to translate the modern

reading *Devinctum . . . Ephialten*; but the old editions read *Devictum.* The Plantin editions give some alternative readings, but not this one. Spenser must have found it elsewhere.

381-385 : Terreor à tantis insistere, terreor Umbris
As Stygias revocatus aquas. Vix ultimus amni
Restat . . . (239-241)

389-392 : Quid, saxum procul adverso qui monte revolvit,
Contempsisse dolor quem Numina vincit acerbus,
Otia quærentem frustra? Vos ite puellæ,

394 : Ite quibus tedas accendit tristis Erinnys. (234-6)

403 : A line of Spenser's own, to explain the allusion.

405 : *Lapwing* is not intended as a translation of *epops.* A more familiar crested bird than the hoopoe is more useful to the Englishman; and the lapwing's voice is a sufficiently desolate sound.

409 : . . . Cadmeo sanguine . . . (254)

414 : . . . infestaque vulnera corpus . . . (255)

425-427 : Alcestis ab omni
Inviolata vacat cura, quod sæva mariti
Ipsa suis fatis Admeti fata morata est. (262-4)

433-434 : Quin misera Eurydice tanto mærore recessit. (268)

443 : Nec mæsta obtentu diro, et ferrigine regna. (274)

449 : Sed fortuna valens audacem fecerat Orphea. (277)

450-456 : Spenser disregards the repetition of *steterantque amnes* in line 281.

461-464 : Spenser omits line 288 :
Non erat in vitam Divæ exorabile numen.

473-480 : Dignus amor venia, parvum si Tartara nossent
Peccatum ignovisse. Sed et vos sede piorum,
Vos manet Heroum contra manus. (294-6)

489-490 : Hunc rapuit serva (300). The name of Hesione is not in the original, but would be given by any commentator. For its form, see our textual notes.

493-494 : Assidet hac iuvenis, sociat quem gloria, fortis,
Acer, inexcussus . . . (301-2)

503-504 : Cum Troes sævi vos Hectoris ira.
Videre . . . (308-9)

505-509 : Ipsa iugis namque Ida potens feritatis, et ipsa
Æqua faces altrix . . . (311-2)

521-523 : Ignibus hic telisque super si classibus Argos
Eripiat reditus. (319-320)
525 : Hoc erat Æacides alter lætatus honore.
528 : An intrusive line, probably a memory of *Æneid*
i, 483 : Ter circum Iliacos raptaverat Hectora muros.
534-536 : Pallade iam lætatur ovans. (329)
538 : Iam Cicones, iam iamque horret Læstrigonas
atros. (330)
542 : illum metuænda Charybdis. (332)
545-546 : Hic et Tantalei generis decus amplus Atrides.
559-560 : A characteristic intrusive couplet; or transferred and generalised from lines 352-3, reading *lætum*.
568 : This passage had troubled Spenser somewhat, and his version is a re-writing from hints rather than a translation.
571 : *Impeach* in Spenser usually means *prevent*, from the French *empêcher*.

580 : Iamque superne
Corruere et Sol iis et sidera cuncta minantur
Ac venit in terras cæli fragor. (350-352)
589-590 : The old editions read *Camilli* for *Metelli* in line 362.
604-605 : Devotum bellis consumsit gurgitis haustus.
(364)
613-616 : Spenser translates the sense rather than the phrases:
Iure igitur talis sedes pietatis honorat
Illi Scipiadæque Duces: devota triumphis
Mœnia quos rapidos Libycæ Carthaginis
horrent. (369-371)
The 1564 Plantin edition reads *honore* in line 369.
625-628 : Ergo iam caussam mortis me dicere vinctæ
Verberibus sævo cogunt ab iudice pœnæ.
(376-7)
632 : Nec tolerabilibus curis hæc immemor audis.
(379)
633-634 : Quæ tamen ut vanis dimittens omnia ventis
Digredior. (380-1)
638 : Et mea diffusas rapiantur dicta per auras: this line follows line 383, not line 380 as in the Oxford text.
642-643 : Interius graviter mentem æger. (386)
666-684 : Spenser deals somewhat loosely with the list of flowers, as he did with the bird-name *epops* in line 405.

666: Et rosa purpureo crescit rubicunda colore. (399)
669: . . . hic est et Spartica myrtus.
670: *Costmarie* probably stands for *acanthus*. (398)
676: *Box* is not *Bocchus ;* this is a sheer eye-translation, and probably never pretended to be anything else. The *old offence* is equally vague.
678: *Oxeye* is *Buphthalmus*, and *patience*, *picris*: correctly enough.

MOTHER HUBBERDS TALE.

Spenser conceived of his own life-work as that of a scholarly and philosophical poet dealing profoundly with Right and Wrong, Virtues and Vices, and he was apt to see in political affairs the manifestations only of these contending powers. In the worldly atmosphere of Leicester's household, however, he was led for once to treat of affairs on the plane of the times, unphilosophically; and for this game of political satire, in which not only opinions were attacked but—though more covertly than in later days—personalities also, he showed himself almost unexpectedly equipped in intelligence, in neatness of style, in wit, and even in humour. Here we have, it may be, a hint of the Spenser that might have been had not fate removed him from the centre of English things. The occupations and adventures of Irish frontier life were so far away from his earlier interests that they rarely became real enough to grow into his poetry. They might provide illustrations and details, but could never be fused into his habitual thought and the circle of his favourite topics. Had he been able to stay in England even after 1590, Irish experiences might one day have been recollected in tranquillity and made valuable to his poetry, but as things fell out they were rarely more than crude disturbances, hopelessly out of key. Many a young scholar felt thus between 1914 and 1918.

This poem, however, was written before Spenser became involved in that inextricable tangle—the only first-rate poet who ever spent all his maturity in such pressure of affairs. Though life in London provoked his satire, though it was more complicated and more abundant in abuses, it had not the deadliness of the Irish struggles, nor did it tempt our poet to dream. His books were still a delight, not yet a refuge. Satire was indeed a respectable form in the eyes of the learned, but Spenser, learning this kind of satire from Chaucer and Langland, learned to look on the world as they did. The didactic, generalised railing of Juvenal was the model of his contemporaries and of the next generation also; *Mother Hubberds Tale* is, in temper and in purport, such satire as England had to wait a hundred years for, until modern party politics bred it after the Restoration. In spite of its disguise in a mediæval fable, it deals with events as they passed before the poet's eyes, with subjects that were exercising the minds of the men of his day; it grew out of the common talk, not out of books and dreams. Comment, accordingly, which attempts to follow the poet's mind, becomes a matter of illustration rather than of sources. If statute-books, Puritan pamphlets, contemporary books are quoted here, it is not that Spenser used them as he used his Ovid or Virgil, but because they are chosen as giving most economically and conveniently the written evidence upon which we have to depend.

The form of the poem indicates clearly enough its literary filiation, and though Spenser could never resist the temptation of an apt literary allusion, the form alone requires literary research, and of that, fortunately, little. The fable—the simplest kind of allegory—was recognised and accepted by contemporary theorists, and came naturally to a reader of the Bible, of Chaucer and Sir Thomas More, and of popular literature. The setting, the diction, and the verse are Chaucerian, if anything. Spenser deliberately roughens his verse in imitation of his master, to observe decorum with the pseudo-ancient tale, and perhaps with some foresight of the principle that was to be rediscovered by his admirer, the next realistic satirist, Dryden:

> This unpolish'd, rugged verse I chose,
> As fittest for discourse, and nearest prose.

It is but another proof of Spenser's brilliance as a metrical artist that he, the incomparable musician, should understand how verse must on occasion approach (but not become) the everyday cadence of prose. Diction and style are simplified in consonance. Any student of the art of writing, or of Spenser's professional competence, may learn from the comparison of this style with that of *Muiopotmos* and *The Ruines of Time*. Spenser knew his trade.

He planned well, and indeed, one may imagine, with ardour; but he was neither careful nor rigid in adherence to a plan once made, and his uncertainty of method infects the conduct of his fable. At first the Ape and the Fox wander in the world of men, and may be visualised in their proper shapes; but soon they become semi-symbolic. The Ape retains his simian form, but the Fox is metamorphosed—or, rather, loses form altogether, so that he can deal among men at least plausibly disguised in human shape. The true method of the beast-fable recurs when they meet the Mule, and the courtiers are referred to for a few lines as beasts, but, too intent on the subject of his satire, Spenser returns to his first method. In the last section the whole system changes, and we find ourselves no longer in the world of men, but in that of *Reynard the Fox*, inhabited only by beasts which symbolise human types after the same mode as the Ape and the Fox themselves. This may be due to revision, or to Spenser's habit of working in patches. One excellent reason there was: he was attacking the central administration under which he lived, and the removal of his tale to a more remote plane of existence allowed an air of innocence, for dangerous identifications were then the reader's affair, and prosecution would be a confession that certain caps fitted.

Every effective satire contains general and personal reflections; the difficulty is, often, to judge how the emphasis lies. *Mother Hubberds Tale* is no exception. It was written by a partisan of Leicester, a Puritan, and so necessarily written with Leicester's opponents and the High Church leaders within range of the guns. Also it is concerned with matters of public policy, regarding which Spenser's position is easily identified with known bodies of opinion. Now any satire conducted with a sufficiency of wit and in an effective style preserves its interest, even after the immediate occasion and the persons concerned have become mere matters of history, partly by the permanent pleasure of good workmanship and just temper, partly because an important controversy and important people always contain something permanently human, so that we read an old satire as we read a novel. Great satire interests us thus, and also by its exhibition of permanent human weaknesses and perpetually recurrent abuses. Every period of commotion throws up its Zimris and Achitophels, though not its Drydens; Saint Michael and Lucifer are eternal antagonists. By this test also *Mother Hubberds Tale* succeeds. Everything Spenser satirises is an abuse of old standing and of long continuance, and if we pride ourselves that we have accomplished much reformation in the last sixty years, we may discover on closer inspection that only names and technical details require alteration to make this *Prosopopoia* as applicable as ever.

This satire-general has four spheres of action: labour, church, court, and administration. In the first Spenser deals with one specific social problem of his time—the body of vagrants, masterless men and sturdy rogues which the break-up of feudal society and the agricultural and other economic conditions left as an ever-recurrent problem to sixteenth-century administrators. As an attempt at complete discussion of that social problem the poem may be considered a failure, because the angle of vision and the mode of treatment have altered. In Spenser's time such things were subjects for popular pamphlets and royal proclamations; the only intellectual efforts to understand their foundations were confused by moralising, confined to the theory of natural rights, and entangled with other controversies, both political and religious, incident upon the revolution from the Middle Ages. Spenser, like Shakespeare, represents the average thought of his time, the line of thought that descends from Langland, conservative and desirous of order; for order was what England required, and the imposition of order by the Tudors made them acceptable. Otherwise the problems of unemployment and labour organisation would never be presented to Spenser's mind as intellectual questions. So this part might be considered dead—were it not that after all the economic discussion and social legislation the same primitive arguments reappear in the armoury of realists and the dreams of romantics.

The next section, dealing with ecclesiastical affairs, is more effective, for here Spenser treats of questions which had aroused strong emotions and prolonged intellectual exertion, especially at Cambridge during his seven years of University life. He does not attempt a complete exposition of Puritan principles, for he has passed from the echoing quadrangles into a larger and more hurried world, and he is too wise to argue on dogma or to labour his points. His satire on ignorant clergy and careless and dishonest patrons is repeated in another Cambridge production, certainly not a Puritan manifesto, *The Returne from Parnassus*; but these abuses were generally complained of, were older than his time, and were attacked by English writers for many a day to come. The Cambridge mark is still upon him, not only in the occasional phrases which smack of the pamphlet, but in his scorn of the moral and intellectual laziness which seemed to men of his kind to shelter behind the episcopal appeals for peace and loyalty and the administrative repression of preaching and discussion. In later years in Ireland, he was a fighter in the conflict between Romanism and Protestantism, a conflict the simpler, intellectually, for its deeper issues and its political implications. Here he is conscious that the enemy is abuse, not uncompromising principle, and the influence of the circle in which he was living suggested a style less emphatic, comparatively detached, even humorous. He does not preach, but, like Chaucer, is content to state. Chaucer's example, indeed, shows itself here in more than form, for the disciple has learned the master's trick of making his victim condemn himself unconsciously out of his own mouth.

Of the Court, the matter of the third episode, Spenser had some small experience by the time he wrote; on the other hand, there was abundant literary precedent for his satirical picture of court life, the evils of which, from Alain Chartier's time and before it, are almost a tradition among vernacular and neo-Latin poets. The insistent question here is that of personal allusion, for we have some notion of the personalities among whom Spenser lived. What actual case suggested the first episode of *Mother Hubberds Tale*, or what experience in the diocese of Rochester the second, we do not know: we should beware, however, of assuming on the one hand that the earlier part of the poem is general satire or on the other that this is particular satire, merely because the records tell us more about one group of people than about another. Commentators have fastened on one passage (lines 891-908) as expressive of Spenser's own feelings aroused by his own experience at Court. It is indeed a telling passage, and contains one line that may refer to his cross at the hands of Burghley:

> To have thy Prince's grace, yet want her Peeres.

This would date the passage as written in 1590; which is quite possible, since the poem was apparently revised before publication. Spenser was not conspicuously unsuccessful as a courtier, except that he presumably wished for employment in England. He seems to have hated court life—it is unlikely that a man of his academic temperament and training would be happy or successful among politicians—and the repetition of his indictment of courtly abuses in *Colin Clouts Come Home Again* almost forces us to believe that his dark picture was painted from personal observation. Yet we must also remember the literary tradition, which would have led him to write in much the same strain whatever his own experience, and we must not be too eager to fix upon particular persons.

> Blame is (quoth he) more blamelesse generall,
> Than that which private errours doth pursew.

The historical transaction with which this passage has naturally been connected is the much-discussed proposal of marriage between Queen Elizabeth and the Duc d'Alençon, to which Leicester and his party were bitterly opposed, while Burghley seems to have favoured it. Alençon's principal agent Simier was in England nearly all the year 1579, and Spenser might well be expected to assist the cause of his party. " My Ape " was the Queen's punning nickname for the accomplished French courtier. Dr. Greenlaw has suggested that Spenser has pressed into service a whole series of animal nicknames with which Elizabeth graced her courtiers ; yet it would be a dangerous matter—quite apart from the obvious discourtesy—for a mere client to parody the Queen's affections in order to satirise her policy. The Alençon courtship was a ticklish business. For addressing a solemn protest to his Royal mistress Philip Sidney suffered exile from her countenance ; Philip Stubbes suffered the loss of his right hand : and despite his powerful protectors Spenser was nearer the degree of Stubbes than that of Sidney. In any case the personal allusion can only have been one in passing. The episode of the Ape at Court may have provoked men to smile and think of Simier, but the Ape cannot represent Simier throughout the poem, nor can Burghley, who in all probability is attacked later under the guise of the Fox, be credited with the part of the Fox in this passage, any more than in the earlier portions of the poem.

Nor need only one person be aimed at. In 1580 Gabriel Harvey published, in his correspondence with Spenser, a " bolde Satyricall Libell . . . *in Gratiam quorundam Illustrium Anglofrancitalorum, hic et ubique apud nos voli-*

tantium." He assures Spenser, "*Nosti homines, tanquam tuam ipsius cutem.*" Harvey's *Speculum Tuscanismi* has much in common with Spenser's courtly Ape; and the Earl of Oxford took it as a satire on himself. Foreigneering newfangledness indeed was a common butt of contemporary satirists of all grades. While keeping Simier in mind, then, we should not assume that the passage is aimed at Simier exclusively. Its moral tone and the didactic element it includes show the more general intention of the poet.

As we have said, the last episode (line 942 to the end) is devised on a different system from the rest, as an Æsopic beast-fable of the ordinary kind. This warns us of a difference in aim, and here we have the most direct attack on Burghley.* The Ape can no longer stand for Simier, though the role may be transferred to Alençon, and the fable be a warning to England of what would happen if Alençon and his supporter Burghley gained supreme power through Alençon's marriage to the Queen. I imagine, however, that the satire lies more in the description of the Fox's behaviour as chief minister than in the story, which may have been invented mainly with an eye to its literary value as a climax. Spenser changes his method cleverly, generalising the form while he particularises the covert purpose, so as to make retaliation difficult. Dr. Greenlaw has shown that the various misdemeanours of the Fox were all committed by Burghley: but unfortunately they were by no means peculiar to him—Leicester's record was decidedly worse. Spenser is playing the old game of attributing to the opposite party the commonplaces of crime, some known by contemporary practice, some traditional, and it is more by side-hits, the Fox's contempt for arms and letters, his thrift, his policy and his plea of experience, that we are led to think of Burghley, the Queen's "Fox." In the episode as a whole there is more literary imitation than in the other parts of the poem. So we must not press interpretation too far. Spenser shifts his ground frequently, and the reader requires a certain agility to follow him. In all his work he had a triple aim: to write delectable poetry, to teach sound and various doctrine and to comment on contemporary affairs: and that is the order of importance.

This discovery of an effective way of satire—one of the many discoveries of the New Poet—was only too complete. Gabriel Harvey disapproved. "Mother Hubbert, in

* See note on line 1144.

heat of choller, forgetting the pure sanguine of her sweete Feary Queene, wilfully over-shott her malcontented self: as elsewhere I have specified at larg, with the good leave of unspotted friendship." (*Foure Letters*, 1592.) Nash, apparently, did not find the allusions easy to interpret after the lapse of ten years—which may excuse us. "Who publikely or of late brought *Mother Hubberd* into question, that thou shouldst by rehearsall rekindle against him the sparkes of displeasure that were quenched? Forgot hee the *pure sanguine of his Fairy Queene*, sayst thou? A *Pure sanguine* sot art thou, that in vaine-glory to have *Spencer* known for thy friend, and that thou hast some interest in him, censurest him worse than his deadliest enemie would do. If any man were undeservedly toucht in it, thou hast revived his disgrace that was so toucht in it, by renaming it, when it was worn out of al mens mouths and minds. Besides, whereas before I thought it a made matter of some malitious moralizers against him, and no substance of slaunder in truth; now, when thou (that proclaimest thyself the only familiar of his bosome, and therefore shouldst know his secretes) gives it out in print that he overshotte himselfe therein, it cannot chuse but be suspected to be so indeed." (*Strange Newes*, 1592.)

It has, indeed, been confidently asserted that *Mother Hubberds Tale* was "called in," but when, or by what authority, is not stated. The question is one of the history of the book, and so is referred to our bibliographical notes. Here it is enough to note the fact—if it be a fact, and if it is only a tradition the point remains good—that Spenser's satire was felt. So, being effective in its own day and interesting in ours, *Mother Hubberds Tale* may be ranked among the few English political poems which possess permanent value.

THE DEDICATION: Anne, fifth daughter of Sir John Spenser of Althorp, the *Phyllis* of *Colin Clouts Come Home Again*, married (1) William Stanley, Lord Mounteagle; (2) Henry, Lord Compton, who died in 1589; (3) on September 4th, 1591, Robert Sackville, who succeeded his father, the poet, as 2nd Earl of Dorset.

THE TITLE *Prosopopoia*—a personification—may mean either that the personages of the poem are to be identified with general abuses, or that Spenser, deprecating too personal an interpretation, wishes us to believe that they are.

1-8: This notation of the time of year by the astronomical signs would of course be familiar to Spenser—Harvey describes him (*Marginalia*, page 162) as Sphæræ, astrolabijque non plane ignarum—but he employed it here probably to create an antique feeling through its Chaucerian reminiscence. Compare *The Shepheardes Calender*, *July*, 17-24, and E.K.'s note. These have been taken as references to the plague of 1577-79: they may be, but in any case Spenser would probably have written something like this, merely following the astronomical poets. The mention of the Dog-Star compels the mention of sickness. In plain prose, it was the month in which the Sun, with the Dog-Star beside him, leaves the House of Leo and enters that of Virgo: that is, August. Virgo is identified with Astræa by Virgil (*Ecl.* iv, 6), Ovid (*Met.* i, 149-150), and by the astronomer-poets generally.

12: *geason:* unusual. *Piers Ploughman*, B-text, xiii, 271.

33-38: This reminds one of Sir Thomas More, *A Dyalogue of Comfort*, II, xiv (*Works*, 1557, page 1183): "My mother had (when I was a little boy) a good old woman that tooke heede to her chyldren, they called her mother Mawde. . . . She was wont when shee sat by the fire wyth us, to tell us (that were children) many childysh tales. But as *Plinius* sayth that ther is no boke lightly so badde, but that some good thing a man maye pyke out therof, so think I that ther is almost no tale so foolysh, but that yet in one matter or other, to some purpose it may hap to serve. For I remember me that among other of her fond tales, she told us once, that the Asse and the Wolfe came upon a tyme to confession to the Foxe. . . ."

THE APE AS SHEPHERD, 45-339.

49: *unhappie witted:* with unlucky, that is, restless minds.

67: *losels:* good-for-nothings. *Piers Ploughman*, vi, 124.

72: *awhape:* confound. Spenser would find the past participle *awhaped* in Chaucer (*Troilus and Criseyde*, i, 316 and elsewhere); no other part of the verb appears before Spenser's use of it here. It is one of his experiments in revival of old words.

78: The expression is proverbial.

85: *Pilgrim, Lymiter:* Chaucerian touches thrown in for their archaic effect.

86 : *Gipsen :* The word is italicised presumably because it was still somewhat strange in English ears. The spelling retains a hint of the early derivation from *Egyptian.*

129-169 : Spenser was a man of the new age, a believer in authority and an opponent of the popular communism of the previous century. Here he cleverly makes the arguments of the other side the arguments of the beggar. Compare Langland, *Piers Ploughman,* B-text, xx. 271-276 :

> Envye herd this . and heet freres to go to scole,
> And lerne logyk and lawe . and eke contemplacioun
> And preche men of Plato . and preve it by Seneca,
> That alle thingis under hevene . ouȝte to ben in comune.
> And ȝit he lyeth, as I leve . that to the lewed so precheth,
> For god made to man a lawe . and Moyses it tauȝte,
> Non cupisces rem proxime tui.

In political questions Spenser follows neither Plato (*Republic,* iii. 415 ff.) nor Seneca (*Epistolæ,* xc), but rather the Cicero of the *de Officiis.* "Non de ea philosophia loquor, quæ civem extra patriam posuit, extra mundum deos." Still more he followed the teaching of the times and of the Church whose 38th Article stands : "The Riches and Goods of Christians are not common, as touching the right, title, and possession of the same, as certain Anabaptists do falsely boast." For the Fox's speech, Spenser probably had in mind the definition of Natural Right in the Institutes of Justinian ; the old idea of the Golden Age in Ovid, Virgil, Lucretius, and Seneca *op. cit. :* "In commune rerum natura fruebantur ; sufficiebat illa ut parens in tutela omnium, hæc erat publicarum opum secura possessio" ; and the famous speech of John Ball, reported by Froissart (ccclxxxi) and reprinted by Holinshed : "A ye good people, the maters gothe nat well to passe in Englande, nor shall nat do tyll every thyng be common ; and that there be no villayns nor gentylmen. . . . What have we deserved, or why shulde we be kept thus in servage ? we be kept thus in servage ? we be all come fro one father and one mother, Adam and Eve : wherby can they say or shewe that they be gretter lordes than we be ? savynge by that they cause us to wyn and labour, for that they dispende

. . . and by that that cometh of our labours they kepe and mayntayne their estates : we be called their bondmen, and without we do redilye them servyce, we be beaten."

151-153 : Compare Thomas Howell, *Devises*, 1581, (ed. Raleigh, p. 53) :

> The golden worlde is past sayth some,
> But nowe say I that worlde is come :
> Now all things may for Golde be had,
> For gayne of Golde, both good and bad . . .
> Then truth to tell, and not to fayne,
> Right now the golden worlde doth raygne.

Either may have been first, but the quip is not so recondite that it may not have occurred to each separately.

183-280 : All vagrants were required to carry a passport or licence issued by the appropriate authority. The important Statute of 1572 (14 Eliz. c.v.) provides in Clause 9 " That Shipmen and Souldiours having Lycense of the next two Justices of the Peace to the Place where they firste happened to land, or where they firste entred into this Realme, shall and may passe accordinge to the Purporte of their Lycense, and Intent of this Acte of Parlyament." Clause 13 provides that this Act does not make frustrate or void " any saufe Conduite Passeporte or Lycense made and granted " by the Lord Deputy of Ireland, Officers Commanding garrisons, and other officers " uppon the dispersing of any Armye onlye, to any Souldiour or Souldiours." The problem of the discharged soldier was not pressing at the moment, though it had been and was to be again, but there was always the stream of discharges from Ireland and the Low Countries, and as Captain Robert Hitchcock put it, " At the breaking up of wars, there are a great number of worthy and valiant soldiers . . . who, through want of living . . . if they tarry in England, hanging is the end of the most part of them." (*A Politic Plot*, 1580, printed in Lang's *Social England*, p.87). Harman knew the type : " The Ruffler . . . hath served in the warres . . . And with stout audacyte, demandeth where he thinketh hee maye be bolde, and circomspecte ynough, as he sethe cause to aske charitie, rufully and lamentably, that it would make a flyntey hart to relent, and pytie his miserable estate, howe he hath bene maymed and broused in the warres ; and, paraventure, some wyll shew you some outward wounde, whiche he gotte at some drunken fraye."

(*A Caveat for Cursetors*, 1567, Shakspere Soc., p. 29.) " If they repayre to a poore husbandmans house [the Upright Man] wyl go a lone, or one with him, and stoutely demand his charytie, eyther shewing how he hath served in the warres, and their maymed, eyther that he sekethe service, and saythe that he woulde be glad to take payne for hys lyvinge, althoughe he meaneth nothinge lesse." (*Ibid.*, p. 31.) It was the gambit also of the " Courtesy Man." See, in *Shakespeare's England*, II. 488, a facsimile of the forged passport of a counterfeit shipwrecked mariner.

192 : *defie* in the French sense—those who are suspicious of beggars.

309 : *javels :* worthless fellows. More, *Works* (1557), p. 1272. D.

THE FOX AS PRIEST : 340-574.

347 : *wyte :* reproach. *Troilus and Criseyde*, i. 825.

348-358 : The Statute 14 Eliz. c.v, clause 5, defining " Rogues Vacaboundes and Sturdye Beggers," includes " all Scollers of the Universityes of Oxford or Cambridge yt goe about begginge, not beinge aucthorysed under the Seale of the said Universities, by the Comyssarye Chauncelour or Vicechauncelour of the same."

379-395 : Here speaks the Cambridge Puritan. Field and Wilcox's *An Admonition to Parliament*, 1572, set out the main tenets of the party, and provided texts for the controversy between Cartwright and Whitgift. In the primitive Church, says the *Admonition*, " the ministers were preachers : now bare readers." (sig. Aiij.) " Appoint to every congregation a learned and diligent preacher. Remove homylies, articles, injunctions, and that prescript order of service made out of the masse booke." (Aiiij). " By the word of God, it is an offyce of preachyng, they make it an offyce of reading . . . they are enjoyned to fede Gods Lambs, and yet with these, such are admitted and accepted, as only are bare readers that are able to say service, and minister a Sacrament according to theyr appoyntment. And that thys is not the feeding that Chryste spake of, the scriptures are plain. For bare reading of the word and single service saying, is bare feeding, yea it is as evil as playing upon a stage, and worse too. For players yet learne theyr partes without boke, and these, a many of them can scarcely read within boke." (B) " Are not the people wel nodifyed thinke you, when the homily of sweping the church is red unto them?" (B b) "In thys booke (the Prayer-Book) also, it is appointed that after the Creede, if there be no sermon, an homily must folowe . . . that which is already set out, being corrupt and straunge, to maintain an unlearned and reading minysterie." (Bij) "The minyster . . . posteth it over, as fast as he can galloppe. For eyther he hath two places to serve, or else there are some games to be playde in the afternoone, as lying for the whetstone, heathenisshe dauncing for the ring, a bear or a bull to be baited, or else Jack an apes to ride on horssback, or an enterlude to be plaide." (Biiij b) Lines 386-391, of course, go back to the controversies begun round the New Testament of Erasmus: but the types are permanent.

404: *eath:* easily. *Troilus and Criseyde*, v. 850.

406: *troad:* way to be followed, footing.

421-424: "Lordly Lords, Archbishops, Bishops, Suffragans, Deanes, Universitie Doctors, and Bachelers of Divinitie, Archdeacons, Chauncelours and the rest of that proud generation." (*Admonition*, sig. A) "And therfore titles, livings and offices by Antichrist devised are given to them, as Metropolitane, Archbishop, Lords Grace, Lord Bishop, Suffragan, Deane, Archdeacon. . . ." (Aiij b) "Bishops, Archdeacons, Chancellors, Offycials, Commissaries, and such like. . . ." (Avii) "The Lorde Bishops, theyr suffraganes, Archdeacons, Chancelors, Officials, proctors, Doctors, sumners, and such ravening rablers . . ." (B v b).

424: *yet spite bites neare:* whatever spiteful men may say.

439-440: Isaiah, liv, 13: "And all thy children shall be taught of the Lord." St. John, vi, 45: "It is written in the Prophets, And they shal be all taught of God." In his ignorance the "formall Priest" refers the text to Aaron.

446-459; 475-478: This comparison with the older Church need not be taken as proof either of recusancy or of inconsistency. The charge against the High Church party is that they have taken from the Roman Church as much as suited them and no more. It is fair criticism, probably by no means confined to Spenser.

452-454: *Complines*, the last service of the day; *Trentals*, series of thirty masses for the dead; *memories*, services—masses, sermons, etc.—at interval of a month, year, or so, in memory of the dead. Spenser, of course, is using merely such technical terms as occur to him and suit his verse.

460-474: This is an echo of the vestments controversy. Spenser gives a version of the High Church argument. The letter of Beza attached to the *Admonition* tells how "theyr ministers beganne to be attired in pretious and Bishopplike, yea, and Emperourlike garments, and all forsothe to honoure the sacrament with all." (Dij) Spenser may also have had in mind the more general complaint voiced by Philip Stubbes in his *Anatomy of Abuses*, 1583: "They cannot contente themselves with cloth, though never so excellent, but they must weare silkes, velvets, satans, damaskes, grograms, taffeties, and the like. I speake not against those that are in authoritie . . . but against those that bee meane pastours and Ministers, that flaunt it out in their saten doblets, taffetie doblets, silke hosen, garded gownes, cloakes, and such like." (Book ii. Shakspere Society ed., p. 108.)

479-544: "Whereas in the olde churche a trial was had, both of their abilitie to instruct, and of their godly conversation also: now, by the letters patent of some one man, noble or other, tag and rag, learned and unlearned, of the basest sort of the people (to the sclaunder of the gospell in the mouthes of the adversaries) are freely receaved . . . now every one picketh out for himselfe some notable good benefyce, he obtaineth the next advowson, by mony or by favoure, and so thinketh himselfe to be suffyciently chosen." (*Admonition*, Aij b) Bishops appoint alone that they may "get benefyces by frendship or mony, or flattery where they can catch them." (Bvj) "Now it is thought sufficient for the certaintie of his conversation if he either have letters dimissorie from one bishop to another . . . or else letters commendatorie from any gentleman, or other, especially if they be of any reputation. If he can get these things, he is likely to speede, I warrant him. Which thing is scarce well, in my judgment. For you knowe one private man or two, or three, or foure may, peradventure either write upon affection, or else bee corrupted with bribes or gifts." (Stubbes, *Anatomy*, ii; Shaks. Soc. ed., p. 91.)

487-540: "The most patrones keepe the fattest morsels to themselves, and give scarcely the crums to their pastors. But if the benefice be woorth an hundred pound, they will hardly give fortie pound. If it be woorth forty pound, it is well if they give ten pound, imploieng the better half to their owne private gaine." (*Anatomy*, ii; p. 80.) The complaint was very common: it is one of the main themes of *The Returne from Parnassus*, Part ii. Holinshed himself notes it, though no Puritan: "But if it were knowne to all, that I know to have beene performed of late in Essex, where a minister taking a benefice (of lesse than twentie pounds in the Queenes bookes so farre as I remember) was inforced to paie to his patrone, twentie quarters of otes, ten quarters of wheat, and sixteene yeerelie of barleie, which he called hawkes meat; and another left the like in farme to his patrone for ten pounds be the yeere, which is well woorth fortie at the least, the cause of our thred-bare gownes would easilie appeare, for such patrons doo scrape the wooll from our clokes."

THE APE AT COURT: 575-942.

582: The Mule is chosen presumably as the traditional mount of rich and self-indulgent potentates.

620: The *wilde beasts* are Elizabeth's fighting captains and courtiers, the *Lyon*, of course, being the Queen.

623-626: Elizabeth believed in keeping her men under control, and liked to have her favourites at court. Her forbidding Sidney, Essex, and other young courtiers to go adventuring is well known.

622-630: There is an obvious break in the sense here, apparently due to hasty revision, either soon after the poem was written or just before publication. A reference to Leicester has been altered or imperfectly excised: all commentators seem agreed that *His late chayne* means his marriage to the Countess of Essex, which was kept a secret from the Queen until Simier revealed it some months later, in 1579. Elizabeth was extremely angry.

656: *aguize:* dress, array. *O.E.D.* gives no earlier example.

671: *what mister wight:* what kind of man. Chaucer, *Knight's Tale*, 852.

672-674: Newfangledness of dress was a constant butt of Elizabethan satire. Nor was it so only in England, as we may judge from Castiglione: "We see infinite variety in it, and some are arayed after the Frenche fashion, some after the Spanyshe attier, an other wyll seeme a Dutcheman. Neyther wante wee of them also that wyl cloth themselves lyke Turkes. . . ."

692-700: Compare Castiglione: "And I recken vautyng of no lesse prayse, which for all it is peynefull and harde, maketh a man more light and quicker then any of the rest: and beside the profite, yf that lightnesse be accompanyed with a good grace, it maketh (in my judgemente) a better showe than anye of the reste. If our Courtyer then be taught these exercises more then indifferently well, I beleve he may sette a syde tumblynge, clymynge upon a corde, and suche other matters that taste somewhat of jugglers crafte, & doe lytle beseeme a Gentleman."

701-710: "But the meerie Pranckes that the Courtier ought to use, must (by myne advyse) be somewhat wyde from immoderate jesting. He ought also to take heed that his Meerie Pranckes tourne not to pilferinge, as we see many naughtipackes, that wander about the world with divers shiftes to gete money, feining now one matter, now an other. And that they be not to bitter."

717-734: "He shall not be yll tunged . . . for it apeereth that there is a storme in courtes that carieth this condicion with it, that alwaies looke who receyveth most benefittes at his Lordes handes, and promoted from very base degree to high astate, he is evermore complaynynge and reporteth woorst of hym: which is an uncomly thing. . . . Oure Courtier shall use no fonde sausiness. He shall be no carier about of trifling newes. . . . He shall be no babbler, not geven to lyghtenesse, no liar, no boaster, no fonde flatterer." "I wyll have oure Courtier also take heede he purchase not the name of a lyar, nor of a vaine person. . . . Therfore in his communicatyon let him be alwayes heedefull not to goe out of the lykelyhood of truth. . . . Other, at the first entringe into a friendshipp wyth a newe friende . . . sweare that there is not a person in the world whom thei love better. . . . Thus bicause they would bee counted to lovynge woormes, they make menne counte them lyars, and fonde flatterers."

735-748: "And therefore will I have him . . . to shewe strength, lightnes, and quickenesse, and to have understandyng in all exercises of the bodie, that belong to a man of warre. And herein I thinke the chief point is to handle well all kynde of weapon both for footeman and horseman, and to know the vauntages in it. . . . I think also it will serve his turne greatly, to know the feat of wrastling, because it goeth much together with all weapon on foote. . . . Also men occupie their weapon oftentimes in tyme of peace aboute sundrie exercises, and gentlemen are seen in open showes. . . . Therefore will I have our Courtyer a perfecte horseman for everye saddle. . . . And because it is the peculyer prayse of us Italians to ryde well, to manege wyth reason, especiallye roughe horses, to runne at the rynge and at tylte, he shall be in this amonge the beste Italyans. At tourneymente, in kepyng a passage, in fightinge at barriers, he shall be good emong the best Frenchmen. . . . There bee also manye other exercises. . . . And of them me thinke huntyng is one of the chiefest, for it hath a certaine lykenesse with warre, & truelye a pastime for great men, & fitte for one lyvyng in courte. . . . It is meete for hym also to have the arte of swimming, to leape, to runne, to cast the stone."

749-752: "These olde men . . . say it is no good sight to see yonge men on horseback aboute the stretes and especially upon Mules." Spenser agrees with the old men and not with the newer fashion to which Castiglione is indulgent. The *Persian pride* looks like a perversion, a false memory, or the memory of a perversion, of Xenophon, *Cyropædia*, IV. iii. 22-23, wherein it is said the Persian nobles were taught to ride continually—not, however out of pride, but so as to keep in training for service as cavalry.

753-759: "You must thinke I am not pleased with the Courtyer if he be not also a musitien, and beside his understanding and conning upon the booke, have skill in lyke maner or sundrye instruments. For yf we waie it well, there is no ease of the labours & medicines of feeble mindes to be found more honeste and more praise worthye in tyme of leyser then it. And princypally in Courtes, where (beside the refreshing of vexacyons that musicke bringeth unto eche man) many thynges are taken in hand to please women withal." With more to the same purpose. The happy recovery of Elizabethan music in late years has reminded everyone of the proper place music held in Spenser's day.

The courtly theme of love is, of course, one of the principal in Castiglione's book.

759-772: See the passages quoted in our commentary on *The Teares of the Muses*, page 207. Castiglione continues: "Retourne againe unto oure Courtier, whom in letters I will have to bee more then indyfferentlye well seene, at the least in those studyes, which they call Humanitie. . . . Let hym much exercise hym selfe in poets, and no lesse in Oratours and Historiographers."

803 : *balliards :* billiards.

810-820 : See notes on *The Teares of the Muses—Erato.*

832-838 : Compare du Bellay's ironical *Le Poete Courtisan—e.g.* lines 60-63 :

> seras estimé entre les mieux disans,
> Non comme ces resveurs, qui rougissent de honte
> Fors entre les scavans, desquels on ne fait compte.

913 : *himselfe will a daw trie :* will prove himself a fool.

THE APE AS KING : 940-1384.

940 : *stound :* This word has several meanings in Spenser : here it means, I think, *time—complaining of the evil time he was experiencing.*

947-8 : Though *at home* they ate hips and drank water.

950 : *rechless :* careless, at random. Had Spenser in mind Chaucer's Monk " whan he is reccheless," *Prologue,* 179 ?

950-1380 : Compare the fable of the Ass in the Lion's Skin. The theft of the skin while the Lion sleeps, the deception of the other beasts, and the Lion's roaring (1352 ff.) suggest that Spenser elaborated much of this episode from that very common fable.

1057-8 : Jortin points to Cicero, *de Officiis,* III. xxi : " Ipse autem socer (*sc.* Cæsar) in ore semper Græcos versus de Phœnissis habebat . . .

> Nam si violandum est ius, regnandi gratia
> Violandum est :

1117-1126 : Like most of his contemporaries, Spenser may have read Machiavelli's *Principe,* but his remark on the use of foreign mercenaries here owes nothing to Machiavelli, who deprecates their use as uncertain in allegiance. He more likely remembers the custom of certain later Roman Emperors, and perhaps the French Kings.

The crocodile and the beaver are " bred of two kinds," since they are amphibious, half beast half fish.

1144 : *Fiaunt :* " A warrant addressed to the Irish Chancery for a grant under the Great Seal."—*O.E.D.* The use of a technical term of Irish administration suggests a later date for the writing or revision of this passage. Yet though the word would become familiar to Spenser in his Irish office, it need not have remained unknown to him earlier. The change in method after line 950, the comparative absence of archaism, and the literary admixture tempt one to think this part was rewritten, perhaps even substituted for a different version; but the evidence is not strong, and I prefer to leave the suggestion here, rather than in the general remarks above, though it might be of importance in connexion with the growth of Spenser's feeling against Burghley.

1155: This may be an echo of the vestments controversy, wherein the symbolism of colours was much discussed: "By the white garment is meant . . . innocency of life."—Whitgift, *Works*, Parker Soc., II, 26.

1189-1192: Compare *The Ruines of Time*, 440-455. All this passage may well be aimed directly at Burghley, but whether Spenser had any particular transactions in mind, either in his general accusations or in the affair of the Sheep and the Wolf, is hard to tell.

1204: *but for availe:* unless it were to his own advantage.

1205-1222: This is a neat variant upon a common tale which may be found among the Reynard stories and among Henryson's fables.

1225-1231: *Æneid*, i. 223-6:

> Et iam finis erat: quum Jupiter æthere summo
> Despiciens mare velivolum terrasque iacentes
> Litoraque et latos populos, sic vertice cœli
> Constitit et Libyæ defixit lumina regis.

The phrase *with his black-lidded eye* seems a Homeric reminiscence. Warton compares *Iliad* i. 528: 'H καὶ κυανέῃσιν 'επ' ὀφρύσι νεῦσε κρονίων, which Spondanus translates, in the version Spenser probably knew, *nigris superciliis annuit Saturnides.* I am uncertain as to Spenser's knowledge of Greek, and I imagine that he, like Chapman, found it useful to have the Latin opposite. He imitated no Greek passage available at that time in Greek alone.

1245: *stal'd:* nor have his punishment postponed.

1246-1299: There may be memories here of *Iliad* xxix. 339-345, but Virgil supplies all that is required:

> Maia genitum demittit ab alto . . .
> Volat ille per æra magnum
> Remigio alarum, ac Libyæ citus adstitit oris. (i. 297, 300-1.)

1279-1290: The hat of darkness belonged to Hades, not to Mercury. Spenser is probably thinking of the story of Perseus, whom Mercury guided to Hades to borrow it.

1291-1299: *Iliad* as above, and *Æneid* iv. 238-246:

> Ille patris magni parere parabat
> Imperio: et primum pedibus talaria nectit
> Aurea, quæ sublimem alis sive æquora supra
> Seu terram rapido pariter cum flamine portant.
> Tum virgam capit; hac animas evocat Orco
> Pallentes, alias sub Tartara tristia mittit;
> Dat somnos adimitque et lumina morte resignat:
> Illa fretus agit ventos, et turbida tranat
> Nubila.

In his commentary on this passage Servius notes *virga: Caduceus*. See also Ovid, *Metamorphoses* i. 671 ff.

1321-1322: There is nothing about this *wicked weed* in the passage (ll. 951-1018) which describes the theft of the royal honours. Clearly all this section of the poem has been revised before publication.

THE RUINES OF ROME.

These translations of Joachim du Bellay's *Antiquites de Rome* are so inexact and careless that Child doubted Spenser's authorship, and Koeppel, in *Englische Studien*, xv, used them as evidence against Spenser's authorship of the sonnets in *A Theatre . . . for Worldlings*. We do not know when Spenser translated these sonnets; but obviously he had not his dictionary by him, wrote in haste, and was more concerned to hammer out a passible English sonnet than to render the niceties of the French original. In no way are these translations to be compared to some that are imbedded in *The Faerie Queene*, or even to *Virgils Gnat*, and though they contain—as they could not fail to—some neat turns of phrase, they may be regarded as part of that process of digestion of foreign poetry that du Bellay recommends in his *Deffence et Illustration de la Langue Francoyse*. The results are to be sought in *The Ruines of Time* rather than here.

1.8: *my shreiking yell:* The original has only *mon cry*. This noisy style resembles that of *The Teares of the Muses*.

9-10: This is none too clear. The original reads:

Trois fois cernant sous le voile des cieux
De vos tumbeaux le tour devotieux.

Spenser has connected *cernant* with the Latin *cernere* whereas du Bellay means "having thrice made the tour of devotion round your tombs." Spenser commits the same error in sonnet 26.

2.2: *steeples:* The original has *vergers l'air*—the hanging gardens of Babylon. Spenser must have known the Seven Wonders of the World, and his perversion of the text is peculiar: it is not only his knowledge of French that is in question.

10: *erect:* the past participle. Compare *Theatre for Worldlings*, v. 5.

3.5: Voy quel orgueil, quelle ruine.

4.3: *More:* Moor, Mauritania.

12: *noysome Esquiline:* The original has *l'eschine Exquilienne*—the Esquiline ridge.

5.3: *In case that:* in modern phrase, *If so be that. . . .*

5.5-7: There is considerable confusion here:

Rome n'est plus; et si l'architecture
Quelque umbre encor de Rome fait revoir,
C'est comme un corps par magique sçavoir
Tiré de nuict hors de sa sepulture.

10-11: Et son esprit rejoindre s'est allé
Au grand esprit de ceste masse ronde.

Spenser has missed the philosophic allusion.

14: *Idole:* from the original, *idole*—εἴδολον, image.

6.6: Stress of rhyme has forced Spenser to omit a point:

de qui le pouvoir
Fut le pouvoir du monde.

7.1: *tragicke sights;* does not translate *sacrez costaux.*

7: *Arcks:* arches, as in *Visions of Bellay*, 4.4.

8.1: *vassals:* an eye-translation—*vaisseaux.*

13-14: Que le chef *deterré* aux fondemens antiques
Qui prindrent nom de luy. . . .

9.3: *by course of kinde:* in the order of nature—a Chaucerian phrase. Du Bellay has *par ordre.*

11.2: Spenser misses the point here. Du Bellay has *l'impuissance humaine.*

11-12: Ce peuple adonc, nouveau fils de la Terre . . .

Ces braves murs accabla sous sa main,
Puis *se* perdit dans le sein de *sa* mere.

13.10: Spenser attempts an embellishment—*snaky-paced* for *tortueux.*

13-14: The translation somewhat spoils the climax:

> Que la grandeur du rien, qu'ilz t'ont laissé,
> Ne face encor' emerveiller le monde.

14.7: *Whetting* has scarcely the visual power of the original *ensanglanter.*

9: *most dastards:* the most dastard—*les moins vaillans.*

12: *Behold* does not convey the strength of the original *accompagner.* Du Bellay means that those now "show boldnesse vaine" who were formerly led captive in the Roman triumphs.

17.6: This does not translate:

> L'aile qui trop se feit la terre basse.

9: Spenser had found and made difficulty by mistaking *feindre* for *fendre:*

> Alors on vid la corneille Germaine
> Se deguisant *feindre* l'aigle Romaine,
> Et vers le ciel s'élever de rechef
> Ces braves monts autrefois mis en poudre,
> Ne voyant plus voler dessus leur chef
> Ce grand oyseau ministre de la foudre.

18.7-8: Spenser has not made this clear:

> Puis l'annuel pouvoir le plus grand se vid estre,
> Et fut encor plus grand le pouvoir de six mois.

Du Bellay refers to the rule of the Consuls, elected for one year, and to that of the Dictators, whose tenure was limited to six months, until Julius Cæsar made it perpetual.

20.1-2: Non autrement qu'on void la pluvieuse nue
Des vapeurs de la terre en l'air se soulever.

4: *Tethys:* The original has *Thetis la chenue.* The 1611 Folio reads Thetys, but Tethys does not make non-sense, so it is left in the text.

9: *shade:* shelter. Du Bellay merely has *ouvrage.*

11: *vade: vadere.* The rhyme shows that Spenser thought of Latin.

22.2: *mear'd:* marched, made a frontier; original, *borna.* See *The Ruines of Time*, 63.

23.11-12: Spenser does not appear to have caught du Bellay's allusion to the strife between Cæsar and Pompey:

> Ce qui advint, quand l'envieux orgueil
> De ne vouloir ny plus grand, ny pareil,
> Rompit l'accord du beaupere et du gendre.

The same reference is missed in sonnet 31.

24.4 : *Armed be with clawes* is a substitute for, not a translation of the original—*qui vont rampant.*

25.10 : This scarcely translates *veu l'ardeur qui m'allume.*

26.7 : *the yerely starre :* the Sun—*l'Astre annuel.*

9 : Du Bellay changes tenses in this line, and Spenser's failure to follow him slightly obscures what follows :

Rome fut tout le monde, et tout le monde est Rome.

27.4 : *arcks :* arches, as before.

10 : Du Bellay is more explicit : *Rome fouillant son antique sejour.*

28.7-8 : Et sans fueille umbrageux, de son poix se support
Sur son tronc noüailleux en cent lieux esbranché.

9-14 : Spenser has missed the point :

Et bien qu'au premier vent il doive sa ruine,
Et maint jeune à l'entour ait ferme la racine,
Du devot populaire estre seul reveré.
Qui tel chesne a peu voir, qu'il imagine encores,
Comme entre les citez, qui florissent ores,
Ce vieil honneur poudreux est le plus honnoré.

29.6 : Spenser seems to have tried to improve on du Bellay's repetitions. As in sonnet 14.4 he has *hope . . . labour* for *espoir . . . espoir*, here he has *wit . . . skill* for *La main d'Apelle, ou la main Phidienne.*

30.12 : *pill :* A transliteration from the French, but already made English by Lord Berners and others.

31.8 : Du Bellay's phrase is

Ny ce brave soldat qui boit le Rhin Gaulois.

Is Spenser thinking of the *furia francese*, and remembering how Gideon chose the most impetuous of his troops ; or is *running* an epithet of Rhine ?

10-11 : As in sonnet 23, Spenser seems to have missed the allusion to the wars of Cæsar and Pompey, and to the battle of Pharsalia :

Qui semant par les champs l'Emathienne horreur,
Armas le propre gendre encontre son beaupere.

32.14 : *people gowned long : peuple à longue robe—gens togata*—the Romans.

L'Envoy : This is, of course, original. Spenser owed a considerable debt to Joachim du Bellay, not only for the pieces translated in this volume and the hints they provided for some of the other poems, but, I believe, for the general direction of his efforts to found a new and ambitious poetry in England. For du

Bellay's *Deffence et Illustration de la Langue Francoyse* not only declared the the principles of the Pleiade, but passed these principles on to Englishmen. Italian poetry has at all times, perhaps, been more influential in England than French poetry, but French criticism has always helped and stimulated English thought. Guillaume Saluste du Bartas, as a Huguenot, met with more appreciation in England than later generations may think he deserved. Spenser, however, borrowed from him, and Milton admired him. His *heavenly Muse* is his poem *L'Uranie;* he is better known for his long poem on the Creation, *La Semaine*.

It seems strange that Spenser did not mention Ronsard. The religious-political causes that helped du Bartas may have militated against public eulogy of Ronsard, a strong Catholic who approved of the Massacre of St. Bartholomew, inveighed against the Huguenots, and fulminated against the executioners of Mary Queen of Scots. Spenser could not fail to know his poems.

MUIOPOTMOS.

This poem also has been interpreted as a complaint against Burghley. It may be; but if it is, it is barely successful, for an allegorist should provide a key lest his meaning remain obscure, and this story of a Butterfly and a Spider is completely self-contained, without any reference—that we can recognise—to anything outside its own limits, from which we might work forward and back to elucidate the whole. We must take the story as a whole and interpret it as a whole: which becomes more and more difficult on examination. The hatred of the Spider for the Butterfly springs from disappointed ambition and envy; the Butterfly reminds the Spider of something he failed to accomplish. Thus, we might say, Spenser suffers from the competition between Burghley and Leicester. It would, however, be a far-fetched device to represent their rivalry as that of competitors in art. And, though the point is not made clear in the poem, the Spider is but the descendent of Arachne, not himself the rival of Pallas. Is the theme, then, Burghley's general objection to the whole race of poets? It can hardly be, for the Spider's hatred of the race of Butterflies is not unmotived. If we dismiss this idea and are content to search for a noble being entrapped and destroyed by an enemy, we shall find enough and to spare. Apart from Spenser himself, the Duke of Norfolk has been suggested, and Sir Walter Raleigh; we might add Gabriel Harvey, with Dr. Perne and the Earl of Oxford as rival claimants to the role of Aragnoll. The Irish wars could surely furnish some useful ambushes and assassinations. And need we confine ourselves to England? Surely Spenser had heard of Bussy d'Amboise, of Egmont, Condé, Ramus, Coligny. Nothing in the poem need invalidate any of these: the amateur is free to back his fancy.

The poem, again, treats, however lightly and fancifully, of one of the main themes of Spenser's book, the evanescence of beauty and strength. Aragnoll may be a symbol of the foul thief Death. The stimulus to Spenser's imagination, on the other hand, may have been a real butterfly caught in the web of a real spider; or he may have invented the whole affair; or some lady's embroidery may have inspired both this and the Bee and Spider of sonnet lxxi of the *Amoretti*—Lady Carey's, perhaps, who has, indeed, been cast for the somewhat ungraceful part of Aragnoll. One thing is certain, if anything can be in this ticklish trade: the man who played with technique as Spenser did in this poem was not living in misery. It is not that the poem is an original companion piece to *Virgils Gnat*, nor that part of it was borrowed direct from Ovid; the theory and practice of the time put that argument for "insincerity" out of court. It is not that Spenser shared with his master Chaucer a humanitarian incapacity for tragedy, and with Gray, his successor among English academic poets, a tendency to wax metaphysical when he wished to be impressive. The whole spirit of the thing is high and light. It is a decorative fancy carried out with a firm clear touch and an obvious zest in the display of dexterity. Spenser was enjoying himself as Pope enjoyed himself in *The Rape of the Lock*. It may have been a holiday from the weighty matter of *The Faerie Queene*. Even the loose ends are evidence of the lack of seriousness, of play. *Lusimus, Octavi . . . ut araneoli tenuem formavimus orsum.*

The butterfly Clarion, halfway between Turnus and Sir Thopas, and the Ovidian spider Aragnoll inhabit a landscape sited in the land of the *Culex* and charted in tapestries and in the margins of manuscripts, a landscape in the realms of a Faerie Queene whose name is neither greatest Gloriana nor chaste Belphœbe, but Mab. Where did this fanciful prettiness come from, which descended to Drayton and Herrick and finds a counterpart at times in Shakespeare? It seems the invention of Elizabeth's England, indulging the light fancy of a happy day. These are the little things of strong men, made for pleasure—pleasure for the reader and pleasure in the doing.

Few theories of art lay stress enough on these aspects of that very complex activity—on play, and on the inspiration that lies in tools. Paris of the Left Bank excites and nourishes half its inspiration for painters through the continual sight of its colour-shops, their sheaves of brushes, and stacks of stretched canvases, and orderly racks of plump tubes. So also with poetry. The delight of words, the timbres and the rhythms of them, their precision, their suggestivenesses, invite their lover to handle them, to put them in use, to make something with them. It is a main virtue of music, that it is pure wilful making, as mathematics is pure thinking, and poetry at times shares this virtue. So strong is the motive power of this element in poetry, that it may even become a snare to the poet, as Keats knew and as Shelley did not. And one of the many queer things about poetry is, that in this happy hour, when the sheer delight of doing seems his only motive, the poet, whose medium is not self-sufficient tone or completely-generalised symbol but words which have an immediate correspondence with things, discovers some new significance in the universe, some strain of thought or feeling which the world accepts and believes for ever. The artist may begin from an intense desire to express, or from an intense desire to do: the miracle is wrought where the two desires meet, as meet they must, and so the creative mystery is accomplished that sets the artist apart, as free maker of things new and unique.

THE DEDICATION: Elizabeth, second daughter of Sir John Spenser of Althorp, married George Carey, who succeeded his father as 2nd Baron Hunsdon in 1596. She appears as *Charillis* in *Colin Clouts Come Home Again*, 540-563, and was honoured, like her father-in-law, with a dedicatory sonnet in *The Faerie Queene*. Lady Carey was evidently the one of the three sisters to whom Spenser was most attached. It has been suggested that the *Amoretti* were originally addressed to her: some of them may have been. Hers was a literary household, and her husband was the Lord Chamberlain who numbered among his servants the famous company of players which had been that of his brother-in-law Lord Strange, and of which Shakespeare was a member.

1-16: Observe the solemn mock-epic opening—Proposition, Invocation, and Narration in proper sequence.

15-16: It is these lines that lead some to suspect a personal allegory in the poem, but they may be read also as a "sentence," one of the wise sayings in which Renaissance poets and their readers delighted, and of which there are several typical examples in this poem.

20: *favourable:* well-favoured.

22: *Clarion:* "the trumpeter." Compare *The Faerie Queene*, II. ix. 16:

> a swarme of Gnats . . .
> Their murmuring small trompets sounden wide.

42: *stie:* mount—an archaism which Spenser uses several times.

69: *spredding:* The active form is used for the passive; or the verb used reflexively.

77: *Bilbo* is, of course, Bilbao, long famous for iron and steel. *Brasse from Corinth fet* (i.e. *fetched*): Pliny, *Nat. Hist.*, 34. 2, 3, writes at some length on the brass of Corinth.

Oricalche: Orichalcum, of which Pliny speaks in the place cited above: it was a kind of brass. That it should come from *Phœnice* seems to be Spenser's own idea: the epithets *costly* and *strange* give the reason—the suggestion of rarity. Servius says, in his note on *Æneid* xii, 87: "Apud majores orichalcum pretiosius metallis omnibus fuit." This leads to one of the passages Spenser probably had in mind, the arming of Turnus:

> Ipse dehinc auro squallentem, alboque orichalco
> Circundat loricam humeris: simul aptat habendo
> Ensemque, clypeumque, et rubræ cornua cristæ.

84: The *Brigandine* was a small galley, armed, like its larger relative, with a ram. Compare *The Faerie Queene*, IV. ii. 6:

> As when two warlike Brigandines at sea,
> With murdrous weapons arm'd to cruell fight,
> Do meete together on the watry lea,
> They stemme ech other with so fell despight. . . .

92-101: Compare the description of the statue of Cupid in *The Faerie Queene*, III. xi. 47:

And wings it had with sundry colours dight,
More sundry colours, then the proud *Pavone*
Bears in his boasted fan, or *Iris* bright,
When her discolourd bow she spreds through heaven height.

Jortin notes Ovid, *Metamorphoses*, xi. 589-90 :

Induitur velamina mille colorum
Iris.

119 : Asterie was changed into a quail by Jupiter : but this is an Asterie of Spenser's own, made as an offshoot of the story of Psyche. The name comes from *Culex*, or from Ovid's allusion in a passage of *Metamorphoses* vi, which Spenser imitated in this poem. The episode is not closely linked with the main story : Astery is presumably the ancestress of Clarion, but the relationship is not stated explicitly.

184 : *weather :* to spread his wings to the air—a falconer's term, such as Spenser liked to introduce. Compare *The Faerie Queene*, V. iv. 42 :

Like to an Eagle in his kingly pride,
Soring through his wide Empire of the aire,
To weather his brode sailes. . . .

187-200 : The catalogue of flowers, like the list of trees in *The Faerie Queene*, I. i. 8, 9, is a regular set piece, to be compared with its original, the close of *Virgils Gnat*. Spenser's botany is decidedly bookish. He displays nothing of Shakespeare's love of flowers or of his firsthand knowledge of them, and seems more interested in their virtues than in their appearance. True, it is a formal garden that he imagines, but he does not seem to have visualised it clearly, and the catalogue is literary rather than pictorial. Some of his epithets are vague enough ; some are evidence of the study of Pliny and of the herbals which were then appearing in some number and in great beauty. The best available to him were William Turner's *New Herball*, first published in 1551, and Lyte's translation of Dodoens : *Niewe Herball*, 1578. Gerarde followed soon after. Sir Thomas Elyot mentions the virtues of Sage, Hyssop, Savory, Coleworts, Parsley, Lettuce, and Rosemary, in his *Castell of Helth*, first published in 1539 and frequently reprinted. Spenser does not mention always the most common or most notable virtue of the herbs, and some of his phrases are devised with more eye to the verse than to the plant.

188 : *Cummin good for eyes :* " Iidem oculis claritatem adferunt," says Pliny (20. 10), and Bartholomeus Anglicus, that it " dissolveth and doth awaye bloudye reume in the eie, if it be wel meddeled with cleare Waxe, and layde oft thereto." (Trevisa's translation.)

189 : Dodoens recommends *Hyssop* for bruises, not for wounds. Culpeper saith : " The green herb bruised and a little sugar put thereto doth quickly heal any cut or green wound, being thereto applied." But this is much later, and may even be a memory of this passage.

191 : *Bees-alluring Thime :* Spenser is probably remembering his Virgil, *Bucolics* v. 77, and *Georgics*, iv. 30-33, 112, etc.

The compound epithets are worthy of notice. This Greek " composition," used by du Bellay, Ronsard, and especially du Bartas, and approved by Sidney, is not noticeably frequent in Spenser : he knew it, and used it, but not extensively. Its comparative frequency in this poem is one sign that Spenser was playing at ease with technical devices.

193 : *Orpine :* the plant Livelong—*Sedum telephium.*

194 : *embathed :* bedewed.

Galingale : Cyperus longus, used as a condiment, *e.g.* by Chaucer's Cook.

195 : *Costmarie : Balsaminum.* " This herbe is also used in meetes as Sage and other herbes, especially in Salades and sawces, for which purpose it is excellent, for it yeeldeth a proper sent and Taste."—Dodoens.

Camomill : Turner says " It is most convenient for the mydriff, and for the paynes under the pappes." Gerarde, more explicit, says it " easeth the peine in the chest comming of winde, and expelleth tough and clammie flegme."

196 : *Setuale :* Setwall, Garden Valerian, according to Dodoens and Turner.

197 : *Verven :* Turner says : " The herbe layd to wyth vinegre, stayeth burning heares, and saint Anthonyes fyre, and stoppeth rotting, and joyneth together woundes, and covereth wyth a skinne and filleth wyth flesh olde woundes."

Dill : Dodoens says : " The seede thereof being well chaffed, and often smelled unto, stayeth the yexe, or hiquet."

198 : *Bazil hartie-hale :* Dodoens says : " The later writers say that it doth fortifie and strengthen the harte,

and the brayne, and that it rejoiceth and recreateth the spirites, & is good against Melancholie and sadnesse."

199: *Perseline:* Parsley; according to Elyot it "is very convenient to the stomacke, and comforteth appetite."

200: *Lettuce* "is cold and moist temperately," saith Elyot.

201: Compare the formula in *Virgils Gnat*, 681 (*Culex*, 410).

206: *Embay:* bathe. This is the earliest example given by the *O.E.D.*

239: *Sprent:* sprinkled; past participle of the verb *to sprenge*.

257-352: This is a version of the story of Arachne, as told by Ovid, *Metamorphoses*, vi. 1-145; and no dishonour to its original. Spenser improves on Ovid's arrangement by describing the work of Arachne before that of Pallas, so as to strengthen the climax.

277-296: An admirable development—so clearly visualised as to suggest that Spenser knew a good picture of the Rape of Europa—of Ovid's lines 103-107:

> Mæonis (*sc.* Arachnes) elusam designat imagine tauri
> Europen: verum taurum, freta vera putares.
> Ipsa videbatur terras spectare relictas,
> Et comites clamare suas, tactumque vereri
> Assilientis aquæ; timidasque reducere plantas.

292: *Spring:* boy.

293: *Teade:* torch.

297-303: Ultima pars telæ, tenui circundata limbo,
Nexilibus flores hederis habet intertextos.
Non illus Pallas, non illud carpere Livor
Possit opus. (127-130)

303-327: Cecropia Pallas scopulum Mavortis in arce
Pingit, et antiquam de terræ nomine litem . . .
. . . Mirarique Deos. (70-82)

311: *eathe:* easy.

327-328: Circuit extremas oleis pacalibus oras. (101)

329-336: A neat addition of Spenser's own, to connect Ovid's myth with his.

337-352: Spenser omits any reference to the suicide of Arachne, or to the curse of the Goddess: his Arachne becomes a poisonous and hideous creature through mere envy—a vice Spenser often denounces.

347: *dryrihed:* sorrow. *Romance of the Rose*, 4728.

349-352: In latere exiles digiti pro cruribus hærent.

Cætera venter habet, de quo tamen illa remittit
Stamen, et antiquas exercet aranea telas.
(143-145)

397-400: The mixture of imagination and observation here contrasts pleasantly with the catalogue of the flowers above.

409-416: Compare *The Teares of the Muses*, 115-120.

420: *raine:* realm—*regnum.*

438-439: An heroic touch to correspond with the opening of the poem: the reader is expected to recognise the allusion to the last line of the *Æneid:*

Vitaque cum gemitu fugit indignata sub umbras.

440: An absolute construction. *Care* means *woe, sorrow.*

VISIONS OF THE WORLDS VANITIE.

Spenser seems to have had a particular interest at one time in visionary or emblematic poetry of this kind. It was not peculiar to himself, but was common at the time, though more on the Continent than in England, and its appearance here is probably due to the influence of the two series of translations which follow. The same interest appears in *The Ruines of Time*, and, as is suggested of some of the Visions in that poem, these may be remnants of the *Dreames* and *Pageants* mentioned in the correspondence of Spenser and Harvey. They are crude examples of Spenser's attempt to solve one of the great problems of art—a problem which always haunted him as it haunted Tasso: the relation between the physical basis and the spiritual end of art. He was to come nearer its solution, fortunately, but he hovered always between the parabolic, the emblematic, the symbolic, and the true myth that succeeds through its pure æsthetic value. These *Visions* —which are not really *visions of the world's vanity*, but parables of the limitations of power—have little but historical interest for us

The single idea they enclose is obvious enough; I can find no line of connexion between the images, except that they all concern animals, as if Spenser had been reading his Æsop, or were attempting, on a larger scale and in verse, a series of similitudes such as were dear to John Lyly. The style is cramped, and lacks the flow of his usual rhythm. Evidently Spenser still found the sonnet-form a constraint.

1.5-8: This is obscure. I take it to mean: "such (poor) things as this age, in which all good is scarce and in which all that is humble and lowly is despised, is able in its decadence to bring forth." Line 8 then is a somewhat irrelevant exclamation on the evils of the age.

10: Compare *The Ruines of Time*, line 489.

13-14: Compare the dedication to Lady Carey. *Take in worth* means *accept graciously*: as we would say, *accept for what they are worth.* This couplet may well be a later addition to the sonnet.

2.2-3: Spenser's picture of the Bull may owe something to Virgil's (*Georgics* i. 218) though the latter refers to the zodiacal sign:

> Candidus auratis aperit cum cornibus annum
> Taurus.

10: *Brize*: or *breeze*, a kind of gadfly. The word is still used by entomologists.

3: Pliny, speaking of the Crocodile, says, *Nat. Hist.* 8.25 (32): "Hunc saturum cibo piscium et semper esculento ore in litore somno datum parva avis quæ trochilos ibi vocatur . . . invitat ad hiandum pabuli sui gratia, os primum eius adsultim repurgans, mox dentes et intus fauces quoque ad hunc scabendi dulcedinem quam maxime hiantes."

7: The form *Tedula*, like the errors in proper names in *Virgils Gnat*, suggests printing from a transcript. The mistake could have arisen if the word were written in an Italian hand; Spenser used both scripts, and the italics of the printer may represent a habit of writing proper names in the Italian hand even though the rest were written in the English. The MSS. of Lord William Howard in Naworth Castle show this practice, which might be a fruitful source of error.

4: Spenser might know this fable in Alciati's *Emblemata*, but his source was evidently the fables of Æsop. He could find it in Froben's edition of 1534, Rampazeti's of 1561, the Lyons edition of 1570, and many others, always with a convenient Latin version attached. As usual he alters his original: by making the Scarabee set fire to the Eagle's nest instead of breaking its eggs.

11-12: It was Jove that was infested with filth, and forced to fling away the Eagle's eggs. Over-compression has played havoc with the pronouns.

5: The combats of the swordfish and the whale are, curiously enough, authentic. Spenser may have in mind

Pliny, 32.2 (6): "Milvago (modern editors read *lolligo*) quotiens cernatur extra aquam volitans tempestates mutari Trebius Niger auctor est. Xiphian, id est gladium, rostoro mucronato esse." This juxtaposition, with a hint of Psalm civ. 26—"that Leviathan, whom thou hast made to play therein"—would account for this sonnet. *Leviathan* is explained as *whale* in the Geneva commentary.

6: Pliny does not mention the enmity of Dragon and Spider, though he has a (quite different) story of how certain spiders kill serpents.

5: *Unequall peare* is a strange phrase. *Equall peares* occurs several times in Spenser. The reason is, probably, constraint of rhyme; the justification, that both Dragon and Spider are venomous beasts.

7: The Cedar of Lebanon may be chosen here not only for its legendary nobility, but from a memory of Bartholomeus Anglicus: "Ceder is never destroyed with mought (*moth*), neyther with *Terredo*, that is the Tree worme." Pliny says no wood is exempt from the *teredo*: Spenser required a superlative, or extreme case.

8: I find no original for the Elephant and the Ant, but Pliny tells how the Elephant suffers from swallowing leeches: inelegant animals to which Spenser may have preferred the proverbially respectable Ant.

9: Pliny (32.1) not only describes the "parvus pisciculus" which "cogit stare navigia," but also appends the moral. Relating how great warships are stopped in their course by this fish, he says: "Heu vanitas humana, cum vostra illa ære ferroque ad ictus armata semipedalis inhibere possit ac tenere devincta pisciculus." Pliny calls the sucker-fish *echenais*, so Spenser was not dependent entirely upon him.

10: I have found no original for the Lion and the Wasp, except the fable of the Lion Tormented by Flies.

11: This is too obvious to require comment.

12.9: Does not this use of the term *ruines* suggest a relation with *The Ruines of Time?* It may have something to do with the origin of that title.

THE VISIONS OF BELLAY.

These sonnets are translated from a *Songe: ou Vision* appended to *Les Antiquites de Rome* of Joachim du Bellay, translated also in this volume. All but sonnets 6, 8, 13, and 14 appeared originally in *A Theatre . . .*

for Worldlings, in 1569, where, however, they were unrhymed. The translations are not conspicuously good, nor conspicuously bad. The adaptation to rhyme has entailed a certain number of parasitic phrases, but it is ingenious and neat, and the strictness of sonnet form forced Spenser to compensate for his expansions by compression elsewhere, as the form of *Virgils Gnat* did not.

1.7: *Whence . . . come:* This is an interpolation of Spenser's, and not very happy.

10: *this great temple:* the heavens.

2.7: *rayons:* The *Theatre* version has *rayes*. The introduction of the French word suggests reference to the original.

9: *parget:* plaster-work; *lambriz* in the original.

3.4: *level:* aim:

Tant qu'un archer pourroit prendre visée.

9: *pight:* fixed, or placed.

4.4: *arke:* arch, as in *The Ruines of Rome*, 7.7.

7: *chayre:* The original has *char—chariot*. The illustration in *A Theatre for Worldlings* shows the chariot, but there also the English text reads *chaire*.

5.1: *Dodonian tree:* the oak of Dodona.

2: *gleame:* The original has *umbrage*, the *Theatre* version, *shade*. We may take *gleame* to be a violent but not uncharacteristic Spenserian perversion of *gloom*—which, however, Spenser does not use elsewhere as a noun. He was evidently hasty in finding a rhyme for *streame*.

5: *addrest* echoes the original *dressé*. The *Theatre* has *erect*. This is another sign that Spenser has the French by him when he revised his old translation.

10: *fone:* a plural form of *foe*, common in Spenser.

12: *wedge:* original *congnée*. Spenser confuses *cognée* (axe) and *coin* (wedge).

14: The Empire and the Papacy.

6.4: This is not clearly understood:

Et d'un col allongé la Louve les lecher.

13: *soyle:* original *sang*. *Soil* as a term of venery means a marshy or wet place where the chase takes refuge; thus *her own soyle* means the place made wet by her own blood: a neat complication of the original.

7.10: *in firie fold:* original *en tourbillon de feu*.

8.3-5: The original is clearer in connexion:

Je le vy tout couvert d'une obscure bruine,
Qui s'eslevoit par l'air en tourbillons fumeux:
Dont se formoit un corps à sept chefz merveilleux.

The seven-headed beast is an obvious memory of the Revelations of St. John.

6: *coure:* cower; original *couvoit.*

7: *foes:* This is intruded to fill up the rhyme:

Les plus doulx animaux, et les plus orgueilleux.

10: *hew* in Spenser's poems usually means *appearance*, not only *colour.*

9.1: *nightly:* nocturnal. The original has *ce monstre nocturne.*

13.1-2.: The *Florentine* is Petrarch. See below, *Visions of Petrarch*, 2.

3: *loast:* lowest—that is, by a latinism, *very low.*

10.5: *this:* original *ceste;* a modern reader would translate it *that.*

11.8: *stie:* to mount up; an archaism fairly common in Spenser.

11: *silver dew:* The *Theatre* version translates accurately the original *pluie doree.* Spenser is thinking visually instead of allegorically. Du Bellay meant to signify the Donation of Charlemagne.

12.3: *grayle:* gravel.

13: *ray:* soil, as at various places in *The Faerie Queene;* the form *beray* is better known.

14.5: *rayse:* graze, as at *Faerie Queene*, III. i. 65; from French *raser.* The original here has *touchast.*

15.4: *Typhœus sister.* The description suggests Bellona, but the genealogy is difficult, even for a Renaissance poem. Du Bellay probably meant Rhea, daughter, as Typhœus was son, of Earth, and one of the patron goddesses of Rome. Ovid, *Fasti* iv. 201 ff.

THE VISIONS OF PETRARCH.

This allegorical meditation on the death of Laura is one of the main origins of all this emblematic poetry. It is a *canzone* in 12-line stanzas, Canzone vi *in Morte di Madonna Laura.* Clement Marot translated it into French, also in 12-line stanzas, and Spenser translated Marot's version for van der Noodt's *Theatre*, where the stanzas are separated and called Epigrams. The first and third in this version consist of fourteen lines, the remainder of twelve, and all are made into sonnets here.

2: Line 10 is added, and line 10 of the *Theatre* version is expanded into lines 11-12.

4: Lines 13-14 are additions to the original version.

5: Line 12 of the original version is expanded into lines 12-13 here; line 14 is an addition.

6: Lines 13-14 are added, as in the fourth sonnet.

The last sonnet is written on the theme of the four-line Envoy which was the coda of the original Canzone. It will be observed that the rhyme-scheme is the distinctively Spenserian one which appears in the dedication of *Virgils Gnat* and in the *Amoretti*.

EPIGRAMS AND SONNETS IN *A THEATRE FOR WORLDLINGS*, 1569.

Spenser's name does not occur in this book, which is an English version of one already published in "the Brabants speache" and in French, and purporting to be translated by Theodore Roest. Roest may have translated the prose, which is much the greater part of the book, but the arguments of those to attempt to disprove Spenser's authorship of these verse translations are not convincing. In *Englishe Studien*, XV, XXVII Kœppel argued that Spenser's later translations from French show diminished accuracy instead of increased knowledge of the language: but there is considerable difference to be expected between a schoolboy's translation and the hasty methods of a formed poet to whom such work is merely an experiment or a diversion. That only *The Visions of Petrarch* should be noted as *formerly translated* does not invalidate *The Visions of Bellay*; it may merely indicate that the two poems were printed from manuscripts of different provenance—as we might expect, since the re-handling of each was so different. If Spenser was not the author of these *Theatre* versions, he committed a monstrous theft in the *Complaints*, and—what is more important to us who know more about his art than about his morals—performed an unprecedented kind of work. We may continue to accept these translations as the first offspring of Spenser's Muse.

BIBLIOGRAPHY.

BIBLIOGRAPHICAL AND TEXTUAL NOTES.

ENTRY IN STATIONERS' REGISTER:

(1590) 29 Decembris. William Ponsonbye. Entred for his Copie under the handes of Doctor Staller and bothe the wardens, A booke entytuled Complaintes conteyninge sondrye smalle Poemes of the worldes vanity.

TITLE-PAGE:

(Within a woodcut border) Complaints./ Containing sundrie/ small Poemes of the/ Worlds Va-/nitie./ Whereof the next Page/ maketh menti-/on./ By Ed.Sp. (device of four hands pointing inwards) London./ Imprinted for William/ Ponsonbie, dwelling in Paules/ Churchyard at the signe of/ the Bishops head./ 1591.

Title-pages with the same border, device, and imprint before *The Teares of the Muses, Mother Hubberds Tale,* and *Muiopotmos.*

Running-title to each poem. On Z_1 a and b, *Visions of the Worlds Vanitie* in error for *Visions of Bellay.*

Quarto. A—Z, in fours unpaged. Z_4 blank.

CONTENTS:

General title as above (A_1 a). A note of the sundrie Poemes contained in this Volume (A_1 b). The Printer to the Gentle Reader (A_2).

The Ruines of Time (A_3—D_4 b). Headtitle, " The Ruine (*sic*) of Time " within an ornament on A_3. Dedication occupies A_3 a and b.

The Teares of the Muses (E—G_4 b). Title-page as above, " The/ Teares of the Mu-/ ses./ By Ed. Sp., 1591 " on E_1 a; E_1 b blank. Dedication on E_2 a and b.

Virgils Gnat (H—K_4 b). Dedicatory sonnet on H_1 a.

Mother Hubberds Tale (L—Q_4 b). Titlepage as above, " Prosopopoia./ Or/ Mother Hubberds Tale./ By Ed. Sp./ Dedicated to the right Honorable/ the Ladie Compton and/ Mountegle, 1591" on L_1 a; L_1 b blank. Running-title, "Mother Hubberds Tale."

The Ruines of Rome (R—S_4 b).

Muiopotmos (T—X_2 a). Title-page as above, "Muiopotmos,/ Or/ The Fate of the Butterflie./ By Ed. Sp./ Dedicated to the most faire and/ vertuous Ladie: the Ladie/ Carey./ 1590" on T_1 a; T_1 b blank. Dedication on T_2 a and b. X_2 b blank.

Visions of the Worlds Vanitie (X_3—Y_1 b).

The Visions of Bellay (Y_2—Z_1 b).

The Visions of Petrarch (Z_2—Z_3 b).

Z_4 blank.

It will be observed that the title-page of *Muiopotmos* is dated 1590, while the others have 1591. The usual uncertainty of date between January 1st and March 25th may have misled a compositor, or the discrepancy may record a change of mind in making up the volume. The order of the poems may be an afterthought: some of the manuscripts, gathered as Ponsonby describes in his preface, may have arrived even after printing was begun. More than one compositor may have been employed, and though *Muiopotmos* comes last in the book as we have it, it need not have been printed last; the title-page would be used first on whatever was ready first.

THE PERSONS CONCERNED:

William Ponsonby is described by Dr. Mackerrow as "the most important bookseller of the Elizabethan period." He was made free of the Stationers' Company on 11th January, 1570/71, was Junior Warden in 1598-99, and died in 1603. He published, among others, Greene's *Mamillia* and *Gwydonius*; Sidney's *Arcadia* and *Apologie for Poetrie*; the Countess of Pembroke's translations; most of Abraham Fraunce's works, and all Spenser's except the first, *The Shepheardes Calender*. The list suggests a regular connexion with the Sidney group, which may have led to the Spenser publications, or *vice versa*.

The printer of *Complaints* was almost certainly Thomas Orwin, who was made free of the Company in 1581, and died in 1593. He printed, *inter alia*, Lyly's *Sappho and Phao*; Fraunce's *The Countess of Pembrokes Ivychurch*, 1591 (for Ponsonby); and Spenser's *Daphnaida*, 1591.

Thomas Staller or Stallard, of C.C.C., Cambridge, matriculated 1562; B.A. 1565/6; Fellow 1567-70; M.A. 1569. Rector of All Hallows, Lombard St. and of St. Mary at Hill; Archdeacon of Rochester, 1593-1605. Appointed one of the licencers of the press by the Archbishop, 1588. Died 1605/6.

VARIANTS:

As usual, copies vary in certain places. The table on the next page gives these, the copies being numbered as under:

(1) The Bodleian copy used by Mr. de Selincourt in his Oxford edition.

(2) The Huth copy, used by Grosart and by Mr. de Selincourt. I have taken the readings of this copy from Grosart and Mr. de Selincourt where they agree. Copy (4) shows many of the same readings.

(3) Copy 103.f.30 in the Signet Library, Edinburgh.

(4) Copy Co.3.19 in the Hunterian Museum of the University of Glasgow. Collier seems to have had a similar copy.

(5) Copy Co.3.20 in the same library.

	Sig.	Copy 1.	Copy 2.	Copy 3.	Copy 4.	Copy 5.
R.T.						
333	C2b	Linus	Linus,	Linus,	Linus,	Linus,
T.M.						
52	E3	Can	Can	Gan	Gan	Can
435	G2	crime	raime	crime	crime	crime
M.H.T.						
169	M1b	anie	anie	anie	anie	anie.
302	M3b	woolley	woolley	woolley	woolley	woolly
304	M3b	dog	dog	dog	dog	dog.
308	M3b	wings	wings	wings	wings	winges
R.R.						
4.6	R1b	Th'old Giants	The old Giants	Th'old Giants	The old Giants	The old Giants
4.14	R1b	Vimnial	Viminall	Vimnial	Viminal	Viminal
Mui.						
196	V2	Dull	(*caret*)	(*caret*)	(*caret*)	Dull
250	V3	dispacing	displacing	displacing	displacing	dispacing
346	V4b	attempted,	attempted.	attempted.	attempted.	attempted,
354	V4b	enfestred	enfested	enfested	enfested	enfestred
370	X1	did slily frame	framde craftily	framde craftily	framde craftily	framde craftily
VWV.						
8.12	X4b	natures	native	native	native	native

The reading *winges* at *M.H.T.* 308 is ascribed by de Selincourt to Hughes (1715). As Hughes reads *woolly dog*, *winges* in the three places on M3b it seems likely that he had a copy like (5)—though Folio also reads *woolly*.

A copy of *R.T.* in Edinburgh University Library agrees with (2) and (4), one in the John Rylands' Library, Manchester, with (1). A copy containing only *M.H.T.*, *Muio.*, and *Visions*, in the National Library of Scotland, agrees with (2) and (4) at *Muio.* 196, 250, 346, 354; but with (1) at 370 and at *V.W.V.* 8.12: and with (5) at *M.H.T.* 169, 302, 304, 308: *i.e.* has signature M like (5), V like (2) and (4), and X like (1).

It is obvious that these copies consist of corrected and uncorrected sheets bound up indiscriminately, with the exception of (5), the correctness of which is apparently accidental, as it is quite undistinguished in appearance and is bound up with other books, which one would scarcely expect if it were a picked copy. Thus no question of different "issues" arises. Corrections have been made twice on signatures R_1b and V_4b.

LATER HISTORY:

The assertion that *Complaints* was suppressed, mentioned on page 232 above, rests on an epigram of John Weever's and on two references by Thomas Middleton. Weever's epigram was written and published in 1599 after Spenser's death; in Dr. Mackerrow's edition page 101:

> *Colin's* gone home, the glorie of his clime,
> The Muses Mirrour, and the Shepheards Saint;
> *Spencer* is ruined, of our latter time
> The fairest ruine, Faëries foulest want:
> Then his *Time-ruines* did our ruine show,
> Which by his ruine we untimely know:
> *Spencer* therfore thy *Ruines* were cal'd in,
> Too soone to sorrow least we should begin.

In *The Black Book*, 1604 (*Works*, ed. Bullen, viii. 31), Middleton calls for "a health half as deep as mother Hubburd's cellar—she that was called in for selling her working bottle-ale to bookbinders, and spurting the froth upon courtiers' noses." And in the preface to *Father Hubburds Tales*, 1604 (Bullen viii, 53-4), he says: "Why I call these *Father Hubburds Tales*, is not to have them called in again, as the *Tale of Mother Hubburd* . . .

for I entreat here neither of ragged bears or apes, no, nor the lamentable downfall of the old wife's platters,—I deal with no such metal."

These seem fairly clear, though Middleton's references to ragged bears and the old wife's platters suggest either that he was thinking of something else or that he had never seen *Mother Hubberds Tale* and was talking at random. But to what period are we to ascribe this calling in? In 1580 Weever was aged about two, and Middleton about ten. By the same reckoning Weever is no first-hand evidence for 1591, though Middleton might be. They may refer to a later reprint of which no record remains: no record remains either of its prohibition. If *Complaints* were called in, it must have been after 1591, or Harvey and Nash would surely have referred to it. The number of copies extant would not lead anyone to suspect suppression. I am inclined to believe that—unless a reprint was suppressed—Weever and Middleton are retailing gossip.

Complaints was never reprinted alone. The poems appear in the Folio *Works* published by Matthew Lownes in 1611, *Mother Hubberds Tale* being printed separately, with the date 1612 or 1613. The Stationers' Register contains no entry of its transfer, but *Complaints*, and the other minor works owned by Ponsonby, were probably held as included in the transfer of *The Faerie Queene* to Waterson on 3rd September, 1604 (Arber, iii. 269), and thence to Lownes on 5th November (Arber, iii. 174).

TEXTUAL NOTES:

One question which must be faced is the weight we must allow to the Folio text of 1611, which shows signs of careful editing. Some of the Folio readings are indubitable improvements, but these are mainly, if not wholly, such as might be made without further authority. Some are equally indubitable corruptions, intentional or unintentional. Some, which regularise metre and modernise spellings, are doubtful: I am not convinced that Spenser did not at times—notably in *Mother Hubberds Tale*—deliberately roughen his verse to suggest Chaucerian antiquity. The general result is, that we cannot accept all the Folio readings. Now if we select some and reject others we depend merely on individual taste. I have therefore preferred to give the Quarto text, from the copy Co.3.20 in the Hunterian Museum (No. 5 above), which copy, as the table on page 266 shows, has the preferable reading in each place where variation occurs. I have restricted my alterations of this text to what I believe to be compositor's or copyist's errors, with a very few changes of punctuation to clarify the sense. A complete list is appended.

THE RUINES OF TIME.

84 : Princesse.) Princesse,
154 : more.) more,
175 : endure.) endure,
214 : men,) men (The comma makes an obscure line a trifle clearer)
259 : give.) give,
363 : covetize) covertize (adopting the Folio reading)
414 : Mausolus) Mansolus
551 : which) with (error probably due to contraction wch.)
574 : worlds) words (Folio reading)
588 : spide !) spide ? The question mark was often used in place of the exclamation, but it is only a typographical point, and not Spenser's, so I remove it for the modern reader.

THE TEARES OF THE MUSES.

113 : anew) This is very possibly a misprint for *in rew*, as at line 173 and the corresponding line of each section. I should have altered it had it not been the first of the series : that is an additional condition of error, but also an additional condition of variation in the MS.
171 : answering,) answering.
232 : singulfs) The 1611 Folio and all later editions alter to *singults*—Latin and Italian *singulti*. Spenser obviously had this word in mind, but he wrote *singulfs* four times, at intervals : here ; *Colin Clouts Come Home Again*, 167 ; *The Faerie Queene*, III. xi. 12 ; and V. vi. 13. Why he invented this form *singulfs* I cannot tell, but apparently he did, so it may as well remain as he wrote it.
256 : night !) night ? (as at *R.T.* 588 above).
310 : wit,) wit.
399 : defaced) defacd (Spenser always spells the disyllabic form *defast* or *defaste*.

432 : compyle,) compyle. The compositor closes the stanza with a period, but syntax demands the continuation of the sentence into the next.

447-8 : The Folio of 1612 widens—and emasculates—the reference :

For, such as now have most the World at will,
Scorne th'one and th'other in their deeper skill.

457 : Folio reads :

Of such as first were raised for vertuous parts . . .
O ! let not those . . .

Whether this prudence was Spenser's or his editor's, we cannot tell.

486 : sovenance) soverance Spenser uses *sovenance* four other times. But the Scottish *soverance—truce*—would make good sense, and is possible.

566 : bee) beee

590 : I have left the semicolon with some misgiving, as an example of what Mr. Percy Simpson calls "the emphasising semicolon." (*Shakespearian Punctuation*, p. 62.)

598 : mone,) mone : }
599 : breake :) breake, }

VIRGILS GNAT.

122 : heart) hear
144 : eate.) eate,
149 : Ascraean) Astraean (*Ascraeo*)

190 : Plaine) Palme Ten years had elapsed between the writing and the printing of this translation, and Ponsonby says that some of the *Complaints* had been out of Spenser's possession. I am inclined to postulate a copyist to take the responsibility of the errors in proper names at line 149 above, and at 490, 511, 588 below, and this *Palme* also. I cannot see how, with *platanus* before his eyes, Spenser could write *Palme*. On the other hand, *Plaine—Palme* is not a difficult error for a copyist or a compositor.

233 : Shepheards) Speheards
308 : creast-front tyre) creast front-tyre
368 : relent.) relent,
387 : throat) threat

490 : Hesione) Ixione See note on line 190 above, Spenser was arbitrary in allusion, but not usually in names ; also though this one is not in the text, he almost certainly

would find it in a commentary and have it before him.

511 : Rhœtean) Rhetæan. See note on line 190.

538 : The Folio reads *subtile surprysall,* which later editors have preferred. This of course gives the right number of syllables in the verse, but does not really improve the rhythm. Also as it stands it *is* a surprise. It is really an æsthetic, not a mathematical question, and the reader is free to choose.

575 : billowes) billowe (Decided by *them* in the next line.)

588 : Heræan) Hercæan *Heræaque . . . litora :* Spenser *may* have written *Hercæan,* but as it is merely a question of copying, the error is more likely to be committed by the man who had not the original text before him.

MOTHER HUBBERDS TALE.

67 : Grosart reads *lifted up,* following his M.S. Folio reads *lifted high.* An alternative may be introduced into the text, or it may be miscopied ; but the alexandrine may be intended, so I leave it.

94 : entice.) entice,
184 : undonne,) undonne.
251 : t'afford,) t'afford.
403 : tride,) tride.
648 : not at all) not all (*At* supplied from Folio.)
658 : successe.) successe,
713 : eare,) eare.
1108 : Conge) Couge
1231 : The) And (J. C. Smith *conj. apud* E. de Selincourt, Oxford.)
1363 : abusion,) abusion.
121 : or) ot
184 : undonne,) undonne,

THE RUINES OF ROME.

2.7 : Mausolus) Mansolus
8 : glorie :) glorie. }
raced.) raced ; }
3.4 : Palaces,) Palaces (adopted from Folio for clarity's sake.)
8.8 : Modern editors omit the comma after *earth ;* I

fancy it is intended to emphasise the rhythm, and so leave it.

11.5 : heate,) heate ;}
6 : fild ;) fild, }

15.14 : Now to) To) (*Now* adopted from Folio : it is not particularly good, but the line is evidently defective, I hesitate to alter, *e.g.*, to *To have become*, merely because of respect to the Folio's age.)

18.5 : ornaments) ornament (Required for rhyme : original has *ornemens.*)

20.4 : Tethys) Folio reads *Thetys*, which agrees with the original : *Thetis la chenue*. But *Tethys* is not nonsense, and Spenser may have written it ; so I keep it, with dubiety.

32.1 : verses) yerses

MUIOPOTMOS.

34 : yongth) yonght
247 : lay,) lay.
391 : those) thoss

VISIONS OF BELLAY.

1.12 : inconstancies,) inconstancies.

2.8 : On) One

4.1 : pilloures) pillowes. I follow de Selincourt, In Spenser's works the word is spelt *pillours* or *pillors*, occasionally *pillers*. *Theatre* has *pillers*.

5.5 : addrest,) addrest.

9.1 : astonied) astoined
nightly) mighty (*Theatre* has *nightly ;* original *nocturne*. The slip may have been made by Spenser's pen, but it is only a slip.)

5 : pot,) pot.

VISIONS OF PETRARCH.

2.13 : moment) monent

EPIGRAMS AND SONETS FROM *A THEATRE FOR WORLDLINGS.*

The text is from the British Museum copy, 224. a. 11.
The last Sonet, 8 : founde.) founde,

POSTSCRIPT.

Thus we have gathered some idea of the reading with which Spenser's mind was filled—reading which formed so large and important a part of the experience of this academically-minded poet; and of his reaction to another important experience, his visits to Court, specially that of 1590 when he stood on his own feet and did not appear merely as one of Leicester's train.

I am indebted to the Librarians of the University of Glasgow, the Scottish National Library, the Signet Library, and the University of Edinburgh for their helpful courtesy; to Professor A. S. Ferguson for many shrewd and learned remarks on the commentary; to Dr. R. B. Mackerrow and Professor D. Nichol Smith and Mr. J. W. Rees for bibliographical points; and especially to Mr. Peter Alexander for collating the proofs with the Quarto.

A few of the notes on *The Ruines of Time* appeared in my *Selections from Spenser*, published by the Oxford Press in 1923.

Armstrong College,
Newcastle-upon-Tyne.
July, 1928.

W. L. RENWICK.

24 JUN 1968
-5 OCT 1957
CANCELLED
-3. JUL. 1970
CANCELLED
-9 JUL 1965
CANCELLED
CANCELLED
17 DEC 1965
WITHDRAWN
CANCELLED
26 APR 1968
20 JUN 1968